Handbook of

COMPUTER MAINTENANCE AND TROUBLESHOOTING

Handbook of
COMPUTER MAINTENANCE AND TROUBLESHOOTING

Byron W. Maguire
USAF, Ret.
Engineer, Litton Industries

RESTON PUBLISHING COMPANY, INC.
A Prentice-Hall Company
Reston, Virginia 22090

Library of Congress Cataloging in Publication Data

Maguire, Byron W   1931-
    Handbook of computer troubleshooting and mainte-
nance.

    1.   Electronic digital computers—Testing.
2.   Electronic digital computers—Maintenance and
repair.   3.   Electronic digital computers—Programming.
I.   Title.
TK7887.M35   621.3819'58'4   73-8932
ISBN   0-87909-324-2

© 1973 by
RESTON PUBLISHING COMPANY, INC.
Box 547
Reston, Virginia 22090
A Prentice-Hall Company

10 9 8 7 6 5 4 3 2 1

Printed in the United States of America.

1763287

This book is dedicated to
My Family
who helped in so many ways
with its preparation.

Preface

This book has been prepared for use by a technician or an engineer working on electronic digital computers, data processing equipment, and digital communications equipment in the field. It presents studies on the maintenance tasks which are currently being performed by personnel in these types of installations. Included in the first four Chapters are the general servicing tasks, routine repairs, and soldering tasks. Chapters five through eight examine tasks which technical managers must understand. The final Chapters, nine through 14, examine tasks used in troubleshooting and maintaining systems operations. These cover programming, troubleshooting, and use of test equipment.

Since most systems can be divided into broad categories according to their function, it can reasonably be assumed that most systems will have Computer Central, Input/Output, Display, and Ancillary Units. The examples presented in the text which illustrate the use of a task or subtask were carefully chosen to provide realism. By studying these examples the reader or student should be able to learn why a task is important and when to use it. The task of alignment, for instance, will normally be used on displays.

This book has been prepared in a manner that guides the reader to an understanding of the simpler tasks through the more difficult. It presents ideas for examination and trial in hopes of providing the reader or student with a greater understanding of the parts that make up a task, its application, and its expected results.

The author expresses his gratitude to General Electric Company and to ITT for their generous help in providing information and photographs or art for this book.

Byron W. Maguire

Contents

1

Performing Servicing Routines, Repairing, and Checking

The general maintenance functions performed by most electronic maintenance men are those of general maintenance and the repairing or replacing of electronic components. Included are such tasks as servicing, inspecting, repairing, replacing, and validating, and the checking associated with these tasks. To help achieve a clear understanding of the job responsibilities in relation to the tasks, it becomes important to analyze why a task is performed and understand the consequences if it is not completed correctly. What are some of the features of maintenance routines? What is accomplished by their performance? What areas of responsibilities are included? What repairs will you need to perform and what problems will you encounter? What repair skills will you need to develop? This text discusses answers to these questions.

1-1 Servicing Routines and Their Checks

Most generally a maintenance routine requires you to clean and service equipment so that optimum equipment operation is obtained. Improper performance of these tasks can and does result in equipment status deterioration, intermittent error problems, and corrosion. In the following pages

1

you will read about situations that arise because these routines are performed haphazardly and when, how, and why repairs are made to components of a system.

You, as an electronic technician, are the only one who can ensure that equipment operates properly. It therefore becomes necessary for you to have a personal feeling of accomplishment about working on the equipment. To best attain this feeling, look closely at the task to be done, analyze the task, and determine that the performance of the task will (1) provide better operational equipment, (2) increase the system reliability by decreasing the chance for failure, and (3) make a more presentable-looking piece of equipment. The visual appearance of the equipment often identifies what type of maintenance is performed. If the equipment is clean, even spotless, it is probably safe to assume that its operational capability will be good. However, if the equipment is dirty, it follows that repair work accomplished will very likely be slovenly, crudely, or poorly accomplished, and eventual system deterioration is inevitable.

1-1.1   Analysis

Perhaps the term *analysis* is new to you. Its meaning as related to performance of tasks must be clearly understood in order for you to fully use the skills of a technician. Fortunately in the electronics career field all steps of analysis are logical; no arbitrary philosophies or generalities exist. So analysis consists of the following steps:

1. Determine the objective. This is accomplished by identifying the task to be accomplished, for example, perform a PMI or replace a lamp.
2. Determine the steps involved in the accomplishment of the task. In preventive maintenance routines the steps are listed. In removal and replacement of components the steps may or may not be listed in the technical reference.
3. Determine what principles, characteristics, or specific requirements must be considered while the task is being performed. These areas include (a) possible impact on the system, such as power requirements, interruption of system operation, partial loss of system capability; (b) physical adjacent subelements involved; (c) removal of other units to facilitate repair; and (d) the use of associated test equipment and testing procedures needed to effect repair.

Many areas are included in this type of work. Many types of devices are used to provide maintenance technicians with indicators to tell them that problem areas are developing. Some of these are visual indications such as lights, fuses, and switches; dirt and corrosion; meters and temperature readings: other indications are audio in nature, such as noisy motors and gears, squeaky belts and doors. Notice that, in these areas of responsibility, the tasks are related to both mechanical and electrical parts of the electronic and mechanical equipment. But you must also understand the equipment operation pertaining to these areas, and where to find the information about them.

1-1.2 Technical References

Since you are on a site and/or in a computer center, you probably know that your work cards (routine instruction cards) are designed and printed on hard card paper instead of on regular paper.

Another technical reference it is important for you to know and be able to identify is the one showing removal and replacement of components. This book is the reference manual, which usually includes a study of the principles of operation. The information and procedures for replacement of components are usually found in a section in the back of the manual.

1-2 Servicing, Inspecting, Replacing, and Validating

As we have discussed, cleanliness and operational readiness of even the smallest component in a system is of paramount importance. It is also necessary for you to be aware of the environmental and physical properties of moving parts that can cause deterioration to the functioning of the system. Let us explore a few applications of this preventative maintenance routine to see if the failure to do them well could result in failure of the entire system.

1-2.1 Cleaning and Lubricating Air-Conditioning Systems

With reference to Figure 1-1 a typical instruction could be *"Step 1. Inspect motor, belt, and attached squirrel cage for cleanliness, proper operation, satisfactory condition, and oil."* A simple enough step, rather routine and unglamorous. But what happens if the squirrel cage becomes clogged with dirt, or the belt dries and cracks, or the motor bearings become dry and burn? Your task is twofold:

1. Visually inspect the unit to determine its cleanliness, inspect the belt for cracks and wear, and listen for dry-running motor operation.

Fig. 1-1. Dirty Squirrel Cage

2. Clean and lubricate the unit. Failure to do the task well often results in equipment downtime.

Following is an analysis of the conditions listed above:

1. Decrease in air flow through the entire cabinet or system results if proper cleaning of the air-conditioning system is not performed. The reduction of air flow causes an increase in ambient temperature throughout the cabinet or system, increasing the possibility for intermittent failures.

2. A broken belt or frozen motor bearing causes equipment failure and results in unscheduled downtime loss.

Your job, then, is to prevent the need for troubleshooting and to prevent a system failure. Perform this routine with care and a definite attitude that the operation of the system depends on it.

The following are typical steps to be taken in servicing an air-conditioning system:

1. Shut off the power.
2. Obtain access to the unit.
3. Clean, inspect, and lubricate.
4. Reinstall and check.
5. Turn on the power.

1-2.2 Cleaning and Inspecting Cabinets, Drawers, and Modules

Again the enemy is dirt and dust, grime and grease. Again your job success depends on your ability to combat these agents (Figure 1-2). The dirty module shown may cause you to remember from your studies of the basic principles what effect these agents had on circuit components. With smaller units such as printed circuit boards, microelectronic circuits, and even the larger units with vacuum-tube circuits, these agents become extremely important. They may act as insulators or conductors or corrosive agents. They can often cause a distorted waveform, cause an oscillator frequency shift, or cause a phase shift in microseconds which could result in intermittent problems and equipment malfunction.

The following are typical steps to be taken in cleaning cabinets and assemblies:

1. Clean component boards, screen filters, air passages, and cables.
2. Vacuum-clean the cabinets to allow complete circulation of air.
3. Clean dirt and grime from the contacts to permit good electrical signal flow.

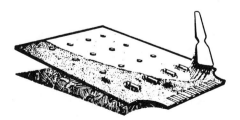

Fig. 1-2. Dirty Module

1-2.3 Inspecting and Servicing Read/Write Heads
Used with Magnetic Devices

A typical instruction could be: "Clean heads daily" or "Lubricate tape drives."

The two most dangerous enemies of magnetic tape/drum systems are:

1. Residue from the tape or drum surface being deposited on the heads.
2. Magnetizing of the heads themselves.

In data-processing systems, some form of storage is generally used. Often these systems employ drums coated with oxide or a magnetic tape unit for use with stored programs. These units require constant cleaning because of the properties of magnetic flux in the heads and the loss of oxide from the tape or drum surfaces to the heads. As the flux or oxide is transferred to the heads and surrounding area, signal loss increases and system signal deterioration rapidly increases. Range data, alert messages, and problem block data are often garbled, incomplete, and of no value.

1-2.4 Magnetic Flux and Oxide Deposits on Heads

What are we talking about? Look at Figure 1-3 and observe what happens as magnetic fields build up; notice how the response falls off. See why, because flux is present, less of the signal is passed into or out of the read/write heads. Again look at the figure and see how a buildup of oxide deposits interferes with the passing of signals into and from the tape when recording or playing.

The following are typical steps to be taken in servicing read/write heads:

1. Clean visually all dirt and oxidation from the heads.
2. Demagnetize heads according to specific instructions with the proper degaussing tool. (Remove built-up magnetic flux.)
3. Lubricate tape drives with the proper chemical agent.
4. Visually examine heads for pitting, cracks, scars, or any other indication that could result in signal loss. (Use a magnifying glass.)
5. Return equipment to operational status.
6. Check operational status.

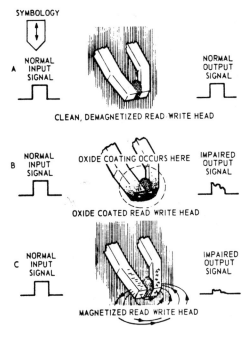

Fig. 1-3. Dirty Heads

We have examined some of the important areas in a data processor where failure of the maintenance man to perform his cleaning and lubricating task could result in the loss of equipment operational capability. The tasks in themselves are not difficult, but analysis of the task as described in this text explains their importance and relates the tasks to the impact these have on the equipment's operational capability. Let us now investigate another area of general maintenance.

1-3 Replacing Lights, Fuses, and Switches

In the system on which you are now working, lights, fuses, and switches are used in abundance. This is true for all data processors. These are of vital importance because they show you the operational capability of the data processor. As more of the systems are changed to solid-state and integrated circuits, quick reliable indicators such as lights or fuses are needed to speed the detection of failure. It then becomes necessary to understand how these indicators are built and installed. Physical features and principles of operation need to be analyzed. The impact on the system during the repair of the unit will be included as a part of the analysis to show the relationship to the task. Logical approaches and basic steps to replacing these components will develop as we study them.

The analysis of this subject includes a study of the types of lamps, their uses, and typical replacement procedures used to restore the circuits to normal operation; the types of fuses normally found in data processors; the types of fuse holders plus typical replacement procedures; and finally an analysis of the switches used on data processors and typical checkout and replacement procedures associated with switches.

1-3.1 *Lamp and Lamp Sockets*

Study Table 1 closely because it includes a description of the most common lamps used in data processors. These lamps come in various voltage ranges, sizes, and shapes. Common lamp nomenclatures are given

	DESCRIPTION	NUMBERS	SYMBOL	SCHEMATIC REF
1		GE 46 6–8V GE 112 1.2V		DS1
2		GE 47 6–8V GE 57 12–16V GE 313 28V GE 1819 28V GE 1820 28V GE 1929 28V GE 1847 6.3V		DS1
3		NE 2 65V START NE 51 65V START NE 2H 65V START	DC LAMP AC LAMP	NE DS1, 2
4		NE 2 65V START NE 2E 65V START NE 68 60V START NE 83 60V START		NE
5		GE 327 28V GE 328 6V GE 330 14V GE 381 6.3V GE 387 28V		DS1, 2

Table 1. Lamps

plus their voltage ratings. These are vital for you to understand in the event that you must replace lamps with substitute lamps. Some lamps even contain resistive and capacitive components internally.

By referring to Table 1 it is easy to see why each lamp requires a special type of socket. Consider the first lamp, the *screw base;* its socket is as shown in Figure 1-4. Since only two wires are used, its removal and

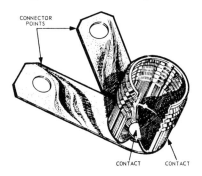

CONNECTOR POINTS

CONTACT   CONTACT

Fig. 1-4. Screw-Base Lamp

installation are relatively simple. Correct wire replacement to the terminals of the new socket must be followed when reinstalling a new lamp socket. Installing the wires on the wrong terminals is a modification of equipment and is not authorized unless directed.

The power must be turned off prior to removing a defective socket and installing a new socket. *Safety first*. Precautions must always be exercised when these units are worked on because, although the lamp may be using only a low-voltage dc or ac source, a shorting of the source voltage to the chassis can result in complete loss of power to the equipment and result in equipment operation loss.

A typical removal and reinstallation procedure:

1. Shut off the power.
2. Label the wires to be removed.
3. Unsolder the wires from the socket.
4. Solder the new socket to the wires.
5. Check continuity with a voltmeter.
6. Secure the socket to the chassis with a washer and a retaining nut.
7. Turn on the power and perform an operational check.

The *off-set prong plug-in lamp* requires a socket, as shown in Figure 1-5. Observe how one side of the socket has a cut higher than the other to accommodate the prongs on the side of the lamp. Also note that this socket usually contains a spring which pushes the base contact up to the lamp

OFFSET PRONG SOCKET

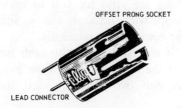

LEAD CONNECTOR

Fig. 1-5. Off-Set Prong Base

when the lamp is seated properly. The spring allows for insertion of the lamp to seat it properly.

1-3.2   *Installation of a Lamp*

1. Align the prongs on the lamp with the slots in the lamp socket.
2. Insert the lamp into the socket, depressing the spring base.
3. Twist the lamp and release it, allowing the prongs on the lamp to seat in the slots.

Removal procedures are the reverse of installation procedures. The replacement procedure for the lamp holder (socket) is the same as for the screw type.

The neon indicator of Table 1 is commonly used in data processors, where counter operations are shown, when error indicators are used and when register operation shows cycling operations. Some of these lamps contain internal resistive and capacitive networks plus lamp filaments. Most of the sockets designed to accommodate this type of lamp are generally two- to four-wire connected units. Refer to Figure 1-6 and observe the type of socket that is used. Replacement of this socket requires strict adherence to identification and replacement of leads when reinstallation is performed.

A typical installation of this lamp is shown in the schematic, Figure 1-7. These NE2 lamps are placed in series with the output of the flip-flops. Internally on these flip-flops the signal swing is from 0 to -30 V, depend-

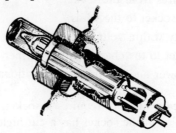

Fig. 1-6. Neon-Lamp Socket

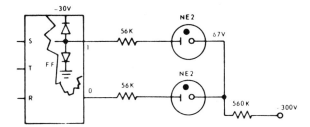

Fig. 1-7. Neon Lamp in a Circuit

ing upon the state of the flip-flop. When the output of the flip-flop is a logic 1 (0 V), there is an approximate 67-V difference of potential across the lamp and its lights. In the zero state, the difference of potential is only approximately 37 V, and ignition of the neon does not occur. The table shows that neon lamps need 65 V to start.

To stress safety in this area, consider that −300 V dc is lethal voltage; extreme caution *must* be exercised when working with this area, and the power *must* be turned off prior to removal and replacement of any lamp socket.

The neon lamp in Table 1 (4) is often part of a power supply, its purpose being regulation of the power supply. It may be a plug-in lamp with stiff leads; however, more commonly it is a lamp with no metal base, and it has flexible lead wires protruding from the glass envelope. In power supplies using this lamp (Figure 1-8), two wells filled with solder are installed to secure the leads of the lamp. Installing and removing consists of heating the envelope with a soldering iron, removing the lamp lead, and then inserting the new lamp lead in the molten solder. Again, any work performed in this area *must* be done with all the power turned off.

The final lamp in Table 1 (5) is a *subminiature lamp*. This lamp is pushed into a glass or plastic lens cover and the lens is then screwed into the socket, as shown in Figure 1-9. This lamp unit usually contains a two-wire connection; however, it may have multiple leads soldered to one of the two connector points. Strict observance of wire placement is necessary whenever you are removing or replacing the lamp base. Use procedures outlined in the description of the basic screw lamp.

Fig. 1-8. Neon Lamp in Solder Well

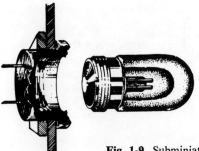

Fig. 1-9. Subminiature Lamp, Lens, and Base

The tasks involved in this area of work are basic and simple, yet a few specific practices do become important when analysis is applied. The steps to follow are:

1. Mark the wires to be removed and installed on the new socket.
2. Exercise care in removing and replacing a lamp from the socket after first determining the type of lamp used.
3. Turn off the power from the unit before starting repair action.
4. Employ proper soldering techniques in all cases.
5. Make a static check with a voltmeter for continuity prior to applying power.
6. Turn on the power and make a dynamic check.

Learn to recognize the various types of lamps from their appearance, size, use, and description on a schematic or wiring diagram and voltage ratings. Above all, observe and practice safety to protect yourself and the equipment. A mistake could burn or kill you. A mistake could also destroy your equipment and cause unscheduled downtime.

1-3.3   *Fuses and Fuse Holders*

We have already identified a fuse as an indicator for the maintenance man which will alert him to a defect or malfunction in the system. The primary use of any fuse is, of course, to protect an electronic unit from destruction by excessive current or voltage. This fact then leads to the analysis of fuse applications in the following terms:

1. Where are fuses normally installed?
2. What are the principles of fuse operation?
3. What sizes and shapes are they and what type holders are provided for them?

4. Finally, what comparisons are there between the removal and re-placement of the holder and those of the lamp holders just discussed?

Typically you will find a fuse in an input power line whether the source of the voltage is ac or dc. They may be installed on a drawer, a rack and a chassis, or in a cabinet. They may be remotely placed and still be wired to the circuits of a given unit. The important thing to know is where the fuse circuits are for your equipment. Air-conditioning systems, motors, and cabinet service lights are also examples of circuits that will be fused to prevent destruction by overload. On a wiring diagram you will probably see a fuse as a symbol like those shown in Figure 1-10. The designation will usually be F followed by a number. On the fuse itself will be a number. It will very likely look like the one shown in Figure 1-11.

The current-carrying element in a fuse melts when heated to temperatures in excess of about 170°F and opens, thereby removing the source voltage from a unit. Two factors are important in this analysis: (1) the type of material used for fusing and its melting properties, and (2) the principles of Ohm's law as applied to circuits using fuses. In the first instance the current-carrying element used in fuses is engineered to

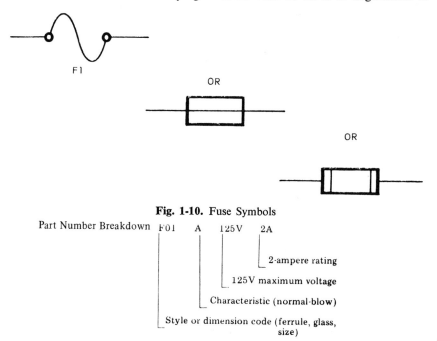

F1

OR

OR

Fig. 1-10. Fuse Symbols

Part Number Breakdown   F01   A   125V   2A

                                                    2-ampere rating

                                 125V maximum voltage

                    Characteristic (normal-blow)

      Style or dimension code (ferrule, glass, size)

Fig. 1-11. Fuse and Its Nomenclature

specific thicknesses, lengths, and widths to carry specific voltage and current loads. This metal will heat and remain intact, provided the applied heat does not exceed the melting point of the metal. Second, basic laws of electronics apply to selection of fuses for specific circuits. These are considerations of:

1. Total energy dissipation.
2. Total amperage needed to maintain circuit operation.
3. Total voltage requirements.

How does Ohm's law apply to fuses?

Ohm's law: $I = E/R$, or $R = E/I$, or $E = IR$, or $P = IE$

where

I = amperes, E = voltage, R = resistance, and P = power.

Consider a unit using a 125-V, 2-A fuse. Consider also that the fuse will blow at exactly 2 A. What effect can an increase in line voltage have on the fuse? Using the formula $I = E/R$, $I = 2$ A, $E = 125$ V, and R is the resistance of the fuse:

$$\uparrow 2 \text{ A} = \frac{125 \uparrow}{R \rightarrow} = \text{blown fuse} \qquad \text{arrows indicate a change}$$

With the resistance of the fuse wire as a constant, an increase in line voltage causes an increase in current, and the fuse melts. Another problem. What effect can a decrease in resistance within the circuits cause? The power formula $P = E^2/R$ is used. A short circuit in the operating unit will very likely lower the total resistance of the unit to almost ground potential and increase the power requirements by increasing current flow. Since power is related to heat, the fuse filament will develop more heat and burn through.

$$P = E^2/R = \text{blown fuse}$$

Another basic principle of electronics is Kirchhoff's law. All energy is dissipated through the circuit. By looking at the schematic in Figure 1-12, observe how the current will flow into the entire circuit through the fuse. It will not flow through the NE2 lamp circuit because of the resistance in the NE lamp. However, if the fuse blows, the current path is through the NE2 lamp. This lamp circuit will draw very little current and no damage

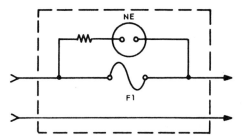

Fig. 1-12. NE Lamp and Fuse Circuit

NO.	TYPE PICTORIAL	SIZE VOLT AMP RATING	DESCRIPTION USES/APPLICATION
1.	FAST BLOW (FB)	125V/250V .01/10A 1-1/4" L X 1/4" Dia. 1" L X 1/4" Dia. 5/8 X 5/64	Metal ends with a glass or ceramic cylinder between the ends. Blows instantly with input surges or shorts.
2.	SLOW BLOW (SB)	125V/250V .01/30A 1-1/4" X 1/4" Dia.	Similar to Fastblow in size, except this fuse is designed to withstand heavy surges for a short time period but will blow instantly on shorts.
3.	FUSE WIRE	125/250V Variable amps depending upon the diameter of the wire.	A strand of malleable wire designed to melt as any other fuse. However, this fuse is usually connected between terminals and not put in a fuse holder. This wire may also be used to repair reparable fuses.
4.	REPARABLE FUSE REMOVABLE ENDS	125/440V Variable to 100 amps, sizes vary with amperage and voltage requirements.	This fuse has screw-type end connectors which, when removed from the center cylinder, allow for replacement of the fuse wire.
5.	SNAP-IN FUSE HOLDER	Size and weight is determined by the size of fuse to be held.	Built to accommodate short and long FB and SB fuses as well as reparable fuses.
6.	FUSE HOLDER WITHOUT LAMP	1-11/32" X 5/8" overall. Voltage ranges to 250V @ 15 amps. 1-5/8" X 5/8"	Fuse holder with a twist ↄp. Top is removed by slight inward pressure and twisting the release. Internal contact is backed by a spring to allow for removal and installation of a fuse.
7.	FUSE HOLDER WITH NEON INDICATOR IN THE CAP	Approximately 2-3/8" L X 5/8" Dia. Voltage ranges 2.5V to 250V @ 20 amps.	Fuse holder with a neon indicator in the cap. This neon lights when the fuse blows (refer to text for description.)

Table 2. Fuse and Fuse Holders

will result to the circuit. This circuit is employed where a visible indicator is used to show a blown fuse.

Refer to Table 2 and study the different types of fuses normally found in data processors, computers, and ancillary equipment. Compare these types with ones used in your system. Compare the holders in your equipment with the ones shown in the table. Prove that fuses in your system are installed where this text states, that symbols are drawn as shown here, and that fuses are labeled as indicated in this text by analyzing your system and technical reference data.

Fuse holders can become damaged and require replacement. The most common causes of damage are heat and mechanical abuse. If holders are corroded, dirty, or they loosely hold the fuse, they will heat. The heat in turn can damage the insulating material in the holder. The heating condition will get worse with time, and the holder will have to be replaced.

By observation of the fuse holders shown in the table it is easy to see that only two connectors will usually have to be unsoldered and resoldered when replacing a fuse holder. The tasks of replacing a fuse holder and the replacement of the lamp socket are so nearly alike that a restatement of the typical steps will apply to almost all work done on a fuse-holder replacement.

The following are typical steps to be taken when removing and replacing a fuse holder:

1. Mark the wires to be removed.
2. Turn off the power before starting any repair action.
3. Exercise care in removing the unit.
4. Employ proper soldering techniques in all cases.
5. Make a static check with a voltmeter for continuity prior to applying power.
6. Insert a new fuse of the proper voltage and amperage rating and size and type.
7. Turn on the power and make a dynamic check.

The analysis has shown that the task of replacing a fuse holder parallels that of replacing lamp sockets. Analysis has also shown that various types of fuses exist for specific purposes. An element in a fuse is designed to carry or handle a specific maximum voltage and current source. Exceeding these values causes the filament to melt, protecting the circuit. Also, the analysis pointed out that a short circuit in the equipment will melt a circuit fuse. An interpretation of this study indicates that exact replacement of a fuse *with both proper voltage* and *current ratings* must be installed. Exact replacement types, such as *fast blow* or *slow blow,* must be used.

1-3.4 Switches

The final subject to be studied in this area of maintenance is the *switch.* We have been using switches all our lives. We turn on lights, appliances, and entertainment devices with them. We know that power is applied to these devices when the switch is turned ON and power is removed when the switch is turned OFF. In computing and processing equipment the same types of switches are used for power ON and OFF. Switches are designed for many other uses. Two broad uses of switches are for (1) digital input and (2) command input.

A switch designed as a *digital input* device will provide the input source with a static level logic 1, a dynamic level 1, or a pulse train. It may even provide the source with an octal input. A switch designed as a *command input* device will provide *preset, reset, advance, repeat cycle,* and other short-duration machine command signals. This study shows how these switches are used and the types of switches usually associated with digital or command inputs. Along with the descriptions of various types of switches are examples of their reference symbols, their schematic symbols, internal functions such as coil operations, and lamp circuits associated with these switches.

Since defects in switches are common to almost all types of switches, the list of tasks about the repairing or replacing of them is explained as a common element instead of individually. Removal and replacement techniques are once again related to the characteristics of lamp- and fuse-replacing procedures.

Following are the types of switches available and their related applications:

TOGGLE SWITCH. The most common switch is the *toggle switch.* Refer to Table 3 (1) for a pictorial description of this switch type. This switch may be designed as a single pole–single throw (SPST) having two fixed conditions, *ON* or *OFF.* However, it may be spring-loaded, as in the case of a *reset switch,* where it can be turned ON and will spring back to OFF when released. The spring-loaded version is usually found in command or control circuitry. This is where a reset pulse must be employed, or a clear pulse or preset pulse is needed. In any use listed, a pulse of relatively short duration is required, and the spring-loaded toggle switch is effective.

SPRING-LOADED PUSHBUTTON MICROSWITCH. A switch used in a manner similar to the toggle switch is the spring-loaded pushbutton micro-

NO.	TYPE AND ILLUSTRATION	DESCRIPTION/USE
1.	Toggle	a. Two position OFF, ON, Normally Open (NO), Normally Closed (NC). b. Two position NO, NC c. SPST, Single Pole Single Throw. d. DPDT, Double Pole Double Throw. (not shown) multiple connectors in series. e. Spring loaded in one direction. f. Primary uses. (1) Control of voltage and current-- ON-OFF. (2) Reset, Preset, Command Control of digital circuits.
2.	Microswitch, circular	a. Two position ON-OFF, spring loaded contactor. b. Command uses, Reset, Preset control of digit circuits.
3.	Pushbutton Switch w/Lamp Indicators	a. Pushbutton switch with: (1) Lamp indicator for either OFF, or ON or both. (2) Contact connectors NO, NC, C. (3) Holding coil for locking in either NO or NC. b. Holding coil may not be used as lock, requiring independent release. c. Lamps may be OFF or ON or may contain dual lamp circuit where one or more lamps will always be on. d. Primary uses: (1) Digital input device, entering codes, bits, presetting wired configurations, advancing. (2) Command uses, transfer, clear, erase, reset.
4.	Microswitch, rectangular cased with Level Contactor	a. A rectangular encased switch with 2 external connectors. b. Connector ball is usually depressed by a spring tension arm assembly. c. Uses--controlling operations of electromechanical devices.

Table 3. Switches

switch. Its description [see Table 3 (2)] is different, but its function is exactly the same as the spring-loaded toggle switch. The schematic symbol and reference designation for both types of switches are shown in Figure 1-13.

PUSHBUTTON WITH LAMP INDICATOR. Another type of switch commonly found in data processors and display consoles is the pushbutton

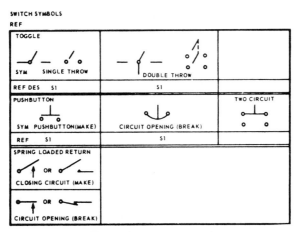

Fig. 1-13. Switch Symbols

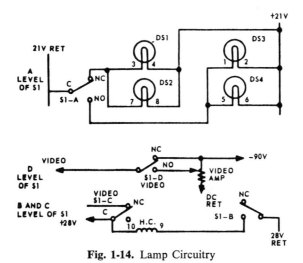

Fig. 1-14. Lamp Circuitry

type of switch with a lamp indicator under the pushing surface [see Table 3 (3)]. This type of switch comes in two types, the nonholding or spring-release return, and the holding type. The holding type employs a holding coil which latches the switch in the ON position when depressed. The second pressing of the switch releases the voltage from the holding coil and returns the switch to its OFF condition. In some applications the holding coil voltage may be removed by another switch remote from the original switch.

In both these types of switches, the holding and nonholding, lamp circuits are employed to identify the condition of the switch, ON or OFF.

Observe the schematic in Figure 1-14 and analyze how two of the lights (DS1 and DS2) are lighted when the switch is OFF and how two different lights (DS3 and DS4) are lighted when the switch is ON. Trace the paths for current flow to prove this analysis. Also observe how the holding coil shown in the schematic is energized and deenergized as a result of the switch action. Trace its current path. Always remember that all circuits function only when the path for current flow is complete.

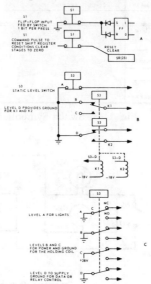

Fig. 1-15. Multilevel Switch

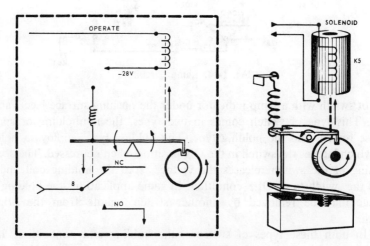

Fig. 1-16. Microswitch in Use

The switch shown in Figure 1-15 is usually employed in digital units. It may be used as shown in part A to enter a static level 1 to register or counter each time it is depressed. Or, as shown in parts B and C, it may be connected to relays to provide a pulse train in binary, binary coded decimal, gray code, octal, or a special code prepared for a specialized circuit.

MICROSWITCH. The *microswitch* used in mechanical devices is another switch commonly found in input/output devices [see Table 3 (4)]. This switch is often placed in a drive unit so that closing its contacts causes a cycle to repeat or stop. Figure 1-16 shows that when the switch is depressed by the pivoted arm of the cam, it breaks the cycle and causes a change in operation. These microswitches are spring-loaded. When the pivot arm is removed, the switch is returned to its normal state.

We have discussed the various switches used in computers and processors. Now let us analyze malfunctions that might be attributed to them. Identify the repairs that are required, and remember that safety starts with *shutting off the power.*

Defects that occur most often are:

1. Defective spring.
2. Broken contact.
3. Burned contact.
4. Shorted contacts.
5. Charred switch body.

Signs of defects are:

1. Sticking spring-loaded switch.
2. No continuity when checked.
3. Loose toggle.
4. Improper placement of microswitch unit.
5. Improper solder connection.
6. Nonoperating holding coil.

Replacing switches is a task similar to replacing lamps or fuse holders. Since switches may have more than two connections, exact replacement of wires is an absolute must. Some switches, such as the push and lock, with lamp circuits and holding coils, have as many as 12 pins. Since these are arranged in rows, they are often designated by A, B, C, D, or 1, 2, 3, 4. Each row could have a normally open (NO), common (C), or normally closed (NC) connector. Identification of wires prior to their removal from the defective unit is a must.

1. Disconnect the power.
2. Carefully label all wires for exact replacement.
3. Remove wires by using proper unsoldering techniques (if soldered).
4. Position and solder the new switch to the leads.
5. Secure the switch to the cabinet.
6. Perform a static check with a voltmeter.
7. Perform a dynamic check with power applied to
    a. Ensure that all lights work properly.
    b. Ensure that the coil holds or the spring releases.
    c. Ensure that the switch is positioned properly.
    d. Ensure that mechanical operation is as specified in the technical order.

1-4   Inspect and Service Electrical and Mechanical Connectors (Jacks, Plugs, Cable Connectors)

Inspection and servicing of connectors is again in the area of general maintenance. You were studing the soldering connections in the case of lights, fuses, and switches. Now you are going to study the solderless connector. The study consists of recognizing the types of connectors and learning which to use when repairing the connectors. It also shows typical problems or defects that can be detected during inspections. Finally, it shows a typical repair procedure.

1-4.1   Types of Connectors

Figure 1-17 shows two examples of connectors used in data-processing equipment. Either connector, although used in different places in the equipment, will perform the same function, which is to connect circuits through electrical connections to transfer data or voltages. The two types of connectors are manufactured for as few as 1 wire connection to as many as 225 wire connections. Each pin in a multiple-pin connector is labeled (see Figure 1-17). Lettering is usually used in preference to numbers, beginning with a through z (i, o, and q are never used) and continuing with aa through zz if necessary. The connector pins in some equipment are labeled with numerals. Numbering on the units usually follows general reading rules. For example, the pins may be designated a and b on row 1 across, c and d on row 2 across, and so on through to the end. Or they

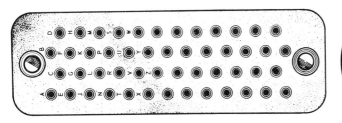 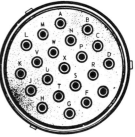

Fig. 1-17. Types of Connectors

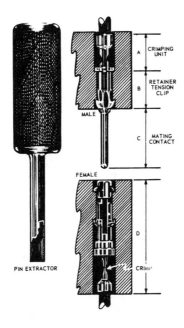

Fig. 1-18. Solderless Connector Pin with Body

may be labeled a, b, c, and so on, clockwise in circular cable connectors.

On the multiple connector bodies, solderless pins, both male and female, are designed to hold a single wire and are designed to be inserted into a connector body (see Figure 1-18). Each pin has three basic sections: A, the wire-retaining section, which is crimped to hold the unit; B, the spring-tension section, which is designed to lock the pin in place in the hole provided in the connector body; and C, the male or female mating unit. Looking at D, the cutaway cross section of a typical connector body, observe how a ridge is employed to accept the spring-tension clip (the B portion of the pin). When inserted in the connector body, the pin locks in place. Removal of this pin requires an extraction tool (see Figure 1-18).

It is designed to slide over the spring-tension clip, compress the spring, and allow removal of the pin.

1-4.2   Types of Crimping Tools

Many companies manufacture crimping tools. However, each crimper is designed to perform the same function—secure a wire to the pin by crimping a portion of the pin around the wire with enough pressure to retain the wire. Crimpers are designed to allow their function to be performed on all sizes of wire and pins. For instance, a crimper used to fasten a pin to #22 wire would have a very small opening (see Figure 1-19), whereas a size #12 wire would require a crimper with a wider opening to accommodate the larger wire and pin.

When removing, replacing, or modifying the jacks, plugs, or connectors on equipment, research the manufacturers's publication to determine which tool is used for each size of wire and pin used in the system.

1-4.3   Inspections

What do you look for when making inspections of jacks, plugs, and cables? In both the metal- and the plastic-body type of connector, certain

Fig. 1-19. Crimping Tool

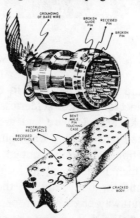

Fig. 1-20. Defective Connectors

defects will be visible. You can use them as indicators of trouble spots. Some of the more prevalent connector problems are (see Figure 1-20):

1. A recessed pin. In this case a male or female pin has either slipped back into the connector body because of a broken clip, lack of a spring-tension clip, or a broken plastic recess catch. It will not mate properly with the male or female connector and intermittent electrical connection occurs. Heat at the point of contact between the male and female connections can result, causing burning or melting of the plastic body used to hold the pins.
2. Loose-fitting pins. This problem occurs when a pin is pushed to one side instead of properly mating. Again intermittent electrical connection or shorts may result and heat builds up.
3. Cracked or broken plastic connectors.
4. Bare-wire contact with the metal casing in metal connectors. Happens especially at the clamp that secures wires that enter the rear of the connector.
5. Defective threads or missing guide pins on metal connectors.

Before analyzing the typical steps involved in removing and replacing jacks, plugs, and cable connectors, let us define the symbology used in the technical data. As outlined in the *Military standards,* and by other agencies, connectors are referenced according to the following rules:

1. "The movable [less fixed] connector of a mating pair shall be designated P. . . ."
2. "The stationary [more fixed] connector of a mating pair shall be designated J or X. . . ."
3. "A connector P on a flexible cable shall mate with a fixed connector designated J rather than X."
4. "If two cables are connected, each of the connectors will be labeled P."
5. "A connector to mount an item . . . shall be designated with an X prefix if its mate is directly mated [not on a flexible cable] to the mounted item. . . ."

Further explanation of these rules then brings out these factors:

1. A plug will be designated P when it is attached to a cable or is the less fixed of two connections. (Refer to rule 1 above.)

2. Jacks J will designate the other unit the plug matches. (Refer to rule 2 above.)

3. No designation is provided to indicate the male or female portions of mating pairs.

4. A printed circuit card (PCB) or similar module will not be labeled P but will have an equipment location number. The receptacle for the PCB will use the X designator before the location number. Example: PCB A3 goes in location XA3. (Refer to rule 5 above.)

1-4.4 Typical Removal and Replacement of Multiple Connectors

One very helpful feature in the manufacture of multiple lead cables is that the cable strands are twist-paired and color-coded. This feature is invaluable in troubleshooting and in marking.

1. Carefully mark each wire position and color code prior to starting any repair. This may be done by using a piece of masking tape on each wire and labeling each wire with its location letter or number designation taken from the old connector. Another method is to prepare a chart with a layout of each pin as seen on the connector. Then write the wire color code adjacent to the pinhole number.

2. Turn off the power before proceeding with any work.

3. Disconnect the connector from the panel (if applicable).

4. Release pins with a pin extractor.

5. Insert pins in the new connector if all pins are in good condition.

6. Replace defective pins.

7. Examine the connector to make sure that pins are properly seated and that there are no cracks or frayed or loose wiring.

8. Secure the connector to the frame (if applicable).

9. Secure the mating unit to the repaired or replaced connector and carefully match the guide pin.

10. Turn on the power and make dynamic checks where applicable.

Inspecting and servicing of connectors is a task that requires a careful, conscientious effort by you. Your attention must focus on the elements listed in this text and peculiar factors of your equipment when looking for trouble spots. You must select a definite method of identification of wires before removing them from the connector to be changed. You must ensure 100 percent accuracy and quality when reinstalling the pins. Further, if you must replace a pin, you must use the correct crimping tool for each size of wire and pin. Finally, you must be able to recognize deficiencies and relate them to symptoms of possible trouble.

TEST QUESTIONS

1. What are two indications of equipment output that would indicate a need for cleaning the equipment?

2. What classification of maintenance is usually given to cleaning tasks?

3. What is usually the first step of any cleaning task?

4. What expected results can a dirty read/write head produce?

5. What results can be expected if while changing a lamp the lamp is shorted to the chassis?

6. Why must an exact replacement fuse be used when one has blown?

7. Is there a difference between replacing a fuse holder and a lamp socket?

8. What are five defects that usually result in replacement of a switch?

9. If a charred socket around a pin within a connector is detected, what was probably the cause?

10. What are at least two tasks used in removing and replacing a connector that are common to removing switches?

2

Soldering Techniques for Replacing Defective Components

All users of computer equipment prefer to have maximum availability of all equipment component spares and units on hand at all times and in serviceable condition. This trend has resulted in a philosophy of maximum on-site repair of electronic equipment and a minimum of depot overhaul. Naturally the maintenance man will have work to perform, but with the proper training and acquisition of skills, the tasks are relatively simple. This study shows how basic the tasks are, and how common maintenance techniques apply to a great variety of the task applications. As you study this text and are given more responsibilities in your work area, you will attain the skill necessary to maintain the equipment. This study:

1. Recaps component replacement and testing techniques previously developed.
2. Identifies where technical data can be obtained for the repair, replacement, and checkout of components.
3. Develops the knowledge needed and lists the tools to be used for soldering and desoldering.
4. Develops typical task lists for repair and replacement of components on a PCB, microelectronic assemblies, and modular repair.
5. Identifies special attention areas within typical applications.

2-1 Replacement Techniques

In the study presented in Chapter 1, typical replacement techniques were identified. These techniques were common for the replacement of electronic and mechanical components, including such items as switches, light sockets, fuse holders, motors, fans, gears, moving cams, belt-driven units, and the dismantling and reinstallation of fixed subassemblies and assemblies. Also identified were two types of testing which must be accomplished in conjunction with repairs. These tests are the static and the dynamic. The *static test* is generally accomplished with visual inspections and continuity checks. The *dynamic test* is usually performed with power applied using a standard performance check, such as a PMI. To help you recall the techniques previously listed, study the following list.

1. Shut off the power.
2. Label any and all wires to be removed.
3. Disconnect any jacks or plugs that may be used on the assembly to be repaired.
4. Unsolder any wires as required.
5. Remove any assembly or subassembly to facilitate access to the defective unit as required.
6. Follow prescribed directions as outlined in technical orders or contractor manuals for removal, repair, and reinstallation.
7. Remove the assembly or component and replace with a serviceable assembly or component.
8. Reinstall all wires, jacks, and accessories.
9. Make a static check.
10. Connect the power and make dynamic checks to ensure that specifications as stated are measured.

By this time in our study of general maintenance it is becoming evident that reference materials are prepared according to their purpose. In the task of soldering and replacing components, certain chapters are used again because they do provide the information necessary to maintain the equipment. The maintenance chapter may contain subjects related to the task, which are (1) disassembly, repair, and replacement, including general parts replacement, and removal and replacement; (2) reassembly and testing; and (3) performance tests.

The illustrated parts section of a reference manual may provide (1) a pictorial view of the component you may have to repair or replace; (2) a part number for ordering the replacement needed; and (3) a category listing telling you if the part is recoverable, may be thrown away, or must be locally manufactured.

A general shop practice manual, if available, may provide information on soldering and repairs. The data pertaining to soldering may parallel reference materials prepared by National Aeronautics and Space Administration (NASA) publications NPC 200-4, NPC 200-4a, and NPC 275-1.

This study of soldering contains explanations of (1) the tools used in soldering; (2) the nature of solder; (3) good and bad solder joints and examination listings; (4) preparation of tools, components, and circuit boards; (5) application of solder to components, wiring, and circuit boards; (6) special applications when using microelectronic circuits; and (7) a list of terms in the glossary.

2-2 Tools

2-2.1 *Insulation Strippers*

Thermal strippers, shown in Figure 2-1, are usually not found in work centers, but, if they are used, their operation requires the placing of the wire to be stripped between the electrodes, which will then melt the insulation. Heat is applied and controlled by the selection switch. A safety factor must be observed when using this unit, which is that an exhaust-hood and fan-ventilation system must be used to exhaust toxic fumes, such as polytetrafluoroethylene (Teflon) or poly (vinyl chloride).

Precision cutting-type strippers, shown in Figure 2-2, are designed to accommodate various sizes of wire normally used in electronics. Use the

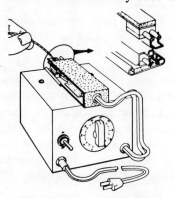

Fig. 2-1. Thermal Strippers

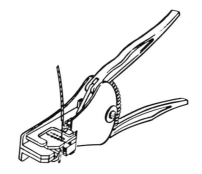

Fig. 2-2. Cutting Strippers

Fig. 2-3. Bending Tools

hole provided for the specific wire size to prevent damage to the wire by nicking.

2-2.2 Bending Tools

Bending tools, as shown in Figure 2-3, are those that have smooth bending surfaces so that no nicking, ringing, or other damage to the component can occur. Nonmetallic tools such as a spedger or soldering aid may be used.

2-2.3 Soldering Irons

Soldering-iron size (tip size and shape, voltage and wattage rating) and temperature should be selected and controlled according to the work to be performed. Temperature may be controlled through the use of a variable power supply, tip selection, or both.

2-2.4 Thermal Shunts

Thermal shunts or *heat sinks* will be used to protect heat-sensitive components such as semiconductors, crystal devices, meter movements, insulating materials, and so on, from damage due to heat while soldering.

FELT-TIPPED TWEEZER

ANTI-WICKING TWEEZERS

Fig. 2-4. Thermal Shunts

These devices, shown in Figure 2-4, are placed or clamped in place so that they prevent the heat from reaching the component while its leads are being soldered.

2-2.5 *Tools and Materials for Cleaning—General*

1. Braided, shielded tool (see Figure 2-5A).
2. Erasers, typewriter (see Figure 2-5B).
3. Eraser shield.
4. Alcohol dispenser.
5. Medium-stiff natural or synthetic bristle brush.
6. Industrial lint-free cleaning tissue.
7. Soldering-iron holder.
8. Single-cut file.
9. Electrician's scissors.
10. Round-nosed pliers (small).
11. Diagonal pliers (small).
12. End-cutting tweezers.
13. Small wire brush.
14. Sponge with holder.
15. Vice, electrical.
16. Solder SN60, SN63.
17. Toenail clippers.
18. Antiwicking tweezers 20, 21, and 22 AWG.

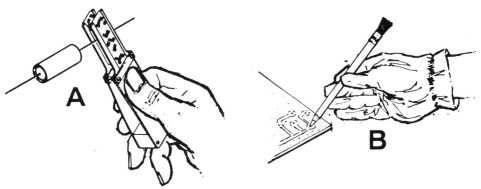

Fig. 2-5. Cleaning Tools

This tool is useful for the removal of gold plating from solder areas.

2-3   The Nature of Solder

Any discussion of soldering techniques should begin with an explanation of solder. This generally accepted substance is thought to be quite simple in nature, and so it is when proper preparation, materials, and techniques are employed.

Ordinary soft solder is a fusible alloy consisting essentially of tin and lead and used for the purpose of joining together two or more metals at temperatures below their melting point. In addition to tin and lead, soft solders occasionally contain varying amounts of antimony, bismuth, cadmium, or silver, which are added for the purpose of varying the physical properties of the alloy. However, some of these elements are present as impurities in many solders. Soft solder secures attachment by virtue of a metal solvent or intermetallic solution action that takes place at a relatively low temperature. The distinction between fusion and solution may be illustrated as follows: Ordinary table salt (sodium chloride) has to be heated to 1,488°F before it melts. However, when a little water is added, it melts easily without any heat. The action of molten solder on a metal like copper or steel may therefore be compared to the action of water on salt; the solder secures attachment by dissolving a small amount of the copper or steel at a temperature considerably below its melting point.

Since the soldering process involves a metallurgical or metal solvent action between the solder and the metal being joined, it is obvious that a solder joint is chemical in character rather than purely physical because the attachment is formed in part by chemical action rather than by mere physical adhesion. The properties of a solder joint are therefore different from those of the original solder, because in the metallurgical process of soldering, the solder, as a result of the action between the respective metals, is partly converted to a new and different alloy, with the formation of a completely new metallic contact.

Thus a soldered connection is continuous in metal continuity while an unsoldered one is discontinuous; when two metals are soldered together, they behave like a single solid metal, but when bolted, wired, or otherwise physically attached, there are still two pieces of metal and, because there is an insulating film of oxide on the surfaces of the metals, they are not even in physical contact.

The permanence as well as the character of the soldered connection is also different. The solder alloy lends itself to stresses and strains due to temperature change without rupture of the joint, while an unsoldered connection becomes more and more loosened by small differential movement from temperature variations and by the gradual accumulation of an increasingly thick film of nonmetallic oxide barrier on the metal surface.

Soldering also provides a different form of attachment from electroplating, in which the metals adhere by physical attachment only. It is important to emphasize that electroplated metals are not successfully soldered by alloying solder to the plating; the metal solvent action must proceed through the thin, physically attached plating to the base metal itself, where the alloy action must form. Plating a metal preserves its soldering quality but does not assist in the soldering itself.

The soldering operation involves the partial creation of a new alloy, but not necessarily the same alloy as that of the original solder. The tensile strength, shear strength, creep strength, and similar physical properties of a soldered connection, therefore, depend on the extent to which alloy formation has taken place during soldering and are subject to wide variation, owing to the important variables in soldering technique. It is important to appreciate that the properties of a soldered connection are not necessarily those of the original solder.

To understand fully alloy or solvent action on molten solder it is essential to consider the tin–lead fusion diagram, Figure 2-6. From the figure you can see that when tin is added to lead, which melts at 621°F, it lowers the melting point of lead along line *AC;* also, when lead is added to tin, which melts at 450°F, it lowers the melting point along line *BC.* At point *C,* where these two lines meet, there is an alloy of the lowest melting point of the metals, tin and lead. The alloy at this point, known as the *eutectic composition,* consists of 63 percent tin and 37 percent lead and has a sharp and distinct melting point, at 361°F.

The characteristic of eutectic (the point at which no plastic state exists) solder is very beneficial to the soldering process. Since the solder

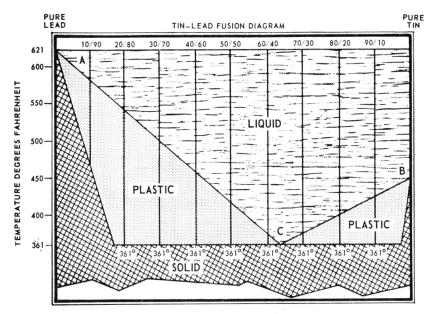

Fig. 2-6. Tin–Lead Fusion Diagram

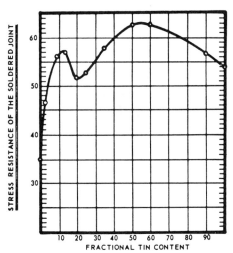

Graph showing the change in joining quality of tin—lead solders
with increase in tin content, based on resistance of the soldered
joint to a simulated bending and torsional stress.

Fig. 2-7. SN63 Solder

melts at a very low temperature and goes from a solid to a liquid at this
point, it is very good for soldering heat-sensitive components or for any
soldering operation in which too much heat could be harmful.

Several other alloys have a eutectic characteristic; however, they also have disadvantages. One example is 62.5 percent tin, 36.1 percent lead, and 1.4 percent silver; this is good solder but expensive. Another example is 97.5 percent lead and 2.5 percent silver; however, this gives a dull gray appearance to the solder joint.

The advantages of SN63 solder are further emphasized by Figure 2-7. From the diagram you can see that the addition of a little tin to lead is reflected in a sharp increase in the quality of the solder joint, which continues until the alloy contains 15 percent tin. Further addition of tin beyond 15 percent lowers the joint quality somewhat, after which it again increases sharply, until the solder contains about 60 percent tin. Beyond 60 percent tin, there is again a slight gradual decrease in the overall joint quality of the soldered connection. Can you see that the maximum points in the alloy quality curve correspond closely to the critical points in the tin–lead fusion diagram, that it is the lowest usable melting point, and that it has the highest pull strength, occurring nearly at the same point?

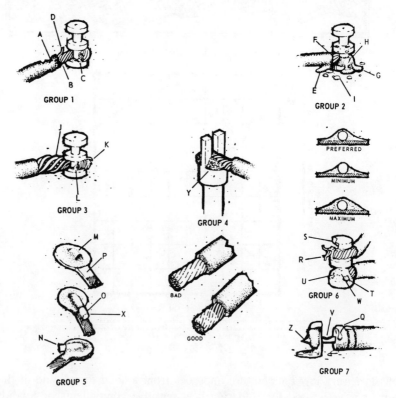

Fig. 2-8. Good and Bad Solder Joints

There is one item which, when present, can destroy a solder joint. Everything, including your iron, parts, wire, and solder, can be affected. They all must be free of dirt and grease. After the joint has been formed, it must be cleansed again. The solder joint isn't any better than what you put into it. If at any point in the operation you carry impurities to the joint, it will not be a good joint. You can go even farther than that and say it will definitely be rejected.

2-4 Flux

Flux is a substance used in soldering and is chemically compatible with the solder core flux.

Table 4. Standards for Soldering

Standard	Title
MIL-S-45743A (M1)	Soldering High-Reliability Electrical Connections
O-E-760b	Alcohol Spec
MIL-F-14256C	Flux Spec
QPL-14256C	Flux Supply List
QPL-QQ-S-571d	Solder Spec
QQ-S-571d	Solder Supply List
MIL-STD-252A	Wired Equipment Classification of Mechanical and Visual Defects
MIL-STD-275B	Printed Wiring for Electrical Equipment
MIL-STD-454A	Standard General Requirements for Electrical Equipment
QQ-R-571b	Rods, Welding, Copper, and Nickel Alloys Spec
MIL-S-006872A	Soldering Process, General Specifications for

2-5 Good and Bad Solder Joints

Figure 2-8 shows the difference between good and bad solder joints. Study these illustrations carefully and learn to recognize the faulty joints by comparison with the good. From your study you should have come to these conclusions about good solder joints:

1. Solder must not cover the entire surface of the unit being soldered so thickly that it obscures the shape of the unit.

2. The solder must be uniformly distributed over the unit and base metal.
3. No residue such as flux or oxide is left on the surfaces.
4. No solder reaches the shield of the wire.

It is a fairly short list for a good solder joint, yet it does cover all the important points of inspection necessary to identify a good solder joint. Now study the list below and identify how many of the soldering defects you can see in Figure 2-8. Select a defect found in the figure and write its corresponding letter in the space provided for it on the list. Stay within each group.

Group 1
___charred insulation
___insulation gap too long
___broken strand
___insufficient solder

Group 2
___melted insulation
___scratches in solder
___spilled solder
___solder or rosin splattered on sur- face
___insulation gap too short

Group 3
___lead improperly formed
___bird caging
___no fillet

Group 4
___fractured joint

Group 5
___insufficient lead length
___bare copper along lead
___bare lead length
___excessive lead length
___lead misplaced

Group 6
___damaged terminal
___foreign material at cut end
___strands misplaced at cut end
___pits in solder
___excess solder

Group 7
___points and/or bumps in solder
___solder splattered on component
___scraped lead

ANSWERS:
GROUP 1: A, B, D, C
GROUP 2 E, H, G, J, F
GROUP 3: K, J, L
GROUP 4: Y
GROUP 5: M, P, O, X, N
GROUP 6: S, T, R, U, W
GROUP 7: Z, Q, V

2-6 Preparation

The tools and the surfaces to be soldered must be prepared properly if a successful solder joint is to be effected. This includes the (1) soldering iron, (2) the component leads that are to be soldered, and (3) the circuit and pad.

2-6.1 *Soldering-Iron Tip*

Every time a soldering iron is to be used, it must be examined to ascertain its condition for use in the soldering task to be performed. It should be:

1. Properly connected or screwed into the holder.
2. Free of oxides.
3. Shaped properly for the task it is to perform.
4. Timed.

If one or more of these items is not as it should be, preparation should proceed as follows:

1. Scale oxides from the tip surface with an abrasive cloth, as in the case of *iron* or *plated tips.*
2. Form the tip into the proper shape by filling. This must be done on *unplated copper tip* because of pitting, burning, and oxidation to the tip surface.
3. Heat the iron to the minimum point at which solder will melt and lightly coat the entire soldering point.

To maintain a clean tip after the iron has been prepared, prepare a wet sponge, either natural or synthetic, and use it to wipe heated tips to remove dirt, grease, flux, oil, or any foreign matter, which could, if allowed to remain, become part of the solder joint and cause the joint to be classed as defective.

2-6.2 *Component*

Each component, wire, or terminal to be installed in a circuit requires physical handling during its manufacturing, processing, and shipping. Further handling by you is required to shape the leads properly, cut the leads, and so on. After all handling is done:

1. Clean the surfaces that are to be soldered with the braided cleaning tool.

2. Dip the stiff bristle brush in alcohol and brush the cleaned surfaces.

3. Dry with an industrial lint-free rag or paper.

2-6.3 Circuit Board

The above list of do's for preparation also applies to circuit boards. However, circuit boards are composed of many substances that can easily be harmed, so the wire braided brush must *not* be used; instead, use a white typewriter eraser. The eraser is very effective because it can be sharpened to a point and easily controlled. Use it to remove dirt, contaminants, gold plating, and any other foreign substances from the pad or pads to be soldered; clean with alcohol and a brush; dry.

2-6.4 Forming

Forming leads from components to properly fit the circuit in which they will be installed requires close examination and careful handling to assure success. To bend the component leads (see Figure 2-9):

1. Use a bending tool in such a manner that the radius of the bend is equal to twice the thickness of the lead wire.

2. Form the bend no closer than $\frac{1}{16}$ inch from the component body.

3. Center the component between its solder connections unless specifications dictate otherwise (Figure 2-9B).

4. Secure the component by bending the protruding lead 45° after insertion into a circuit board. The bending tool is used [Figure 2-9B (2) and (3)].

5. Cut the lead so that no portion when bent flat exceeds the perimeter of the pad (Figure 2-9D).

6. Press the cut lead firmly against the lead [Figure 2-9B (3) and D].

7. On a turret, cut the lead so that the wrap around the turret will reach 180° past the first point of contact with the turret (Figure 2-9C).

8. On a joint where the lead is not bent, cut the lead to the thickness of an AWG #20 wire.

In all cases, whether it be wires or leads from components, forming provides two main functions: (1) securing the lead to the circuit and (2) providing proper stress relief. This relief is needed to prevent rupture of the component lead from the component, or, in the case of a wire, to allow it to move slightly without rupturing the turret or terminal or to prevent a stress pull on the solder joint and rupture of the wire strands.

The preparation of tools and components is probably the most critical of all phases in the removal and replacement of components. The variety of situations and tools makes it extremely important for you to exercise care and comply strictly with the rules herein. These are not all the rules, but they are the most essential to general applications in the area of maintenance. Cleanliness is crucial.

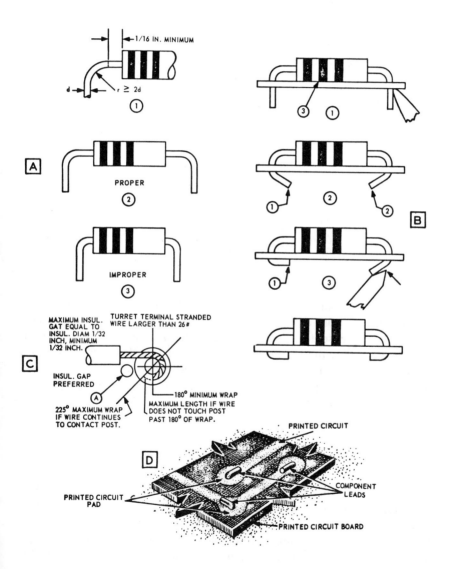

Fig. 2-9. Bending Component Leads

2-7   Application of Solder

Each component, wire, or terminal prepared for soldering in the manner discussed previously must have the solder applied in such a manner that:

1. The solder will form a bond.
2. It will flow readily, providing the complete immersion of all elements of the joint.
3. It will cool and solidify into a bright, flake-free surface.
4. There will be no obscuring of the shape of the elements in the joint.

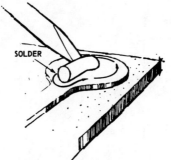

SOLDER

Fig. 2-10. Applying Solder

To best accomplish these ends, place the iron at a 45° angle, with the tip touching both or as many elements of the joint as possible (Figure 2-10). Start the solder flow near the iron, pass the solder around the joint, and end near the iron. Remove the iron and let the solder still present in the area just vacated by the iron flow into that place completely, covering the elements of the joint with solder. This technique is applicable for almost all soldering applications except for those involving certain integrated circuit (IC) units.

2-8   Special Applications

Certain ICs are designed as shown in Figure 2-11. This type of IC does not require forming and does not protrude through a printed circuit card. It is normally soldered to the component side of the card as shown in Figure 2-12. This soldering is accomplished by more than one technique, the electric arc, or an electrode supplying current. The suggested method for repairing these defective circuit modules is shown in Figure 2-12. The iron. is placed near the tip of the IC lead and onto the pad. The heat will allow the solder to flow under the IC tip and lead and form a bond. This technique is called *bridging*.

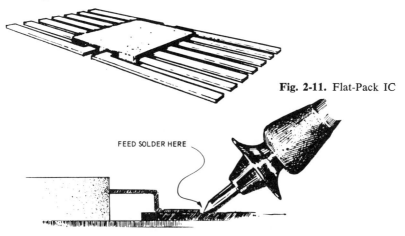

Fig. 2-11. Flat-Pack IC

FEED SOLDER HERE

Fig. 2-12. Bridging

2-9 Replacing Components

Let's examine the replacing of components from two viewpoints: (1) that of the general tasks associated with the preparation and work prior to desoldering and soldering, and (2) that of the soldering itself.

2-9.1 *General Tasks List*

Observe and record how the component is placed before removing it by observing polarity, placement angle, positioning, insulating requirements, and adjacent heat-sensitive components or substances.

1. Label the elements to be removed.
2. Remove any assemblies that will facilitate repair.
3. Locate replacement procedures in technical orders (TOs) or manufacturers' manuals.
4. Turn off the power (if applicable).
5. Prepare the work area by removing obstructions, obtaining sufficient light, and obtaining the tools necessary for the job.
6. Examine and prepare tools, irons, and so on.

2-9.2   Removing the Component Task List

1. Use a chemical agent to remove any hermetic sealer from the soldered joint that is to be worked on. Refer to instructions in the TO for the name of the proper chemical agent. Look for the military or federal specification listing.
2. Clean with isopropyl alcohol.
3. Wick solder from the joint, using either the wick or sniffer technique.
4. Remove elements from the joint.
5. Clean the joint.

2-9.3   Replacing the Component Task List

1. Clean leads of new elements with a cleaning tool, such as a braided tool; use abrasives if required.
2. If a wire lead, remove the insulation.
3. If multiple strands, form the strands.
4. Tin to ⅛ inch from insulation.
5. Form the element.
6. Clean with isopropyl alcohol.
7. Tin the elements.
8. Place the elements in a joint.
9. Fasten heat sinks to protect heat-sensitive items.
10. Apply the soldering iron to the joint.
11. Feed solder into the joint, covering all elements to provide a complete seal. Do not use so much solder that the shapes of the elements in the joint are obscured.
12. Remove the soldering iron and feed solder into the space occupied by the joint.
13. Allow to cool and solidify. Do not disturb.
14. Clean with isopropyl alcohol.
15. Apply hermetic sealer if applicable.

2-9.4   Checks

Perform a static check before the hermetic seal is applied. (Refer to the TO for the appropriate sealer.) Perform the check with a voltmeter by measuring for resistance on the lowest scale. Do this by touching the solder with one voltmeter lead and the wire or component lead with the other.

Any reading except a short reveals a defective joint. After completing the static check on all joints repaired, clean the surfaces again with isopropyl alcohol, and seal. Perform dynamic checks in accordance with specified standards, or, in the case of PCB, by insertion in the circuit, or, in the case of lamp fuse and switch replacement, by the application of power.

2-10 Special-Attention Area

Components needing special attention include crystal-type semiconductors, solid transistors, and microelectronic IC circuit components (Figure 2-13). Heat is destructive to all these components. A heat sink must always be used while soldering. Observe how an IC is formed by studying Figure 2-14. Note that it is composed of layers or strata of semiconductor material. During the formation of the circuit, each layer is designed to perform a portion of the circuit as a P or N type of material or resistive coupling, bias junction, and so on, and from these points wire of extremely

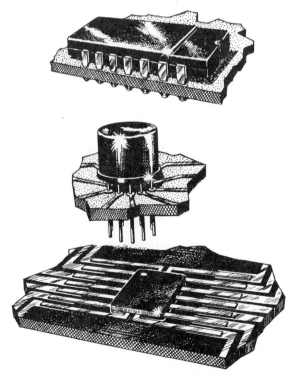

Fig. 2-13. Integrated Circuit Design

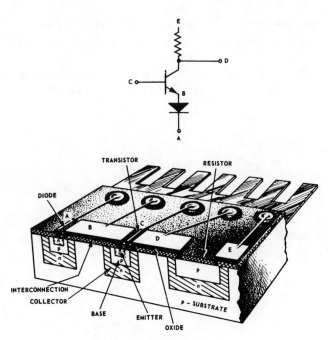

Fig. 2-14. IC Makeup

fine AWG thickness is affixed and fed to one of the external connecting wires or leads that you will solder to. If the IC is fairly large and the conductors are side-mounted to pass through a PCB, as shown in Figure 2-13, the heat sink may be easily fastened to the component side of the card. On a round IC, the heat sink is usually applied to the case when the leads are passed through the PCB. There is not room to place a heat sink on each connector lead. If a flat-pack IC is used, a heat sink may be laid close to the body of the IC. The solder flow from the bridging is effective, and there will be no heat damage to the internal connections of the IC. These general rules also apply to crystal units.

If you work on equipment having components like these, you must study the specifications of allowable soldering iron sizes, voltage ranges, and other factors so that you thoroughly understand the damage you can do if you repair a unit improperly.

2-11   Conclusions

Replacement techniques always include safety, removal, replacement, and testing. Turn off the power, mark the wires to be removed, remove the component leads, and remove the component. Clean the leads and connector, replace the defective component with a good one, install the leads, and check your repair work by both static and dynamic means. Be able to identify the location in the technical reference manual of the section dealing with repair and replacement techniques. Also remember that there is a list of components by part number and that this shows its placement in the circuit.

Secure the proper tools for performing the task, include soldering irons of the proper voltage and wattage, bending tools, cleaning tools and alcohol, and the proper rosin flux. Recall that SH63 is the best type of solder for soldering electronic components; SN60 is acceptable, however. Recognize defective solder joints, those that are cracked, pitted, cold, or stressed, have excessive flux, or have impure solder.

Apply sufficient heat to allow the solder to flow, and apply the solder so that it completely covers the joint, but does not obscure the definition of the component leads in the joint.

On crystal devices and microelectronic circuit elements, use heat sinks to protect the semiconductor structures when soldering whether you are using the component lead to pad type of solder joint or the bridging technique.

2-12   Desoldering

Although various techniques can be used in desoldering, we shall analyze only the "wicking" and "sniffing" techniques. Each technique is very effective in desoldering. In each process the principle employed is that of removing solder from a previously soldered joint. Some physical force or attraction must be employed. In this analysis the principles are examined, and the steps needed to accomplish the task are listed.

2-12.1   *Wicking*

Refer to Figure 2-15 and observe where a typical source of wicking material can be obtained. A wicking solder-removal unit may consist of a braided shield wire with the core removed, or it may be a piece of wire containing many strands.

The preparations for making an effective wick from these types of material are as follows (see Figure 2-15B):

1. After removing the core materials, flatten the shield with a bending tool.
2. Dip the wick in liquid solder flux of the same type of rosin as was or will be used in repair opreations, to a depth of about 2 inches.
3. Tin the end of the wick with the solder and a hot iron.

4. If using a multistrand wire, strip the cover back about 4 inches.

5. Flatten the wire slightly, keeping the strands uniformly in place.

6. Dip the wire into the liquid rosin.

7. Tin the end of the wick.

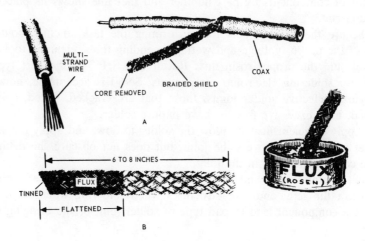

Fig. 2-15. Wicking Tools

The basic principle of wicking is that by the application of a heated wick well saturated with rosin, the solder will flow readily into the rosin area, leaving the terminal to which it was previously affixed. It is almost as if by osmosis that the solder travels into the saturated wick.

When preparing the wicking unit, use a wire size no larger in diameter than the pad size from which you will be wicking the solder. This is most important because if allowed to touch the board, the wick will cause frog eyeing of the material on the board. Refer to Figure 2-16 for a pictorial representation of wicking following these steps:

1. Place the wick on top of the solder joint to be removed.

2. Place the iron tip on top of the wick. The heat of the iron will melt the solder and the solder will flow into the wick.

3. Clip off the wick containing the removed solder, and repeat the operation until all the solder is removed from the joint.

2-12.2   *Sniffing*

In sniffing, a syringe-like tool is used (Figure 2-17). The tool is made from a substance that does not form a bond with a solder. Sniffing is not as highly recommended as wicking, but it is effective.

The sniffer, or "solder sucker" as it is sometimes called, uses the force of air pressure to accomplish the sniffing, which is the removal of solder. This is accomplished by (see Figure 2-16):

1. Squeezing the air out of the rubber ball at one end of the sniffer.
2. While keeping the ball depressed, place the pointed end of the sniffer tube next to the solder to be removed.
3. Heat the solder with a soldering iron, keeping the tip of the iron in the solder and *not* on the sniffer.
4. Slowly release the pressure on the sniffer ball, allowing air to enter

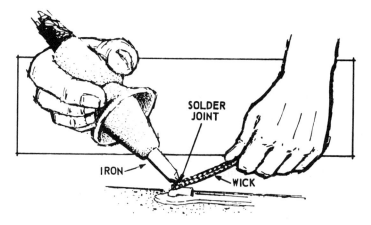

Fig. 2-16. Wicking

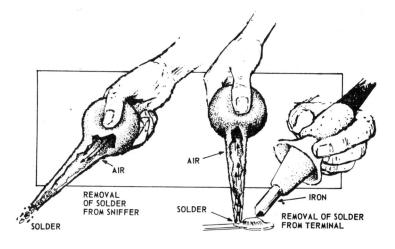

Fig. 2-17. Sniffing

the ball through the sniffer tube. As the air enters, it will pull the molten solder into the tube with it.

5. After the solder has been pulled into the sniffer, remove the sniffer from the joint and, by depressing the ball again, force the collected solder from the sniffer tube.

Wicking and sniffing are both effective for removal of solder from a joint. But caution must always be used because the heat required may damage the base materials and adjacent components. Prepare the work area and tools properly so that a minimum amount of heat is used during the desoldering process.

TEST QUESTIONS

1. What is a primary requirement for a bending tool?

2. What are the characteristics of a soldered joint that make it different from a wire-wrapped joint?

3. What percentage of tin and lead combine to form a liquid state from a solid without having a plastic state?

4. What is the purpose of flux?

5. Why is the forming part of a soldering job so important?

6. What are the characteristics of a solder joint that would be approved by experts?

7. What is the soldering technique called that is used when replacing a new flat pack on a PCB?

8. To keep from destroying semiconductor material, where is the heat sink placed on an IC that is in a round case?

9. What are the two ways to desolder a component? Explain each.

3

Performance Checks

This chapter presents an analysis of tasks associated with the performance of checks on the operation of equipment. As we are learning, equipment is becoming more reliable. Components are being manufactured with greater skill because of major breakthroughs in engineering. The adoption of solid-state devices, using crystal structures, silicon and quartz, thin film, doping, and the techniques used in the manufacturing of these devices, have led to the development of maintenance techniques that you must understand if you are to properly maintain the equipment. Maintenance techniques that were applicable in the past but which have been eliminated or deemphasized include:

1. Checking the equipment frequently to discover weak links:
2. Aligning the circuits on a close-interval basis, even though no indications of malalignment exist.
3. Using test problems at regular intervals to check operational capability.
4. Interrupting the power stability with such marginal checks as power increase and decrease, and conversion to other power units.

There were problems inherent in this approach:

1. There was a decrease in operational availability.
2. There was an increase in the chance for human error, such as the shorting of components.
3. There were great temperature variations in environmentally controlled cabinets.
4. There was a lot of just plain tinkering.

However, the approach did have its good points. The primary ones were that training was maintained at a fairly high level and that engineering data of significant value were collected. Analysis of these data resulted in the present approach, which, as we stated, involves elimination of all but essential maintenance tasks. We covered the service tasks in Chapter 1. Here we are more concerned with the operational tasks, which are the tasks related to data movement.

Operational/performance checks are made in various ways:

1. By use of meters.
2. By use of an oscilloscope.
3. By use of display cathode-ray tubes.
4. By use of printouts.
5. By interpretation of lamps, audio alarms, and internal tests.
6. By visual examination of mechanical assemblies.

Once again, there is a basic technical publication that describes this type of task. This publication contains preventive maintenance instructions. The instructions have periods that range from daily to annually, the time interval being based upon statistical data accumulated through maintenance documentation and engineering data

During the analysis of tasks related to performance,

1. Preferred methods of doing the task are identified.
2. The reason a check is made at certain specific points is determined.
3. Technical data about the task or circuit being tested are examined.

To make this text more meaningful, the tasks that are analyzed are further identified as pertaining to:

1. System input (I).

2. System output (O).
3. Input and output (I/O).
4. System central (C).

Within the following discussion these alpha characters identify the unit where the task will likely be found, but first we need to look at some of the sources of data we will be checking.

3-1 Sources of Data Affecting Operational Checks

3-1.1 *Radar and Beacon*

The operational checks normally associated with this type of system input require the use of hands-on methods and test equipment. These tasks must determine the validity of the return and the quality and accuracy of the return. What return? Well, let's examine a few of the basic principles of radar and beacon so that we can appreciate why operational checks are needed and performed.

Radar means *ra*dio *d*irection *a*nd *r*anging and came into being during World War II. Its concept is related to an echo in sound. When you have heard your voice echo back to you, the delayed response of your voice repeated your original statement. The echo is called the *return*. The delay encountered is measurable in time and distance. Since sound waves travel at 1,100 ft/s, and since the time you say the word until it comes back as an echo return is measurable, the distance to the resounding backdrop, usually a cliff, can be determined.

3-1.2 *Radio-Wave Reflection*

All radar sets work on a principle very much like that described for sound waves. In radar sets, however, a radio wave or signal of an extremely high frequency is used instead of a sound wave. The words *wave* and *signal* have the same meaning. The energy sent out by a radar set is similar to that sent out by an ordinary radio transmitter. The radar set, however, has one outstanding difference in that it picks up its own signals. It transmits a short pulse and receives its echos. This out-and-back cycle is repeated from 60 to 4,000 times per second, depending upon the design of the set. If the outgoing signal is sent into clear space, no energy is reflected back to the receiver. The signal and the energy it carries travel out into space and are for all practical purposes lost.

From Figures 3-1 and 3-2 you can see that if the signal strikes an object such as an airplane, a ship, a building, or a hill, some of the energy is sent back as a reflected signal. If the object is a good conductor of

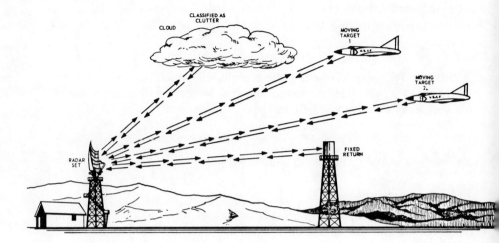

Fig. 3-1. Radar Return

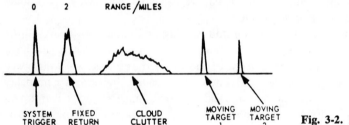

Fig. 3-2. Radar Display

electricity and is large, a strong echo is returned to the antenna. If the object is a poor conductor or is small, the reflected energy is small and the echo is weak.

Radio waves/signals travel in straight lines at a speed of approximately 186,000 mi/s (the speed of light) as compared to 1,100 ft/s for sound waves. Accordingly, there will be an extremely short time interval between the sending of the pulse and the reception of its echo. It is possible to measure the interval of elapsed time between the transmitted and received pulse with great accuracy—to as little as one ten-millionth of a second.

The directional antennas used by radar transmit and receive the energy in a more or less sharply defined beam. Therefore, when a signal is picked up, the antenna can be rotated until the received signal is at its maximum strength. The direction of the target is then determined by the position of the antenna.

The radar return is fed to the input unit of certain electronic data processors in the forms of raw (or normal) video and processed video after each has been amplified by the radar receiver. The returns may be raw (normal) video or processed video. Raw or normal video is that type of return which is merely amplified along with the noise returns. Processed video, however, may be in various forms. One such form is moving target indicator (MTI) video. This form is obtained by comparing a return with the last return for the same target and, if it shows a change in *position* (representing velocity), the circuit performing the comparison generates a pulse. Another type of processed video is main lobe indicator (MLI) video. This type of presentation is generated by a circuit that processes the strongest return from a target (main lobe) and suppresses the weaker returns (side lobes) from the same target. Then there are other types of video which are processed to be used in jamming situations and to eliminate clutter, such as clouds and electrical disturbances.

3-1.3 *Beacon*

Just as radar scans the skies for aircraft, beacon scans the skies for aircraft fitted with transmitters or transponders, as they are called, which transmit coded beacon replies to ground stations. Where radar only locates an object in the sky, beacon, through its processing, is capable of identifying the type of aircraft in the sky. The aircraft may belong to friend or foe. The aircraft may belong to civilian airlines fitted with IFF (Identification Friend or Foe) transmitters, which allow ground stations to identify them, or they may be military aircraft or missiles fitted with SIF (Selective Identification Feature) transmitters, which allow ground stations to identify which type of military aircraft is in the air.

Beacon replies differ from radar returns. In beacon two pulses (a bracket) are generated 20.3 μs apart. Between these two pulses is room for 13 additional pulses, and these pulses are formed into codes. To help you distinguish which type of beacon reply your equipment is processing, the term "mode" is used. Each mode is associated with particular types of

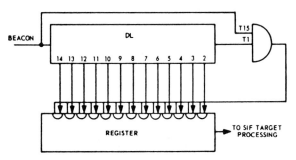

Fig. 3-3. Beacon Detector

replies, such as IFF, SIF, or special military codes. Each return or reply is stored within a half-mile-range block memory. Since a code is bracketed, a detection circuit must be designed to sample the first and last (fifteenth) pulse while the intervening pulses are temporarily stored. To effectively do this, a delay line in conjunction with an AND gate is used (refer to Figure 3-3). With detection of both the first and last pulse a parallel shift is generated, causing data bits 2 through 13 and parity bit 14 to be loaded into a decoder unit.

3-2   Height-Finder Returns

Data-acquisition systems employ height-finder radar returns. These returns are similar to search video. Processing and amplification of these returns are similar to those described in the text. Therefore, operational and performance checks usually are the same. Now let's examine another part of radar, where we must be concerned with operational checks.

3-2.1   Radar Antenna

Search radar and beacon radar usually scan the skies by rotating an antenna assembly upon a fixed pedestal. Height-finder radars usually scan the skies by having the antenna nod up and down, much like shaking your head when you agree with a statement. Height-finder radar is also capable of horizontal movement, but this movement is usually controlled and exercised only upon the demand of an operator or automatic machine operation.

3-2.2   Determining Proper Orientation of Radar Rotation

Does the radar always maintain its proper orientation with respect to north? To find the answer an automatic change pulse (ACP) counter is inserted in data processors. This counts the ACPs from the time of receipt of a main pulse as the orientation signal, and, when the radar personnel orient the radar to north, the pulse can be generated. Since the pulse is generated at north, the pulse may be at *true north* or *magnetic north*. Electronic data processors (EDPs) may use north to determine position; therefore, an ACP counter is installed to count the positional changes of a search radar starting with north pulses. The increment of change is often established at 0.088° per change and a total of 4,096 pulses equals one revolution of a radar antenna scan. The increments may be larger or smaller, depending upon circuit design and antenna rotation speed. The performance check requires measurements of the output of the counter with *north* mark pulse for coincidence. If coincidence does not occur, a problem may be identified. If the EDP uses *true north* and the radar uses *magnetic north* as references, then a preset number of ACPs equivalent to the angular difference between true and magnetic north must be programmed into the ACP counter. A switch or a series of switches will provide this capability.

3-2.3 Determining Proper Orientation of Height-Finder Nod

You must perform a check, usually with an oscilloscope at the input unit, which determines that the nod voltage change is at the proper amplitude, phase, and angle, and that it is coincident with the nod positions at, for instance, 0°, 5°, 10°, and 30°. Radar personnel will provide certain signals to your system which will aid you. A circuit in the radar generates a pulse each time the antenna increases or decreases its nod by 5°. This signal is called "angle mark." Its occurrence, through circuit design and compensation circuit variations, is measurable at selected ranges and altitudes. For instance (refer to Figure 3-4), if the angle mark at 0 with earth-curvature correction (ECC) does not intersect the 200-mi range mark at 31,000 ft (plus or minus a specified amount), then operationally the system is malfunctioning and alignment is required. If coincidence occurs at some points but not at others, nonlinearity is evident and alignment is required. In the operational checks in these areas, the data-processing system and radar positioning are examined, and if errors are discovered, the apparatus must be aligned.

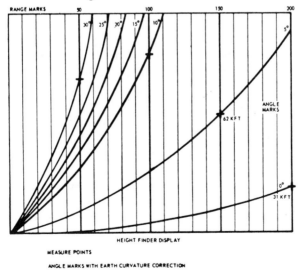

Fig. 3-4. Angle Mark Display

3-3 Keyboards

A keyboard is basically a typewriter with a digital encoder attached that converts the action of depressing a key to a digital code. By this means it is possible to insert data into a digital machine in the machine's language—digital code. In this case, the keyboard and its encoder function as an interpreter between man and machine. Figure 3-5 shows the function of a typical keyboard when it is used as an input device. Each time a key is depressed, an cight-bit binary code is inserted into the transmitter. The transmitter converts these parallel data into a series message that is transmitted over a telephone line. At the other end, a receiver converts the serial data back to parallel and applies them to a printer. The printer decodes the digital data and prints out the character that was inserted by the keyboard.

Note that there are eight parallel lines leading from the keyboard to the transmitter and that each line shows a voltage level that represents a ZERO or a ONE. Also note that each line is labeled with a bit number (D0 through D7). The binary configuration generated in this example is

D7	D6	D5	D4	D3	D2	D1	D0
0	1	0	1	0	0	1	0
Parity bit	Control bit			Character Code			

Now let us see how the mechanical movement of a typewriter key produces an eight-bit binary code. Look at Figure 3-6. There are eight 2-position switches in the code generator mechanically connected to the typewriter. In the figure it is assumed that the M key has been depressed. The mechanical analog-to-digital converter has positioned the switches so that the voltage output of a switch is either −12 V (logic ONE) or 0 V (logic ZERO). In Figure 3-6, switches S1, S3, S4, S6, and S8 are switched to their 0-V positions; therefore, the output code is D0—0 1 0 0 1 0 1 0—D7, which is the fieldata code for M.

As the operator depresses each key, the keyboard prints each character just like a typewriter and, at the same time, generates the fieldata code. Operational accuracy requires that the letter M be typed on the paper by the letter M on the typewriter. If the character is not printed, the keyboard must be aligned or adjusted by using the appropriate technical reference and instructions. If an incorrect fieldata code is developed by the switches and/or electronic logic packages that are part of the keyboard unit, a parity error will very likely be generated. Each parity error is visually indicated by a light. Back-spacing

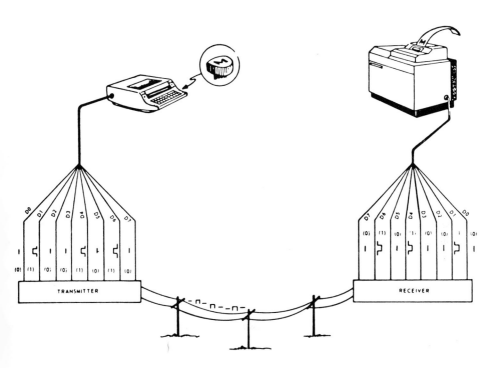

Fig. 3-5. Keyboard System

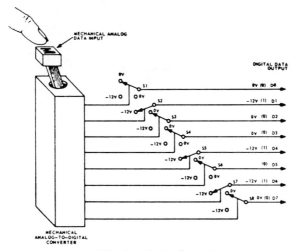

Fig. 3-6. Code Generator

(a machine operation) will erase the fieldata code but will not correct the problem. Troubleshooting with special test equipment in an off-line mode (bench) is indicated.

This keyboard is also used to write data onto magnetic tape. The electronic package when programmed by an external control unit (Figure 3-7) places the fieldata code for each character onto the tape in the sequence in which it is typed. Operational checks of this keyboard also require that compatibility with the tape unit be checked. If data cannot be loaded properly, then the control signals fed to the machine, the timing of the machine, or the development of data from the machine may be incorrect, in which case corrective repair action is indicated.

The keyboard is also used as an output device when checking the availability of taped program data and for control of signals called for from the control panel. By selection of a file on the control panel with the selection knobs in callout (2) (Figure 3-7) and the command signal in search, the keyboard will select the proper key through its electronic package and cause it to print. At the time in the printing of a program that a control signal from the operator is called for, the program stops and a control panel light lights [in the callout (1) area], identifying the operator action that is called for. The operator completes

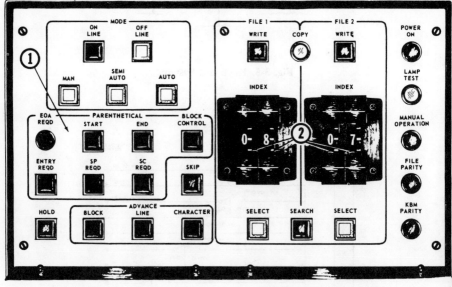

2 FILE SELECTION KNOBS

1 EOA = END OF ADDRESS
SP REQD = SEND PARTIAL REQUIRED
SC REQD = SEND COMPLETE REQUIRED

Fig. 3-7. Control Unit

the operation and the program continues. The final action on a message or program will be an operator action called *send complete* (SC REQD). This action provides the command signal to transmit.

3-4 Tape Transport Units

Let's briefly identify tape-drive units and discover what we should look for during operational checks. Refer to Figure 3-8, the block diagram of a tape unit, and observe that the tape unit is usually an external part of a data-processing or computer system. This unit provides flexibility in the uses of the EDPs, because many programs may be stored on individual tapes and may, at the discretion of the user, be inserted. The data and control functions are fed through and controlled by the interface unit between the data processor and tape-drive unit. Some error checking may also be accomplished by the control unit.

Mechanically the tape-drive unit consists of two units, the tape reel and the takeup reel, plus servo units to control each reel assembly, a vacuum pump (on many models), photocells for tape orientation and control (on some models), and a motor-drive unit and power-supply unit. When the servos are supplied an electrical error voltage, they cause the reel assemblies to rotate until the error voltage (induced voltage) is nulled. The rotation and velocity of the reel assembly is dependent upon the phase angle and magnitude of the applied error voltage. (For a

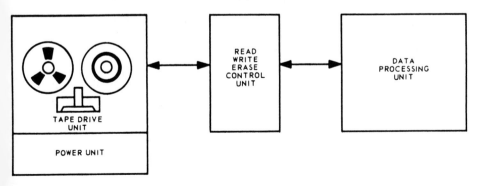

Fig. 3-8. Tape-Unit Block Diagram

detailed explanation of servo units, refer to the servo unit in Chapter 5.) Look at Figure 3-9 and see that the servos do, in fact, control the reel assemblies and that external voltages in the form of error voltages provide the drive force necessary for tape movement. Now that we have briefly discussed some of the general characteristics of tape transport units, let's identify how the units are considered during performance of operational checks.

Mechanical and electrical elements usually examined include:

1. Servos.
2. Motors.
3. Vacuum pumps.
4. Reel assemblies.
5. Tape-head positioning.
6. Photocells.
7. Voltages and currents.
8. Tape tension.

Data-flow elements usually verified by checkout include:

1. Read, write, and erase.
2. Control signals.
3. Diagnostics:
   (a) All 1s check.
   (b) All 0s check.
   (c) Cross-talk check.
4. Reliability check between tape transport and data processor.
5. Error check and circuits check.

The above listings point out each area in which an operational breakdown may occur. These areas are significant enough to have performance routines prepared and performed. Some may be daily, such as the diagnostic check, servo-unit check, photocell check, or vacuum-pump check; others may be scheduled as infrequently as every 180 days.

3-5 Transmission Line

System inputs and outputs require the use of indicator, meters, and switches. To aid in understanding why and how performance checks are

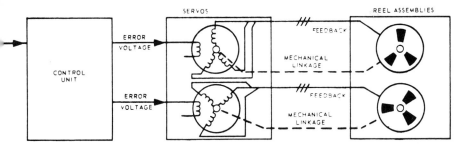

Fig. 3-9. Tape Servo Unit

carried out in this area, let's first explore what is required for data to be transmitted and received. Then let's identify how the input/output equipment can sense the correctness of data and detect errors in data.

Any time data are accumulated at a station, it may be of value to higher headquarters. That is why almost all command and control systems and EDPs have data links. For the most part, these data links are conventional telephone (TELCO) lines or microwave units of the telephone company. In overseas areas and under tactical situations in the United States, military equipment replaces commercial company equipment.

Since data must be transmitted and received over these media, a problem arises in that any signal entered into a long wire loses power. The reason for this is that wire has a resistance that impedes the flow of the signal. To compensate for this, refer to Figure 3-10 and see that

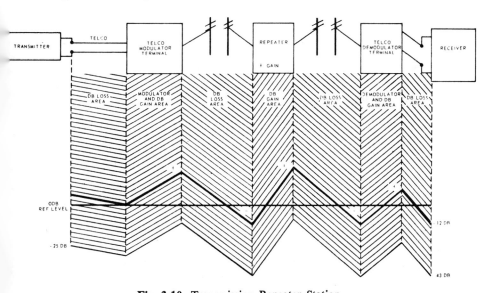

Fig. 3-10. Transmission Repeater Station

TELCO places repeater stations every 6 or 7 mi with capabilities of taking in a very small signal and boosting it to a high-enough power rating to reach the next repeater station. The amplifiers in the repeater station are linear-type amplifiers with automatic frequency and gain control built in. They can raise the power level of the output signal with no loss of signal data.

To properly get the data to a TELCO line you may have a modulator or transmitter included in the input/output unit. This unit prepares the digital data for the line. In one system it may change the digital data to dipole data. Referring to Figure 3-11, dipole data show that a change of binary 1 to 0 to 1 in a message results in a change from a pulse to a level to a pulse. Further examination of Figure 3-11 shows that each binary 1 results one cycle pulse. Another system currently in use uses two audio frequencies. A change in frequency represents a binary 1. No change in frequency for successive time periods represents binary 0s. This method is called *frequency shift keying* (FSK) (Figure 3-12).

3-5.1   Line Quality

Selection of the bit rate of a message is determined by the quality of the local TELCO lines. If the noise levels, cross-talk, or other factors related to audio transmission cause the line quality to be low, data must be transmitted at the slowest rate possible. On the other hand, a noise-free, interference-free line, called a high-quality line, can handle data at a fast bit rate.

3-5.2   Decibel

Now we need one final bit of information; then we can complete this discussion. The decibel (dB) and (dBm) are the terms. The dB is a unit of power ratio, whereas the dBm is a measure of absolute power as compared with a reference level of 1 mW. One milliwatt of power is equal to 0 dBm. Look at Figure 3-13. As you can see, the line loss from the transmitter (west line) is 10 dB—transmitter output equals 0 dBm, repeater input equals −10 dBm. This loss of 10 dB represents a power loss of 90 percent, so if the signal injected into a line was 1 mW of power, the repeater would receive a $\frac{1}{10}$ (0.1)-mW signal. The repeater amplifiers are adjusted to provide a 30-dB gain. This provides a power-ratio factor of 1,000 and the output is $1,000 \times 0.1 = 100$, or a 20-dBm signal, since a power-ratio factor of $100 = 20$ dB. The east loss is −10 dB and the receiver input is 10 dBm.

3-5.3   Transmission Path

Refer again to Figure 3-10 and follow along. The transmitted signal

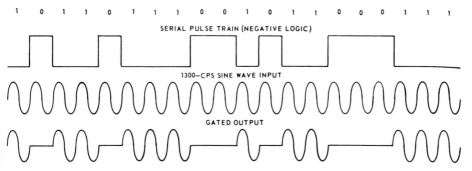

Fig. 3-11. Dipole Data

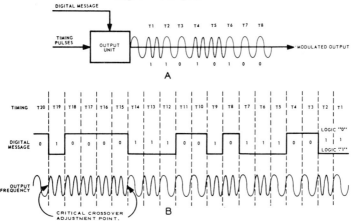

Fig. 3-12. Frequency Shift Keying

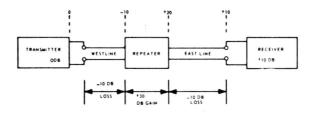

Fig. 3-13. Decibel Levels

enters the phone line from the modulator or transmitter at a fixed decibel level, usually between +6 and −25 dB. It may pass through one or more repeaters until it reaches the high-frequency terminal equipment. Here the data are modulated onto a high-frequency carrier and sped on their way to the receiver. Periodically along the line repeater stations amplify the signal so that it has sufficient power to reach the next station. At the receiving end, the high-frequency carrier is removed and the audio-frequency data are fed to the receiver at the proper decibel level. The receiver demodulates the signal by a reversal of the process used to modulate it—dipole to digital and FSK to digital are examples. Processing within the equipment then commences.

3-6   Printers

Operational checks on printers generally are performed by making the printer produce a printed copy. This makes for a reliable check because a good printout indicates that the printer is operationally satis-factory since the check is reliable for various types of printers. Identifica-tion of subelements within the printers which could cause an improperly printed message and visual tasks associated with these are discussed.

3-6.1   Subelements

SWITCHES. Various types of switches provide for control of the printer. These may be start, cycle, paper feed, advance, and electronic switches (solenoid) for selection of relays; during a print cycle any or all may be used. Failure of one results in improper operation, which can be visually determined.

POWER. Improper power-supply voltage output affects operation. In-dication of improper voltage may result in an insufficient number of printed lines per minute, improper spacing between lines, and missing or overlapped printed characters.

CHARACTER FORMATION. Missing or incomplete character formation is the most common problem. Understanding the principles of printers aids in quick evaluation of malfunction. For instance, if an amplifier fails such as is shown in Figure 3-14, a row of dots would be missing on each letter of the printed message on the electrographic printer. Or if a character failed to print when using the impact printer, a hammer driver (refer to Figure 3-15) could be defective. Each of these examples shows the usefulness of the printout in locating the defect.

MECHANICAL. A defective printout could also be caused by a me-chanical malfunction. Audio noises emitting from motors, drive units, and so on, may be identified when review of the printout shows defects in operation.

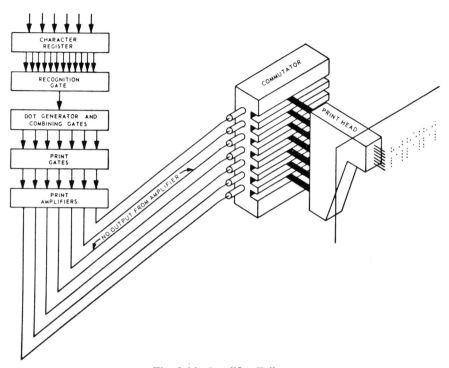

Fig. 3-14. Amplifier Failure

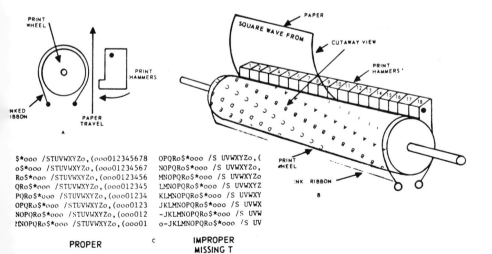

Fig. 3-15. Defective Hammer

3-6.2 *Printout*

To summarize, printer operational checks can be accomplished reliably by use of the maintenance diagnostic printout. Depending upon the type of printer, electrographic or impact, the test should include checks of as many subelements of the machine as possible. Characters, paper advance, switch operation (external and internal), mechanical units, and power supplies are some of the most important areas to be exercised during maintenance testing operational reliability.

3-7 Cathode-Ray-Tube Display

The method most adaptable to performance checks of the cathode-ray-tube (CRT) display is the visual method, using switches and controls. The visual display available most often can be selected by switch action from the console in which the CRT is located.

3-7.1 *Parts of a Display Unit*

Refer to Figure 3-16. Almost all display systems require four basic units for operation. These are the vertical drive unit; the horizontal drive unit, both of which control the sweep display; the intensity unblanking unit, sometimes called the Z axis, where intensification, blanking, video or symbol analog data and high voltage are applied to the CRT; and finally a basic timing unit for controlled generation of all timing signals necessary for CRT display.

3-7.2 *Analysis*

By simple analysis of the video and control selection of data during

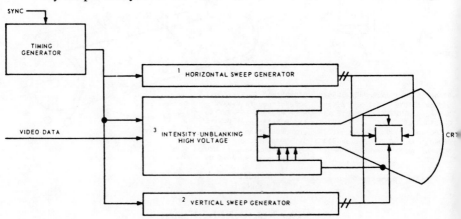

Fig. 3-16. Display Block Diagram

callup, performance checks can pinpoint the defects in any one of these four areas. As an example, suppose the focus is fuzzy. High voltage to the focus anode could be the problem if the variable control did not correct the focus. Linearity problems can be traced to horizontal or vertical sweep circuits. A blackened screen could lack timing or unblanking or even high voltage. So you can see that performance checks do check quality of the display and readily point to trouble spots.

3-8 Central Processor

A fault and facility panel, a confidence indicator, or error lights associated with on-line and off-line testing are the primary devices used to check performance in central processor units. The checks are primarily designed to validate the quality of data transfer in formation, storage, and erasure at specific times with specific known data inputs.

In every test the successful end result validates the quality of the central processing (CP) unit. These tests quite often must encompass I/O devices and peripheral equipment because the data needed come from these units or must go to these units and return. To give you an example, consider the following sequence of events for processing data through the communication center:

1. Input fed from I/O keyboard
   through the
2. Central processor
   through the
3. Modems (modulator)
   and back into the
4. Modem (demodulator) station-to-station operation,
   or to a
5. Headquarters central
   and back into the
6. Modem (demodulator)
   through the
7. CP
   and to the
8. Printer (O) unit.

Another example might be checking the validity of data through the CP of a command and control system by using the central storage unit and by selecting a message for cross-tell, but having the message processor wired for back-to-back operation. The message would:

1. Process through the storage unit to
2. The data link central, where the data are formatted for transmission to
3. The message processor (MP), where it converts the data back to FSK and transmits.
4. Back-to-back operation causes decoding of FSK data in the MP (demodulator) into digital data for
5. Processing by the data link central for
6. Storage in the memory unit.

You can see by these simple examples that exercising the CP does provide reliable checks.

Interruption in data flow usually can be detected by observation of lamp indications on equipment and on confidence panels. Provided you know and understand the full data content of a message and data flow within the CP, you will have very little difficulty interpreting data transmission and processing quality.

3-9   Power Supplies

Electronic power supplies are the units that supply the necessary voltage, power, and current for the operation of EDP equipment. Whether you are working on solid-state or electronic-tube equipment, you will find that a well-regulated source of power is of primary importance. Performance checks are done on these units to verify their proper operation.

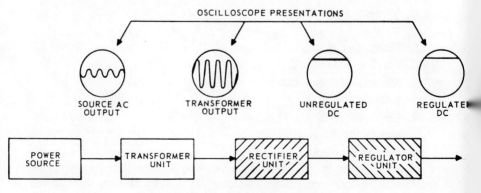

Fig. 3-17. Power-Supply Block Diagram

A review of general power-supply construction identifies that most units have four elements. These are shown in Figure 3-17 and explained in the following text.

3-9.1 Alternating-Current Source

Depending on the particular computer, the ac source may be the output of the motor-generator set, or 60-Hz commercial power.

3-9.2 Transformer Unit

A dc power supply does not always have an input transformer; the input could be taken directly from the ac source. An obvious advantage of an input transformer is that the ac source can be isolated from the load and either stepped up or down within the transformer secondary.

3-9.3 Rectifier Unit

The rectifier unit converts ac to pulsating dc. Therefore, within the rectifier unit there must be some type of rectifying device, such as half- or full-wave rectifiers or bridge rectifiers made from various electronic components, such as diodes, saturable reactors, or transistors.

3-9.4 Regulator Unit

Although the unregulated output of a power supply may be satis-factory for some applications, a regulated output is necessary for the majority of computer circuits. Regulating dc means keeping the output of the dc power supply constant. This is of critical importance for the majority of circuit applications. Some regulator circuits may be quite simply designed, with the use of a single thermistor or Zener diode. On the other hand, complicated units will use an array of solid-state devices to attain proper regulation. Although solid-state regulators are functionally similar to electron-tube regulators, they can be utilized in more ways. The fact that either *NPN* or *PNP* transistors can be used permits con-siderable diversity in design. Regulation of a power supply involves the control of either voltage or current or both. The type of regulations most commonly used are:

1. Shunt-voltage regulation has, as shown in Figure 3-18, a limiting resistor in series with the load and a variable resistance in parallel (shunt) with the load.
2. Series-voltage regulation has, as shown in Figure 3-19, a variable resistance in series with the load. The thermistor, used as the variable component because of its negative temperature co-

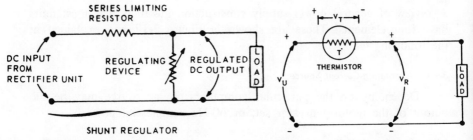

Fig. 3-18. Shunt Regulator   **Fig. 3-19.** Series Regulator

efficient, regulates the voltage as the lead changes, thereby regulating the output voltage.

3. Constant current regulation has, as shown in Figure 3-20, the capability to regulate the current rather than the voltage output. This is accomplished by variation of the bias on the transistor. The transistor resists the current change.

Each power supply generally provides a visual display to identify its status. The display may be voltage or current meters, or indicator lamps in various colors. Some lamps represent proper operation (green);

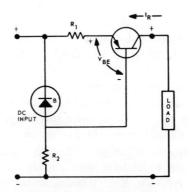

Fig. 3-20. Current Regulator

others represent overload (amber or red) or failure (red) conditions.

3-10 Devices Used To Accomplish Performance Checks

In this section we attempt to identify which methods and devices are used in the performance of operational checks in specific sections of computer and data-processing units. After studying each discussion, complete that part of Form 1 (DPC and Performance Check Devices) by placing an X under each part of the system which uses that method or device.

3-10.1 *Meters*

The performance checks accomplished in various areas using ac volt-meters (rms), dc voltmeters, and differential voltmeters are examined in the following sections.

LINE DATA (I/O). A method for determining line or data quality is by use of an ac voltmeter (decibel meter). This unit is usually connected to the lines or at the common point in the modulators and demodulators. Reading the meter (dBm scale) and comparing the value to prescribed values for transmitting and receiving, it is easy to determine line quality. Refer to Figure 3-21. You can see that it is relatively easy to connect the unit. One important factor to remember here is that the sensitivity of the meter must be very good or attenuation of the input and output signal will occur and as much as 3 dB loss can occur. A loss of 3 dB results in a 50 percent power loss and can easily interrupt data.

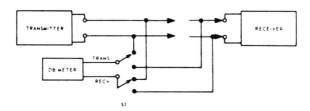

Fig. 3-21. Measuring Line Quality

POWER SUPPLIES (I/O/C). The performance checks used with power supplies require the use of dc meters for measurement of output am-plitudes of dc power supplies and ac meters for ac power-supply output measurements. It may use a current (MA or mA) meter to measure current load output. The power supply may be equipped with a differential (null) dc meter where the output voltage is measured against an internal refer-ence voltage. A deviation voltage reading from the null indicates improper output voltage.

REFERENCE VOLTAGES (C). Within many data processors and com-puters, selected circuits generate dc reference voltages in order to ensure proper linear circuit operation. These are generators other than power supplies. Performance checks on these voltage sources require the use of dc voltmeters and differential meters.

3-10.2 *Oscilloscopes*

The following is a discussion on performance in operating checks by use of oscilloscopes.

LINE DATA (I/O). Oscilloscopes may be required to perform operational checks on modulators and demodulators, especially where a system is using an FSK or frequency-modulation system, or where data, sync, and timing pulses are transmitted separately. A critical point of inspection for FSK is at the coincidence point (see Figure 3-22), where one frequency of FSK meets the other frequency. The crossover point must be at 0V, and the first frequency must be ending a cycle while the second frequency must be starting a cycle.

CRT DISPLAYS (C). Oscilloscopes are frequently used in performance checks of CRT displays to measure waveforms such as ramps, generator outputs, timing circuits, deflection and intensity circuits, and input signal data to the CRT. Check that each signal measured contains all the elements of the waveform and compare the waveform to a standard if possible. Some of the elements may be:

1. Pulse width.
2. Amplitude.
3. Linearity of ramp signals, sine waves.
4. Operating voltage levels.
5. PRT.
6. Proper waveform (i.e., no over- or undershoot of square wave).
7. Ringing.

SERVO UNITS (I/O). The oscilloscope is used to validate waveform data from servos for nulling operations and reference voltage checks. Polarity, phase, and amplitude measurements must be determined and compared with standards. Feedback-loop signals may be measured for phase and amplitude.

RADAR DATA (I). Oscilloscopes are the primary measurement tool for determination of accuracy and content of radar data. Common defects or missing components of a waveform as shown in Figure 3-23 can only be detected with a scope. The defects may be: (1) no system trigger; (2) no noise, or improper level of noise; (3) no video (hit) returns; and (4) excessive noise (clutter or jamming). The circuits that first receive radar inputs are usually the point of inspection. In these circuits you must establish that video is present and that it is of the proper amplitude and polarity. Therefore, the operational check usually contains instructions to:

1. Identify the points to measure and controls to adjust.

2. Measure the input level of the returns at various ranges.
3. Measure and adjust the circuit output for a desired level and phase or polarity.

They may provide a video return drawing which looks similar to Figure 3-2. If the regulating circuit is designed to adjust the amplitude of the video return by resistive means, weak signals and noise signals will be amplified or attenuated in the same way as strong signals. If the circuit is designed to adjust the amplitude of the video return by capacitive means, amplification or attenuation of weak signals and noise can be controlled more than strong signals. This condition exists because a weak return may be only slightly stronger than the noise being received. Both these components of the video return consist of sharp spikes of very narrow pulse width, and a pulse with a narrow pulse width may be expressed as a high-frequency pulse, especially when taken in relationship to the time for one radar trigger period. So we must be conscious of which type of control we are using when examining and adjusting these inputs.

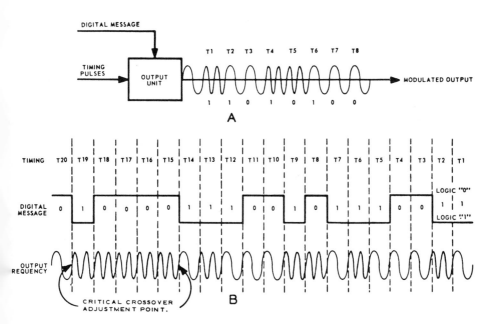

Fig. 3-22. FSK System

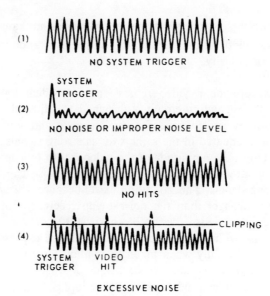

Fig. 3-23. Defective Radar Displays

VIDEO AMPLIFIER CIRCUIT. An oscilloscope is used to measure video amplification, and performance checks show where the likely measurable points are. Look at Figure 3-24. You will see that video is fed to a differential amplifier through a coaxial cable. The shield of the cable is connected to the other input to the differential amplifier. These signals at the output. A variable-current source is used to supply sufficient current for amplification and drive. This current-source control is *resistive*. The video output is then fed to an amplifier circuit, where a *capacitive* control is installed in the emitter portion of the circuit and is called "peaking adj." Since capacitors control high-frequency pulses more than low-frequency pulses, as was previously stated, this control can, if misaligned, eliminate weak returns. The output of the amplifier is then fed to an emitter follower

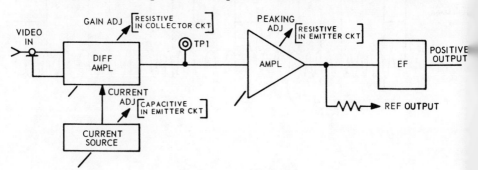

Fig. 3-24. Video Amplifier

(EF), which supplies a current gain, no voltage gain, and no signal inversion. The EF output is routed to a gated amplifier, which provides a control over the intensity of the video through a video-intensity control. Therefore, a video return can be attenuated by three means—two are resistive and one is capacitive. The object, of course, is to establish a desired video output with sufficient amplitude and current to present a reasonably strong signal to a display CRT or to a detection circuit which is designed to store these pulses. Let us now consider another type of input unit, which processes raw (normal) radar video.

QUANTIZER VIDEO. A quantizer (Figure 3-25) transforms video information from radar returns into distinguishable pulses for target determination. An oscilloscope is used to verify signal amplitudes. Performance

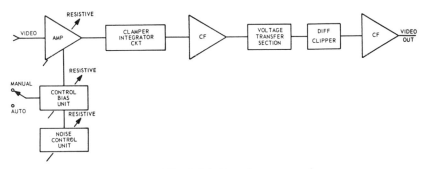

Fig. 3-25. Quantizer

checks require adjustment of various controls in selected portions of the quantizer. The unit contains elements that aid in the detection of video and in the elimination of noise, clutter, and jamming. It provides a digitized video pulse output. There are various quantizers designed using vacuum tubes, solid-state devices, and integrated circuits; however, their functions are similar. Each uses a noise meter to establish an acceptable level of noise which must be present to ensure that weak video returns are not eliminated from processing. The first control in the circuit is a video amplifier *resistive* control. Since the quantizers may be operated in a manual or automatic mode, bias-level controls are included in these circuits and they are resistive. These bias adjustments cause amplifiers to pass only selected peak amplitudes of returns, but they must be adjusted to include a percentage of noise.

One final point about the use of a noise meter is that once its threshold has been exceeded, it blocks all video returns for the remainder of the radar period and part of the next radar period. The obvious conclusion is that the noise-meter circuit can:

1. Affect valid video returns by elimination.
2. Be very effective during a jamming situation.
3. Control the noise level of all video being processed.

RADAR ORIENTATION VALIDATION (I). Oscilloscopes are used as co-incidence detectors for ensuring that north mark and the prescribed number of ACPs occur. The scope is also used to check phase and amplitude signals from radar servos, which are compared to a standard established for the system.

3-10.3 Cathode-Ray-Tube Displays (C)

Video or symbol or digital displays have examinations performed during operation. These checks quickly pinpoint defects. Refer to Figure 3-26 for some of the operational steps that must be included in the checks:

1. Use of CRT voltage controls for intensity, focus, positioning, and astigmatism.
2. Symmetry of range marks and linearity of range marks.
3. Callup operations of console.
4. Printing capability of the digital display by use of a tent pattern.

This test, if completed, also exercises all character generators.

3-10.4 Printouts (O)

The following discussion covers the use of printouts as a check for operational quality.

ELECTROGRAPHIC PRINTERS (O). The printout determines the operational capability of this printer. An accurate printout satisfies performance requirements for quality and accuracy. A defective printout such as that shown in Figure 3-27 indicates (1) improper starting position of com-

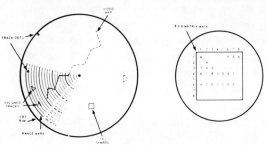

Fig. 3-26. CRT Displays

mutator lead, (2) defective paper feed, (3) defective line amplifiers or a broken commutator lead, or (4) defective decoder unit.

IMPACT PRINTER (O). Printouts that display all characters and numbers validate operational quality. Print-selection circuits, mechanical assemblies, and character-decoding circuits are the most frequent sources of trouble.

CENTRAL-PROCESSOR DATA (C). Printouts that are generated as a result of data taken from peripheral equipment or I/O equipment and which process through the DPC may be used to validate DPC operational quality.

3-10.5 Lamps and Audio Alarms (I/O/C)

The following text is a discussion of the use of lamps and audio alarms.

LINE DATA LIGHTS (I/O). Interpretation of lamps and alarms usually verifies that sync-group (audio-signal data preceding the data message) signals are present or absent. They may be called busy-bit, sync-group, or no-message characters. A synchronization circuit samples sync bits and provides visual-lamp failure indications and audio-tone failure indications.

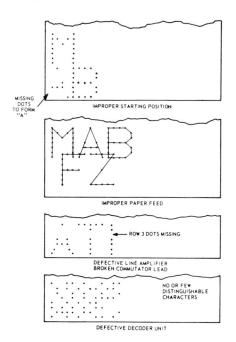

Fig. 3-27. Defective Printer Output

PARITY LIGHTS (I/O/C). The lamps provided for these circuits show that a circuit designed to count each bit of an incoming or outgoing message detects overall correct parity. Failure may be indicated on fault facility panels or confidence indicator units or other convenient panels where lamp and audio indicators alert the personnel to failure.

POWER SUPPLIES (I/C). Lamps indicate operational quality; green or white are for power on, amber for overload, and red for voltage failure.

CENTRAL PROCESSING UNITS (C). Lamps indicate counter operations, sequences, data flow (yellow or white), and failure (red). Sampling circuits may use live data or test data, depending upon design.

TAPE TRANSPORT UNITS (I/O). Sequence lamps, failure lamps, and command and control lamps indicate the status of the unit. Interpretation of lamps may relate to specific areas in which operation ceases.

3-10.6 *Visual Examination of Mechanical Assemblies (I/O/C)*

The following text gives some examples of visual examination to find defects.

SERVO UNITS (I/O). Noisy or binding gear trains are the only visual examinations possible on these units.

ELECTROGRAPHIC PRINTER (O). Noisy drive unit or clutch assemblies and improper paper feed are all signs of visual defects.

IMPACT PRINTER (O). Visual indications of improper or proper operations of cams, motors, paper feed, impact hammers, and related units provide reliable performance data.

TAPE UNITS (I/O). Proper orientation of tape, operation of servos, takeup reel tension, and photo-lamp illumination or vacuum-pump operation are all visual indications of proper or improper operational performance.

3-10.7 *Conclusions*

The examinations of operational checks performed on some of the various input/output and DPC units bring certain factors into focus. These are:

1. The checks require the use of visual indicators, such as lamps,

readout prints, meter readouts, mechanical movements, and meters
and test equipment.

2. The checks often can be accomplished by exercising the machine
operationally and analyzing the output product.

Input, output, and DPC units require that specific tasks and specific equipment be used to perform the operational performance check. When you completed Form 1, you identified which part of the system used specific pieces of test equipment and indicators. Listed below in column 1 are the units. In column 2 are listed the most appropriate methods used to perform operational checks. A comparison of this listing with the form you completed should reinforce the concepts you learned while studying this chapter. Figure 3-28 shows Form 1 filled in. Should you find significantly different indications within your form, restudy the text.

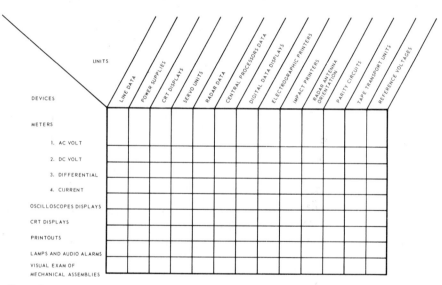

Form 1   Performance checking devices and units

Unit Data	Subtask Check
1. Radar, beacon	a. Hands-on method.
	b. Use oscilloscope.
	c. Measure input amplitude phase and polarity.
2. Radar antenna orientation	a. Hands-on method.
	b. Use display equipment.
	c. Use oscilloscope.
	d. Measure and adjust ACP counter output, north pulse.
	e. Correct for error of ECC.

3. Keyboard

    a. Operational check.
    b. Check for proper orientation of keyboard characters, fieldata codes.
    c. Use with tape unit.
    d. Perform electrical check.
    e. Interpret error indication.

4. Tape and tape drive

    a. Operational check.
    b. Mechanical check.
    c. Cause advance, reverse, read, and write.
    d. Evaluate printout of tape.
    e. Check all 1s, all 0s, cross-talk.

5. Line data

    a. Use meter readings for line quality.
    b. Transmit and receive.
    c. Interpret visual indication.
    d. Examine data for quality on a bit-rate ratio basis.

6. Printers

    a. Operational check with printout.
    b. Visual check of mechanical movement.
    c. Interpret noise, impedance, poor-quality printout.
    d. Interpret lamp indicator.

7. CRT display

    a. Visual inspection using video, symbol modes.
    b. Examine for definition of details.
    c. Operate display with controls and switches.
    d. Interpret indications.
    e. Locate defects in digital information displays.

8. Servos

    a. Use oscilloscope, display consoles, rms and dc meters.
    b. Check null.
    c. Check servo versus antenna rotation.
    d. Check servo position.

9. Power supplies

    a. Use current and voltage meters.
    b. Use differential meter.
    c. Interpret lamps.

10. Central processor

    a. Use fault-indicator panel.
    b. Use confidence indicators.
    c. Interpret reference indicator lamps (counters, data transfer).

11. Reference voltage

    a. Use same procedures as for power supplies.
    b. Use meters.
    c. Interpret lamp indicators.

TEST QUESTIONS

1. What were the gains to a computer system by limiting the operational maintenance tasks?

2. What does "radar" mean?

3. What is the difference in antenna movement between search and height-finder radars?

4. While using the angle mark on a height-finder radar, what would indicate that alignment is required?

5. What feature of a keyboard code generator can alert the operation of an incorrect code?

6. Are the read, write, and erase functions of a tape system used to verify its operation?

7. What is a TELCO repeater station and how does it perform its function?

8. What is frequency shift keying?

9. What is a highly reliable operational check commonly used on printers?

10. What is the most useful way that a display console can be verified as operationally ready for use?

11. Central processors can be verified as operationally ready by different methods. What are two of these methods and what results would you expect from their use?

12. What simple check usually verifies the power-supply output?

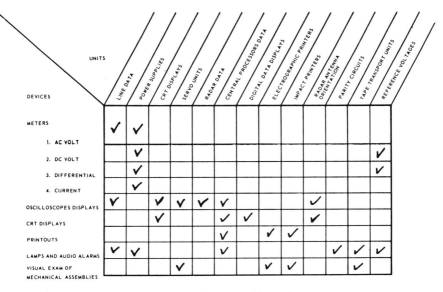

DEVICES / UNITS	LINE DATA	POWER SUPPLIES	CRT DISPLAYS	SERVO UNITS	RADAR DATA	CENTRAL PROCESSORS DATA	DIGITAL DATA DISPLAYS	ELECTROGRAPHIC PRINTERS	IMPACT PRINTERS	RADAR ANTENNA ORIENTATION	PARITY CIRCUITS	TAPE TRANSPORT UNITS	REFERENCE VOLTAGES
METERS 1. AC VOLT	✓	✓											
2. DC VOLT		✓											✓
3. DIFFERENTIAL		✓											✓
4. CURRENT		✓											
OSCILLOSCOPES DISPLAYS	✓		✓	✓	✓	✓					✓		
CRT DISPLAYS		✓				✓	✓				✓		
PRINTOUTS						✓		✓	✓				
LAMPS AND AUDIO ALARMS	✓	✓				✓					✓	✓	✓
VISUAL EXAM OF MECHANICAL ASSEMBLIES			✓					✓	✓		✓		

Fig. 3-28. Completed Form 1

4

Adjustments

Each of you has, during your training in a computer center, performed a task called "adjustment." In all probability you were shown the control to adjust and given a standard to meet. You turned the control in one direction or the other until a specified standard was indicated on a measuring device. Some of you were very cautious in turning the controls and others were not. Since your arrival and training period, you should have realized that indiscriminate control manipulation often produces disastrous results. Circuit misalignment can result in loss of equipment operation, cause unnecessary work problems, and upset supervisors.

Each adjustment must be made with care for the circuit operation. Often, these adjustable components are set very near the proper point. It helps if you know the proper direction to turn the control. However, if you have to guess the direction, you have a 50:50 chance of disturbing the circuit operation and causing it to operate worse than before. Then you will have an extreme adjustment to make. In many circuits, reactive components are the adjustable units, and when these are arbitrarily turned, extreme results are produced. Selected frequencies may be attenuated or lost; waveforms may be distorted, causing improper data flow and loss of digital data quality; and operating levels may be affected, causing a shift in amplifier operation.

84

This chapter identifies reactive controls, gives their characteristics, and shows how they are used in various circuits. The definitions below will help you distinguish the difference between adjustments and alignments.

An *adjustment* is an act whereby a device is used to alter a condition to make it fit or correspond to a standard. This means, for the purposes of the discussion, the physical change of a variable component to make the circuit provide a discrete output. The word *alignment* means to bring into line. In Chapter 5 the adjustments are combined within a functional unit to provide a discrete output.

4-1 Characteristics of Variable Controls

Characteristics are explained by purpose, type, and principle of operation.

4-1.1 Purpose

Each time a variable control is included in a circuit, it serves a distinct function in the operation of that circuit. It is a compensation device used because the inputs to the circuit are variable signals which must be regulated to provide a specific output. Within the circuit, this may cause increase or decrease in bias voltage or current, a change in frequency, or a shift in frequency. Any one of these changes causes the circuit to operate outside its designed operating level. The signal may be affected by distortion, limiting, attenuation, or amplification. Variable controls are used to alter the output waveform to meet specifications. However, if the input signal strength causes the circuit to operate beyond the control of the variable device, no amount of adjustment can correct the output waveform. This is a significant factor to consider when studying the purpose of a variable control.

4-1.2 Types

Study the illustrations in Figure 4-1. Each of these is a variable control even though physical appearances vary. Two common types of *variable capacitors* are the tubular type (A), which has an adjustable core, and the button type (B), which has a variable rotor. In either case different values of capacitors are obtained by varying overcoupling of the plates. For most frequencies up to 30 MHz, these are adequate. For frequencies above 30 MHz, the variable capacitor must be constructed so that no radio-frequency (RF) voltage is developed. This is often accomplished by having the external circuit connected to two sets of stator plates

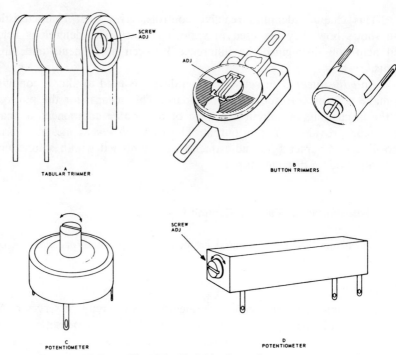

Fig. 4-1. Variable Controls

and using the rotor to increase or decrease the total capacitance between the plates. In this arrangement, no RF current flowed since the rotor is not a link between the stator plates. Figure 4-1C shows a typical *potentiometer*. This control uses a rotor; however, the rotor is in contact with the resistive element. The output voltage or current is tapped off at the point of contact. Figure 4-1D is an example of a potentiometer commonly found on printed circuit cards. Its control is a screw-type shaft which, when turned, causes a contact point on the screw to mate with the resistive element. This provides an output voltage or current proportional to its wiper-arm position. The control shown usually has from 8 to 26 full turns.

Inductors and coils may be variable and are used extensively in electronic equipment. However, variable coils are seldom used in data processing and computer circuitry, so we shall not discuss them further.

4-1.3 *Principles of Operation*

Variable capacitors are manufactured using as dielectrics a variety of materials, including ceramic, mica, glass (for the piston), polystyrene, Teflon, and air. Each of these materials has a different dielectric constant.

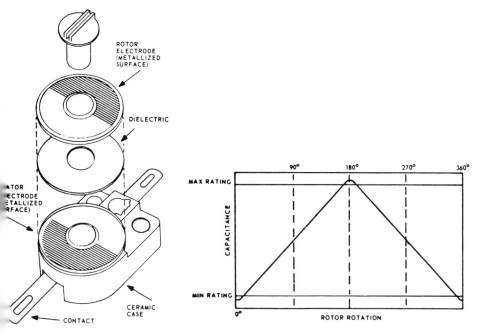

Fig. 4-2. Variable Capacitor   **Fig. 4-3.** Linear Rotation of Trimmer Capacitor

The basic principle of a variable capacitor involves positioning the rotor with respect to the stator. The area of the electrode (plate) is fixed. Turning the rotor from 0 to 180° varies the amount of plate surface exposed, thereby varying the amount of capacitance. Note in Figure 4-2 that the metallized rotor surface may overlap any part of the metallized stator surface. With this arrangement, the capacitance varies, depending upon the amount of metallized plate overlapping and the dielectric constant. To vary the capacitance one can vary the dielectric or vary the overcoupling of the electrode plates.

In most trimmer capacitors used in computer and data-processing circuits, the variable change in capacitance is linear throughout its rotation (see Figure 4-3). The figure shows linear increase and decrease in capacitance through 360° of rotor rotation. Variable capacitors or trimmers are frequently used as filters in oscillators and as attentuations in displays and counters. Let's review some of their characteristics.

1. Most ceramic capacitors have a maximum life of 250 turns. Some tubular types with tuning wands have a life of 1,000 or more turns, since most trimmers connect the stator or rotor to the end frame or turning screw. Placing a metal screwdriver on

the turning screw changes the effective area of the metal-plated surface of either the rotor (usually) or the stator, thereby altering the characteristics of the capacitor.

2. The size of these capacitors has been reduced to meet increased demand for microelectronics. As a result, the voltage breakdown values have been reduced drastically.

3. Tubular-type variable capacitors (Figure 4-4) presently satisfy industry's requirements for microelectronics. These capacitors possess a characteristic not unlike potentiometers (see Figure 4-4). The sliding action of the rotor, controlled by the screw, changes the plate area opposite the stator and thereby varies the capacitance.

Later in this chapter, applications of these capacitors will be explained. Let us now review the principles of potentiometer operation.

Potentiometers are variable-resistance components. They may be either carbon-pile or wire-wound. Wire-wound potentiometers are usually used as rheostats rather than as potentiometers. To see the difference

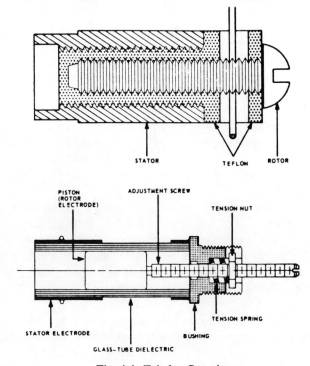

STATOR   TEFLON   ROTOR

PISTON
(ROTOR
ELECTRODE)   ADJUSTMENT SCREW

TENSION NUT

TENSION SPRING

STATOR ELECTRODE   BUSHING

GLASS-TUBE DIELECTRIC

Fig. 4-4. Tubular Capacitor

between the two, look at Figure 4-5. Part A is a schematic symbol for a rheostat. Note that the resistor element is connected to the circuit at each end, and the slider arm, which is used as the pickoff point, is connected to one of the ends. However, in Figure 4-5B, the potentiometer is connected with the entire resistance in a series configuration and the slider is connected to an external circuit. It may be used like a rheostat and still be called a potentiometer.

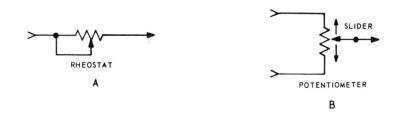

Fig. 4-5. Potentiometer and Rheostat

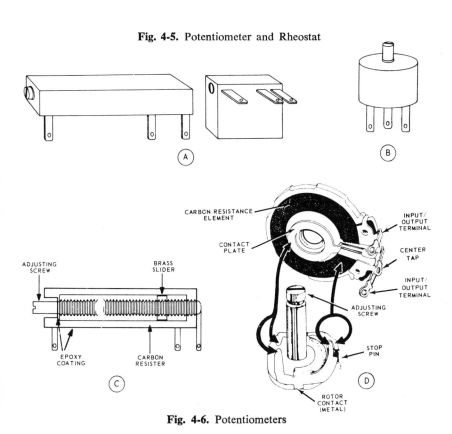

Fig. 4-6. Potentiometers

Potentiometers (known generally as "pots") are used extensively in computer and data-processing equipment. Usually they are made of carbon and look like those in Figure 4-6A and B. Notice that Figure 4-6C indicates that a brass slider is positioned by the turning screw to some point along its path of travel. Its position is manually selected and the resultant output voltage is fed to these units. In the manufacturing of these units, the adjusting screw is isolated from the carbon resistor and the metal turning shaft by a nonconductive substance of the pot shown in Figure 4-6D. Notice that the resistive element is circular in shape and that each end is connected to an external terminal. The variable slider or wiper is pressed against the resistor by spring action and is isolated from the turning screw. The slider has continuity to the third terminal through the circular ring. Two factors must be identified and explained here. First, when the turning device of the rectangular pot is turned to its end, it may make an audible clicking sound, signifying that no further turning in that direction is possible. Second, the pot shown in Figure 4-5D *usually* has a mechanical stop at each end of the resistor, and further turning of the screw results in shearing the stop pin, destroying the pot screw, or both.

Since we are discussing the adjustment of circuit components and the variable resistor, we must recognize another manufacturing characteristic of these components. Variable resistors and pots are made linear in shape and tapered. The linear pot is made so that its resistance is distributed evenly over its entire length. When use is made of an ohmmeter to measure its resistance, the wiper-arm output resistance causes an even deflection of the meter needle for the entire length of the resistor. The tapered pot is made so that $1/10$ of the total resistance is available between one extreme and the midpoint of the adjustment cycle, and the other 90 percent of resistance is available between the midpoint and the other extreme of the adjustment cycle. If you use an ohmmeter to measure the resistance of a tapered pot, placing one lead on the input terminal and the other lead on the wiper (rotor) terminal, you will see that as you turn the wiper, the resistance increases (from zero) very slowly and gradually until you reach a point midway on the pot. From the midpoint on, as you continue to turn the wiper shaft, the resistance will increase much more rapidly in comparison with the first half of the pot-rotor rotation.

4-2   Technical References

Typically, adjustment instructions are found in prevention maintenance routines and in the chapter of the service manual entitled "Maintenance." These instructions seldom explain why adjustment is required. Compliance with the instructions is not very difficult; however, if you cannot comply, what do you do? The answer is that you must study the theory of operation of the circuit or function so that you can apply a logical and accurate solution in a minimum amount of time and, by having a thorough understanding of variable components and their design and application, ensure greater success. Speaking of applications, let's explore some of the most typical areas where we might make adjustments.

4-3 Adjusting Meters and Dials

Adjustments you can perform on meters and dials are usually restricted to centering the needle and calibrating the meter with the calibrating voltage and adjustment control. The only exceptions to these adjustments are those made while working on military equipment, where you are required to perform Category 1 or 2 test procedures for test equipment.

4-3.1 *Balancing*

Positioning the needle on a meter or dial requires that you use a small screwdriver and carefully adjust the screw until the pointer aligns with the proper mark on the meter face. Refer to Figure 4-7 and you will see that this adjustment is mechanical; no voltage or current is involved. You merely twist the control and position the pointer, which is pressed onto the shaft, to the correct position. Balancing the meter needle requires disassembly of the meter and repositioning the weights on the needle shaft, and these adjustments are performed by PME laboratory personnel.

4-3.2 *Centering*

Adjusting a meter prior to its use requires a check of internal electrical components. This is called *zeroing in the meter*. For ohm-adjusting, short the two probes together. This should cause 100 percent deflection of the needle. A potentiometer in the meter circuit will adjust current from the battery to cause 100 percent needle deflection. When you change ohm scales on your meter, you can change the sensitivity of the meter. Therefore, you must adjust the needle deflection again by use of the adjustment of zero pot. To adjust a meter such as a differential voltmeter, apply a source voltage to the balancing circuit. Most differential voltmeters work on the same principle. Refer to Figure 4-8 for a simplified circuit of a differential voltmeter application. Notice how simple the unit is. As you

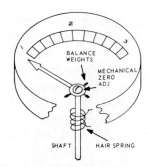

Fig. 4-7. Mechanical Adjustment

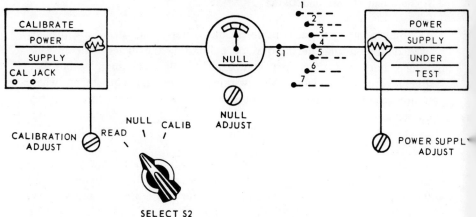

SELECT S2
Fig. 4-8. Null Meter in Use

can see, the calibrated power supply is very similar to an 801B differential voltmeter except that this power supply is permanently installed as part of the equipment. It feeds its output to one side of the meter. The power supply under test has its ouput sampled under load conditions, and if both voltages are exactly the same, there is no deflection of the null-meter needle.

Two factors become important to the analysis:

1. Before the power supply can be used as a standard, it must be calibrated. Remember from your study of test-equipment calibration that some equipment is calibrated by PME for use as a shop standard. An 801B (differential meter), for instance, can be used to calibrate the power supply. Then you can use the power supply as an equipment standard.

2. Having a calibrated source voltage available in the equipment allows an accurate check of all power supplies using that voltage.

By use of a selection switch (S2 in Figure 4-8) any or all units can be tested rapidly.

4-3.3 Application

Figure 4-9 shows an application of potentiometers. R17 is a 7.5-kΩ potentiometer connected as a rheostat. It can, by variation, change the output voltage for the full range of the 7.5-kΩ potentiometer because when the wiper arm is at point *a,* the full resistance is in the circuit. If the wiper is moved to point *b,* all the resistance is removed from the circuit. R2 in Figure 4-8 is a 2.5-kΩ potentiometer used to pick off a

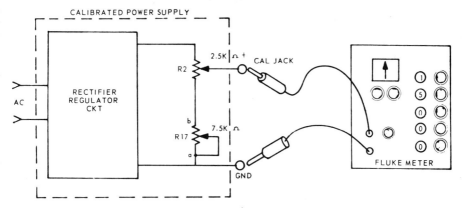

Fig. 4-9. Using a Pot

portion of the voltage depending upon its position. R2 and R17 combine to make a voltage divider.

By plugging in a differential voltmeter and setting it for the exact output voltage, adjustment of R2 and R17 can provide an output that can act as the standard.

4-3.4 Null Adjustment Pot

In Figure 4-10 the null adjustment pot incorporates a centertap pot, and in this application the centertap is grounded. The variable control then has the ability to select not only voltage, but polarity also. This is possible because of the conduction of diodes D1 and D2. The *pickoff* voltage is matched against the algebraic sum of the load voltages of the power supply under test.

Finally, the power supply under test is adjusted to the calibrated voltage power supply. This is accomplished by switching to the read position, as shown in Figure 4-8, and the power-supply voltage under test is fed to the meter. If deflection occurs outside the limits prescribed in the technical orders, adjustment of the pot for that supply increases or decreases the voltage to the null meter and effectively calibrates the power supply to the preset calibrated value.

4-3.5   *Ohmmeter Adjustment Pot*

Refer to Figure 4-11, the meter zero circuit of a typical voltmeter. This meter incorporates two voltage sources for measuring resistance: the

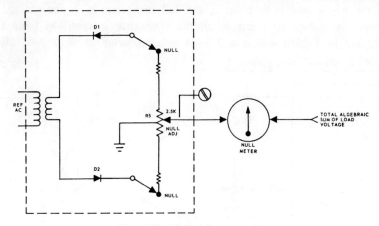

Fig. 4-10. Null Adjustment Pot

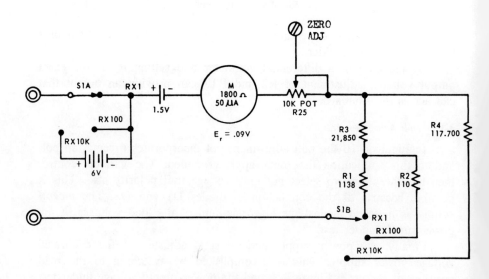

Fig. 4-11. Ohmmeter Adjustment Pot

1.5-V battery for the RX1 and RX100 scales, and the 6-V + 1.5-V batteries (for a total of 7.5 V) for the RX10K scale. In each case the meter, which has an internal resistance of 1.8 kΩ and requires a current of 50 μA for the full scale deflection, uses only 0.09 V of the battery source. The remaining voltage and current are dropped within the circuits when zeroing the meter.

By examining the three modes of operation, RX1, RX100, and RX10K, you can see that the RT for each mode is different. RX1 has an RT of 29,788 ± 5 kΩ. RX100 has an RT of 28,760 ± 5 kΩ. They are almost alike, except that in RX100, R2 is substituted for R1. Finally, the RT for RX10K mode has a total resistance of 124.5 ± 5 kΩ. This mode has an additional voltage source of 6 V, making a total of 7.5 V. The three modes are now calculated to show RT and ET:

$$\begin{aligned}
\text{RX1 path} &= \text{M} + \text{R3 and R1} \\
&= 1{,}800 + 10 \text{ k}\Omega + 21{,}850 + 1{,}138 \\
\text{RT} &= 29{,}788 \pm 5 \text{ k}\Omega \\
\text{ET} &= 1.5 \text{ V} \\
\text{RX100 path} &= \text{M} + \text{R25} + \text{R3 and R2} \\
&= 1{,}800 + 10 \text{ k}\Omega + 21{,}850 + 110 \\
\text{RT} &= 28{,}760 \pm 5 \text{ k}\Omega \\
\text{ET} &= 1.5 \text{ V} \\
\text{RX10K path} &= \text{M} + \text{R25} + \text{R4} \\
&= 1.8 \text{ k}\Omega + 10 \text{ k}\Omega + 117.700 \\
\text{RT} &= 124.5 \pm 5 \text{ k}\Omega \\
\text{ET} &= 7.5 \text{ V}
\end{aligned}$$

In addition to these factors, consider R25, the 10-kΩ pot. Its quality is established at an accuracy of only ±30 percent. Finally, the voltage source must be taken into account. If it is weak, it will not provide the current required for proper circuit operation. With all these conditions you can see the importance of the role the pot plays in providing a control in the variables for accurate use of the meter.

These two examples identify the versatility of the potentiometer. Each example shows how the pot acts as a resistance factor. They show that the wiper arm selects a voltage proportional to its position. You can see that meters and dials require use of potentiometer adjustments and screws to prepare them for use as measuring devices.

4-4 Adjusting Amplifiers and Pulse Generators

In many cases, amplifiers and pulse generators incorporate variable components. The primary objectives of variable components in these circuits are to (1) alter the gain ratio of the circuit, (2) control the pulse duration, or (3) act as phase-shifting devices. To understand these uses of the pot or variable capacitor, examine the basic amplifier and relate its principles to some of the more complex circuits.

4-4.1 *Operational-Amplifier Adjustment*

An operational amplifier is a circuit consisting of three basic parts: (1) an input resistance, (2) a high-gain amplifier, and (3) a feedback resistance. Refer to Figure 4-12A and note that R_{in} is the input resistance and has an assigned value of 100 kΩ, and R_{fb} in the feedback loop has an assigned value of 100 kΩ; therefore, the circuit has a gain of unity (R_{fb}/R_{in} = gain). For example, a 5-V signal into R_{in} results in a 5-V signal output from the amplifier. Now look at Figure 4-12B. By the insertion of a 10-kΩ pot, the circuit is made to provide a variable amplitude output. Apply a 5-V 60-Hz signal into the amplifier and see what effect the pot will have.

First, establish the parameters of the circuit. R_{in} = 100 kΩ; R_{fb} = 100 kΩ $\pm$ R2, 10 kΩ. Therefore, the gain of the circuit is from unity in the case where the wiper of R2 is at point A, or 10 percent where the full pot is in series with R_{fb}. With 5 V input and the pot at minimum or point A, the output equals 5 V PP—unity. Consider the full pot in the circuit. The feedback loop equals 110 kΩ; R_{in} = 100 kΩ. Therefore,

$$\frac{R_{fb}}{R_{in}} = \frac{110}{100} = 1.1 \text{ gain}$$

Therefore, 5 V PP $\times$ gain of 1.1 = output of 5.5 V PP, or a gain of 0.5 V PP.

Based on these conditions, the maximum variation the circuit can

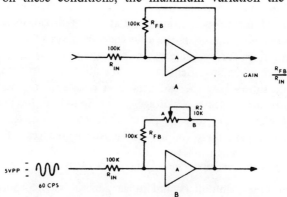

Fig. 4-12. Operational-Amplifier Adjustment

have is 0.5 V PP. Change the size of any component and apply the formula and you can obtain the maximum and minimum gain.

4-4.2 Miller-Circuit Adjustment

Now, alter the basic circuit again and this time replace R_{fb} with a fixed capacitor. This simple change results in the development of a Miller integrator circuit. Refer to Figure 4-13A and see that a rectangular wave input produces a sawtooth output. The Miller integrator is a special amplifier, using a feedback capacitor instead of a resistor. It provides a linear rising (or falling) output voltage when the input level is suddenly decreased or increased. This circuit is basically an RC circuit with the time constant increased by the amplifier gain. Since long time constants can be obtained by using high gain, the output is very linear.

Now refer to Figure 4-13B and see that by replacing the fixed capacitor with a variable capacitor, the capacitor provides a capability for altering the overall time constants of the circuit. Selecting any position of the variable capacitor affects the amplitude of the output waveform since the input pulse is constant. All RC networks contain specific time restricted as in our example; any change in capacitance results in a charge being accumulated on the capacitor for the same time duration in each cycle. Study the following example:

$$T = RC$$

where

$$R = 1,000$$
$$C = 6 = 45 \ \mu F$$

therefore,

(1)
$$T = 1 \times 10^3 \times 6 \times 10^{-6}$$
$$= 6 \times 10^{-3}$$
$$= 0.006 \text{ s or } 6 \text{ ms}$$

or (2)
$$T = 1 \times 10^3 \times 45 \times 10^{-6}$$
$$= 45 \times 10^{-3}$$
$$= 0.045 \text{ s or } 45 \text{ ms}$$

The output waveform can be altered to have one time period for charge from 6 ms to a maximum of 45 ms. Now, by applying a fixed input waveform to control the output, as shown in Figure 4-14, can can see that the output waveform becomes a sawtooth. Also, by studying the graph you can see that for a pulse duration of 1 ms:

1. The circuit with a capacitance of 6 μF allows a charge of 20 percent before discharge begins.

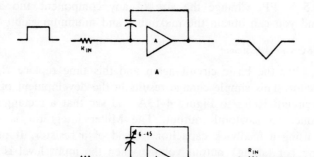

Fig. 4-13. Miller Integrator Adjustment

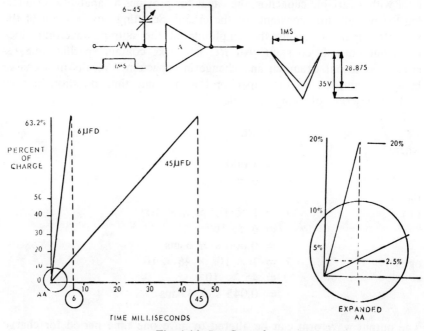

Fig. 4-14. Pot Control

2. The circuit with a capacitance of 45 μF allows a charge of 2.5 percent before discharge begins. From these conclusions, then, the output waveform varies in amplitude depending upon the position of the variable capacitor.

To go one step further, you can calculate the maximum and minimum

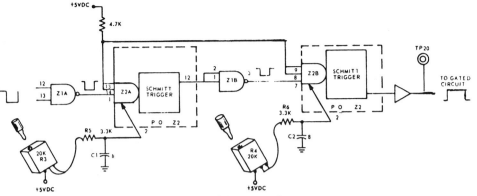

Fig. 4-15. Miniature Pot in Use

points or the maximum variable gain. Assume that the output can have a maximum voltage of 35 V with a control input gate of 1 ms. This would mean that the variable capacitor would have a capacitance of 6 μF. Turning the control to the other end, or 45 μF, decreases the amplitude 17.5 percent, to 2.5 percent of charge. Therefore,

$$17.5\% \text{ of } 35 \text{ V } = 6.125 \text{ V change}$$
$$\text{min to max range } = 28,875 \text{ to } 35 \text{ V}$$

4-4.3 Pulse-Generator Adjustment

A pulse generator, such as a one-shot, single-shot, or monostable multivibrator, can be designed to provide a variable-pulse-width output signal. Most frequently, the device used is a pot. The pot may be installed in the input circuit or in the output circuit. It is frequently incorporated in monostable and bistable multivibrators (MV). Its primary function is to alter the *RC* time constant of the circuit, thereby causing a shorter or longer decay time. This allows the circuit to provide a varied or adjustable output pulse width. Most of these circuits require a trigger input to cause a change in states. From a quiescent state a trigger may be applied to either the base or collector to cut off the conducting transistor or bring into conduction the cutoff transistor. This action causes the MV to switch states. The decay time of the *RC* circuit controls the conduction period of the entire circuit by maintaining bias values until the voltages decay through circuit *RC* components to the point where the circuit reverts to its original state.

Refer to Figure 4-15 for an example of miniature potentiometers being used with an integrated circuit. The operation of pots R3 or R4 is very similar to the uses already described. Their primary function is, once again, variable control; when each is used with a 3.3-kΩ resistor and an 8-pF capacitor, an *RC* network is formed. Study Figure 4-15 closely during the discussion of pots used in pulse generators.

4-4.4 Integrated Circuit with RC Pulse-Width Control

The circuit consists of integrated units Z1 and Z2m; external to the ICs are pots R3 and R4, both 20 kΩ. Resistors R5 and R6 are 3.3 kΩ each and capacitors C1 and C2 are 8 pF. On each half of the IC, Z2 is a Schmitt trigger circuit. The primary function of a Schmitt trigger is to provide a rectangular waveform output whenever the input is caused to change states. If the input is a low-frequency ac signal (e.g., 60 Hz) the input circuit delays its reactions to the input until the controlling slope of the signal reaches an amplitude sufficient for the change to occur. No change in output results until reaction occurs.

For instance, if the input waveform takes 50 μs to rise high enough to bring the input circuit out of cutoff, the output has no reaction until the change takes place. On the other hand, if the input is rectangular and the rise time is 20 ns or faster, the output reacts almost instantaneously. Considering these factors, examination of the circuit in Figure 4-15 shows that the input AND gate Z2A requires three high inputs on pins 1, 13, and 14, plus a high from pot R3. Since this AND gate has pins 13 and 14 tied to ± 5 V dc, pin 1 causes the Schmitt trigger to start operation. R3, R5, and C1 form an *RC* network for pulse-width control. The maximum and minimum times derived from the formula $T = RC$ reveal two conditions: (1) a time of 20 ns with the pot effectively removed, and (2) a time of 187 ns with the full pot in the circuit. This variable component controls the conduction of the input circuit of the Schmitt trigger and consequently delays the completion of the rectangular output waveform.

The ZIA NAND gate provides a pulse when the inputs to pins 12 and 13 are high. A negative pulse is fed to pin 1 of IC Z2 AND gate Z2A. On the rise of the output signal from NAND gate ZIA, the trigger is turned on, and an output is generated from the Schmitt trigger. The length or pulse width of the output pulse is dependent upon the value of the *RC* circuit, consisting of R3, R5, and C1. Their sizes provide a time constant value, which causes the Schmitt trigger to stay in its ON state. The delay resulting effectively stretches the pulse. R4, R6, and C2 and the second Schmitt trigger units do the same.

With this understanding of the circuit operation, performance of the following adjustment routine has meaning: Set up the scope for 5 V at 0.1 ns for each channel. Adjust trailing-edge control R3 fully clockwise. Adjust leading-edge control R4 for maximum value (as near 600 ns as possible) while looking at TP20 on channel 1 of the oscilloscope. This is a primary example of the simplicity of instruction taken from an alignment routine, and it focuses on the point of this discussion—that a knowledge of circuit operation is needed if for any reason the pulse width does not measure 600 ns.

4-5 Adjusting Power Supplies

"Adjust power supply control R25 for a 15 V $\pm$ 0.01 V output."
"Adjust R8 for a meter reading of −15 V dc."
"Adjust the 390 V dc power supply for 390 V + 0.5 V."
"Adjust R16 for a voltmeter reading of 15 V dc."

The above quotes from PMIs show the simplicity of power-supply-adjustment instructions. The first and third examples reflect an exact percentage of deviation and, because they do, the use of a differential voltmeter is required. On the other hand, the second and fourth instructions specify voltage taken from a meter installed on the power unit. The adjustment of any of these pots consists of varying the resistance to the load at the output of the supply. By varying the component, conduction in the circuit is varied and output voltage indications show the new value.

If adjustments are made using a differential meter, the output of the power supply is measured against the output of the calibrated meter, and the adjustment potentiometer on the supply provides the control.

Most regulated power supplies are complex units and require extensive study. For this discussion of adjustments, a brief review of their makeup provides the basis for understanding. The output of a regulated supply is distributed to many circuits. The output voltage is usually adjustable within limits. The output current may or may not be adjustable and visually measured; however, its value is considerable. It may be as much as 100 A.

4-5.1 *Low Voltage*

To have this much current at the low voltage required for transistor and integrated circuit operation necessitates the use of extensive front-end circuitry. Common electronic components, such as *silicon-controlled rectifiers, Zener diodes, thermistors,* and *thyratron semiconductor devices,* are all used to provide current and voltage regulation. Filtering is accomplished by extensive use of coils, capacitors, and resistors. Finally, the source input is frequently 400 Hz instead of 60 Hz because it is easier to filter.

In Figure 4-16, VR1 and VR2 are Zener diodes used in conjunction with R1 and a 500-Ω pot. They provide a variable +15-V signal to one

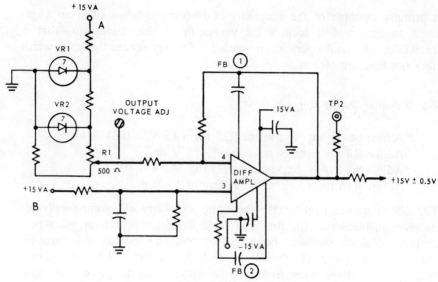

Fig. 4-16. Input-Controlled Power Supply

input of a differential amplifier. The other input (pin 4), also a +15-V
signal, is inverted in the first stage of the circuit. The output is regulated
by developing a difference between the two inputs, which, when added to
the gain of the amplifier, regulates the output voltage to +15 ± 0.5 V.
The *RC* network provides filtering for high frequency induced by amplification of noise. In this example the control is included in the input
circuitry. This illustration again points out the usefulness of potentiometers
and the variations of their arrangement in circuits.

4-5.2 *High Voltage*

Most high-voltage power-supply test points and adjustment controls

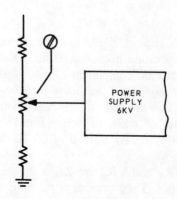

Fig. 4-17. Pot in High-Voltage Power Supply

are isolated. Frequently the potentiometer is connected to a voltage divider network from infinity on one end to ground on the other (see Figure 4-17). The wiper arm, however, has a very high potential since it has a voltage equivalent to the power supply. Caution must be used because of the high voltage present, even though the controls and test points are isolated.

4-6   Adjusting Timing Devices

Almost without exception, timing units incorporate crystals. The extremely high stability of these solid-state structures has accounted for remarkable advancements in newer computer equipment. Many crystals are encased in ovens to assure proper operating frequencies. Many crystals are cut for negative or positive coefficients which require engineering solutions. Advanced technology and manufacturing skills have provided solutions to most of industry's demands, and the result is that the newer computers require little maintenance of their timing units.

4-6.1   Time and Frequency

One of the oldest data processors in use in defense of the United States is the AN/FST-2B. It is used to collect and process data for use in the SAGE system. It transmits the data by controlled timing from a pulsed Hartley oscillator. When properly adjusted, pulses from the oscillator are generated each 3.09 μs. In adjusting the frequency of the oscillator the output of the circuit encompassing the crystal is measured. When its amplitude is at peak, the circuit is operating at the frequency of 323.44 kHz.

A newer air weapons-control system uses a basic 1-MHz crystal-controlled clock. The output feeds local clocks, which, in turn, divide this timing generator output into 64 reference pulses of various pulse widths and pulse repetition times. Timing adjustments in this system are extensive and are made with potentiometers. The master clock circuitry provides for adjustments of the output frequency by trimmer capacitors. The calibrated output must be measured with a frequency counter and must be 1 MHz ± 1 Hz.

The AN/FSQ-7 uses a 2-MHz crystal-controlled reference generator. Its output-frequency variation is exacting also.

One of the newest defense systems, the BUIC system, uses a 3-MHz timing reference generator. Its crystal-controlled timing is set by tubular capacitor adjustment to 3 MHz + 100 Hz. Referring to Figure 4-18, the block diagram of the clock-generation circuit of the BUIC, you can see that:

1. The computer master clock (CMC) is set by the adjustable capacitor to a frequency of 3,00,100 ± 10 Hz.

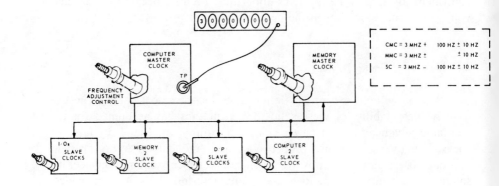

Fig. 4-18. Timing Unit

2. Each slave clock (SC) is set for a frequency of 2,999,900 ± 10 Hz.

3. The memory clock (MMC) is set for exactly 3 MHz ± 10 Hz.

With these frequency variations, it becomes easy to see that CMC does all controlling when operative and causes the slave clocks to speed up to 3 MHz. If the CMC clock fails, the MMC clock, which is still running faster than the slaves, causes the slaves to speed up, and the system still runs at 3MHz. If both MMC and CMC fail, the system fails; however, the SCs are used for local testing.

A modem used with the Strategic Air Command employs a crystal-controlled reference generator. This unit uses ovens for frequency stability. It requires a stability of ±1 Hz. Adjustable trimmer capacitors (button type) are included for frequency adjustment.

Another modem used in tactical control equipment also uses a crystal encased in an oven. However, this crystal and associated circuit have no frequency-compensation controls. Its crystals are cut to oscillate at frequencies as high as 10.36 MHz. The crystals feed frequency dividers which are manufactured with variable pulse width and amplitude resistive controls.

Whereas the T2 and BUIC have reference clocks for central timing, the last example, the modem and its associated equipment, uses many different clocks. In addition to the central or master timing, many other timing circuits are used. Some of these are:

1. Free-running oscillators.

2. One-shot multivibrators.

3. Blocking oscillators.

4. Time-sharing circuits for displays.

5. Automatic gate-length generators for use with radar returns.

In each case a variable control is usually incorporated, and frequently it is resistive to control voltage amplitude.

Let's look at the facts we have covered so far. First, variable capacitors of both the button and tubular type are used for controlling frequency. These are normally found in circuits for master timing and are often found in display timing units. Second, resistive variable controls in master timing units are usually in the output for amplitude control. They are also used in other timing circuits to control *pulse width, pulse-repetition rates,* and *amplitude.*

4-6.2 Timing Routines

Timing routines fall in two broad categories:

1. The frequency adjustment of a crystal-controlled oscillator.

2. The duty-cycle adjustment.

The *frequency adjustment* is made with a frequency counter externally connected to the oscillator output. The frequency control is adjusted until the counter reads the precise value of the performance standards.

The *duty-cycle adjustment* is usually measured on an oscilloscope. A basic reference pulse is usually displayed on either the A or B trace, and the waveform of the circuit to be adjusted is displayed on the other trace. The waveform is calibrated and the duty cycle is adjusted by altering the variable component in the circuit under measurement. If an amplitude variable is included, the instructions usually specify the amplitude plus or minus a specified deviation.

4-7 Adjusting Memory Devices

During a study made of storage devices and their adjustments, a significant factor developed. The adjustments performed were divided into two separate and significantly different subtasks. One was *mechanical adjustment* and the other was *electrical adjustment* using an electronic component. One might say that any adjustment, even a pot, is mechanical, and in the truest sense he would be correct. In this study mechanical adjustment indicates the physical altering of components to a specific distance, even though the distance is measured in voltage amplitudes. Electrical adjustment is constructed to mean a variation of a pot or capacitor to provide a standard waveform or level.

Based on these premises, mechanical adjustment can be readily associated with drum systems, tape systems, and disc systems, since each has the same principle of depositing and extracting data through a magnetic head. The electrical adjustments can be associated with the systems listed above; also core systems, thin film, electrostatic-tube storage systems, delay-line storage systems, and some integrated-circuit storage systems. In these systems, electrical adjustments are performed on components external to the storage device in almost every case. During this study you will see that this is true.

4-8 Mechanical Adjustment Principles

The *drum-storage device* consists of many channels; each channel has read/write heads and usually an erase bar. Each head is secured to a frame

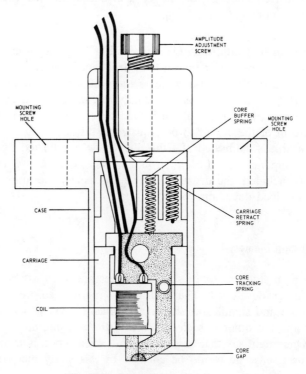

Fig. 4-19. Read/Write Head

that is designed to place the head very close to the drum surface. The read/write head assembly, shown in Figure 4-19, is similar to one used on two different computer systems. You can see that a screen controls the positioning of the carriage assembly.

4-8.1   Drum-Head Adjustment

The physical size of the assembly is approximately 1¼ inches by ⅜ inch. It contains two mounting screw holes on the flanges and internal coil, the heart of the unit. The amplitude adjustment screw allows the carriage to move up or down, closer to or farther away from the drum surface. The adjustment routines require that data in the form of a binary 1 be written onto the drum channel ebbing adjusted. Measurement of the pulse is made on a dual-trace oscilloscope with one trace measuring the input waveform and the other trace measuring the output waveform. Adjustment of the head for the Q7 requires that an output voltage be measured at 125 to 150 mV peak to peak. The steps to arrive at this voltage output are such that the head is lowered to the stopped drum surface and then raised until 75 percent of the voltage waveform is displayed on the scope.

Ten years of progress and advanced technology have brought simplification to the drum-head units, as shown in Figure 4-20. This BUIC

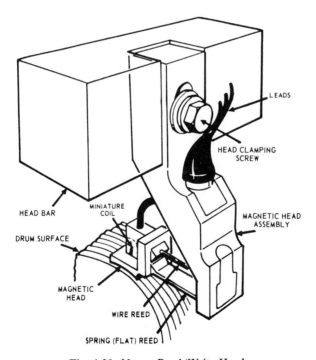

Fig. 4-20. Newer Read/Write Head

read/write head is smaller, simpler, and uses spring steel (spring flat reed) to hold the recording head near the drum. It incorporates a miniature coil measuring approximately ⅛ inch square. The techniques of adjustment are similar to the older models in that a binary 1 is written into the channel and the read-out voltage is measured while adjustments are being made. Special tools are required to adjust this system. The pivot screw shown on the left in Figure 4-21 secures the adjustment tool to the head mounting bar, and the adjustment screw controls the positioning of the head. The head clamping screw is tightened and the task is complete.

4-8.2 Tape-Drive Adjustment

On tape-drive systems, mechanical adjustments are usually associated with the drive mechanism rather than with the heads. Most heads are installed in a metal container and are recessed from the outer surface of the container 3 to 7 one-thousandths of an inch, thereby providing the required gap for magnetizing the tape. Some tape systems use shims to raise the tape 0.003 to 0.005 inch from the tape head.

Mechanical adjustments vary according to their design features; how-

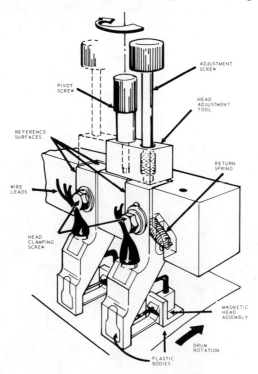

Fig. 4-21. Read/Write Head Adjustment Tool

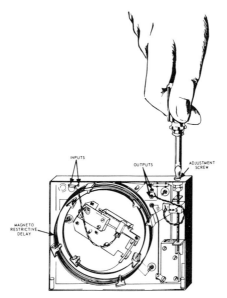

Fig. 4-22. Magneto Restrictive Delay Line

ever, they are common in that the proper drive speed, stop, start, and tension must be maintained. For instance, in the format message composer of a communications system, there is a sprocket adjustment which provides the required tension for the tape as it passes over the read/write head.

On the other drive units, a pinch roller may be adjusted by use of shims, and so may its brakes. Its vacuum-pump adjustment is made so that the water gauge shows a reading of 40 ± 5 inches, and any adjustments that are made to belt-driven assemblies are usually performed at the time recommended for corrective maintenance. These adjustments involve the driven capstan, vacuum-pump motors, and rewind motors.

4-8.3 Delay-Line Adjustment

The magneto restrictive delay-line storage system incorporates a mechanical adjustment device tunable to a precise position. The principle of storage for this device is shown in Figure 4-22. A silver wire is used as the storage element with approximately the last 16 μs variable. Current in the form of a pulse of short duration is put into the wire at one end. It travels down the wire at the rate of approximately 1,100 ft/s. Since its rate of travel is linear, the selection of a precise length then identifies two facts: (1) the time delay of the pulse if known by the length of the wire times the rate of travel, and (2) if the pulse (data bit) occupies a precise measurement of length along the wire, a specific number of data bits or words may be stored. Access to data at the output is sequential and any selection data can be sampled provided their entry time and the total length of the storage line are known. The adjustment of the last few microseconds becomes a critical factor and the timing must be precise. Two methods are used in making the adjustments. First, an oscilloscope using two traces may be used. The input pulse is shown on one trace; the output pulse is shown on the other. Since these are the same pulse, the measurement of the time between input and output reveals the delay or storage time. Adjustment can be made to display a precise known delay storage time. The second method is performed by using a test setup designed and built for adjusting these storage devices. The principle used is that switches program the tester's internal circuits, thereby providing pulses and measuring pulses at specific times. The pulses are then displayed by use of neon lights. The first light to come on is interpreted to indicate that a close setting has been achieved, and the second light indicates an exact setting.

4-8.4   Disc-Memory Adjustment

The disc-memory system is related to a juke box in that the disc rotates and the heads are placed above and below the recording disc. Figure 4-23 shows a cutaway view of a disc-memory unit. As with other storage devices using magnetic recording, there are mechanical and electrical adjustments. The mechanical head assemblies are adjusted by screws installed in pivot arms. These are shown in the breakout in Figure 4-23. The heads are adjusted with shims and the use of a micrometer. From Figure 4-23 you can see that the heads are placed in various positions around the disc. By examination of callout 1 of Figure 4-23 you can see that the head bar has an adjustment called a *pivot screw*. The head bar is shown more clearly in callout 2 of Figure 4-23. Once again, extensive use of mechanical adjustment is made on storage devices.

4-8.5   Electrical Adjustment Principles

Current is required to write a 1 onto a storage device and all systems use drivers to accomplish this action. The current is almost always the result of the decoding action of data. A binary 1 will usually cause a circuit action, which converts the digital 1 into a current pulse of the proper polarity for use in a magnetic storage medium. The device most generally used is the write amplifier.

4-8.6   Read/Write Amplifier Adjustment

Almost all systems use write amplifiers and read amplifiers. These amplifiers usually have potentiometers installed for fine adjustment. They may be current-limiting, voltage-limiting, or both. They are usually adjusted specifications as PM routines. This study also reveals that all tape

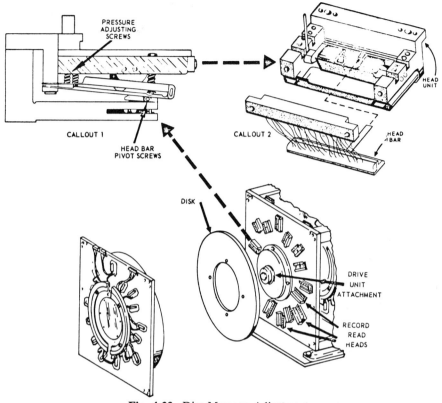

Fig. 4-23. Disc-Memory Adjustment

storage units have either a read amplifier or a write amplifier adjustment pot, but some storage systems have neither. One drum system uses a current-limiting memory protection circuit with adjustment pots to regulate the current requirements for the entire drum unit.

4-8.7 Thin-Film Circuit Adjustment

Thin-film memory systems provide a nondestructive readout after storage of data. This is accomplished by reading a current amplitude of slightly less than switching current or hard state, as shown in Figure 4-24. The adjustments associated with this memory system are made on the read/write amplifier units. Coincidence of two pulses is required to provide the switching current necessary for storage of data.

The principle for write needs a coincident address current plus a write current sufficient to cause switching. To read requires a coincident current, but one not so high in amplitude that it causes switching. The diagonal dashed line in Figure 4-24 is the read value for either a 1 or a 0.

The makeup of a thin-film storage unit is shown in Figure 4-25. The

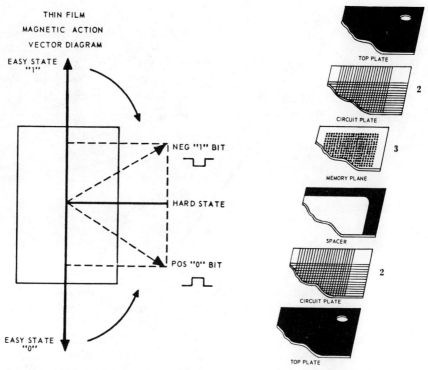

Fig. 4-24. Thin-Film Memory Switching   **Fig. 4-25.** Thin-Film Unit

storage area consists of dots of magnetic deposits (3) within a grid of co-incident connectors (2). Each dot is capable of acting as a core and is addressed in a similar manner. The primary differences are the physical makeup and the nondestruct readout of data from loss of power.

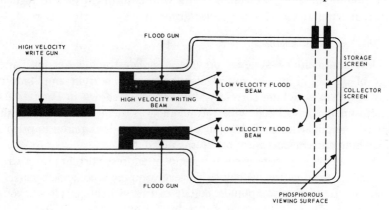

Fig. 4-26. Storage Tube

4-8.8 *Storage-Tube Adjustment*

The electrostatic storage tube is a device using a modified cathode-ray tube (CRT) to allow operators to view its stored data. There are variations of this tube you may use. One is called the memo scope. The principle of operation is shown in Figure 4-26. Data are written by the high-velocity write gun through the collector screen onto the storage screen. The flow guns scan the screen and every point on the storage screen where data are present (+ voltage). The flood voltage penetrates and illuminates the CRT phospher. As in drums and core storage, the applied voltage and current are controlled by pots. They control scanning, unblanking, video data levels, flow gun intensity, and storage and collector screen erase.

4-8.9 *Integrated-Circuit-Display (CRT) Adjustment*

One system previously using the storage tube had the circuit redesigned to use a simpler more modern design. Chart 1 (DID control unit) shows a view of the control panel, including all the potentiometers; a view of the CRT and integrated circuit packages; and logic and circuit diagrams. This simplified circuit eliminated the older storage scope with its six mechanical centering controls for pitch and yaw, its eight stepping voltage adjustments (four for horizontal and four for vertical), and its two intensity controls. The new system operates on the principle of storaging the data to be displayed in a recycling storage buffer (not shown in Chart 1). The data from the buffer programs the memory IC storage (B in Chart 1), which provides an output to digital-to-analog converters 1 and 2 (D in Chart 1). The character voltage from the digital-to-analog (D/A) converter is added to a vertical and horizontal stepping voltage, and these voltages are applied to the deflection plates. During intensity time, the character is painted. The controls, all pots, adjust for (refer to A in Chart 1):

1. Character width and height.
2. Position vertical and horizontal.
3. Character spacing vertical and horizontal.
4. Intensity.

Let's study *A*, the alignment panel of the DID unit. The upper third contains three potentiometers, all contained in a serial voltage divider network with one end tied to source voltage +13 V and the other end to ground. Tracing back to its use, each wiper arm feeds to the D/A converter board. R11, the vertical gain, feeds to an amplifier (shown in 2, the D/A computer) to the high-order bits decoder. The symbols shown are really transistors acting as switches. The output voltage of the high-order bits is determined by the binary-count input. It may be 0 through

15. Each count biases one or more of the transistors and the algebraic sum of the four, plus or minus the variable gain of R11, projected through the amplifier provides a deflection voltage for the vertical deflection plates. The unit is capable of providing 16 stepping voltages; however, by looking at C in Chart 1, you will see that only 10 vertical positions are used.

The next in the series of pots is the *character-height pot.* It permits increase and decrease in the vertical size of the individual characters. The voltage from the pot is fed to the lower bits decoder. Variation in size is therefore restricted by the allowable parameter of the decoder.

The third control (vertical position) voltage is fed to the differential amplifier. This control determines when the difference output occurs. It does not alter the character size. It provides a control for positioning the characters in a particular position on the CRT.

To show you the effects of the pot as displayed on the CRT, look at callouts 1, 2, and 3 of C in Chart 1. Callout 1, the vertical gain, alters the stepping voltage to the plates. Therefore, it provides more or less stepping voltage and causes the display to vary as shown. Callout 2, the character-height pot, controls the size of the character within the space allotted for the character. The difference in size is shown in callout 2 of C in Chart 1. Callout 3, the vertical-position control, moves the display up and down as shown in C of Chart 1 but does not affect the size.

Returning again to the schematic of the alignment panel (Chart 1A), the upper shaded area of the panel shows a similar arrangement for horizontal control of characters. Notice, though, that R5 is 2.5 kΩ, where R11 in the vertical unit was 1 kΩ. The additional variable resistance is provided because the display is wider across than down, and more stepping voltages (16) are generated. The controls provide the same function as the vertical controls.

The right side of the alignment panel (Foldout 1A) shows a rim (panel) light-control knob and an intensity amplitude control for overall brightness of the CRT display.

From this study of adjustments you can see that adjustments are many and varied. The final area of application in this study is adjustment of data input and output circuits.

4-9 Adjusting Data Input and Output Circuits

Both potentiometers and variable capacitors are used in establishing the correct data levels within the input and output circuits of the computer, data processing, and communications systems. Since some systems use more than one type of data entry or exit, this discussion shows where typical adjustments are made according to type of data. The data inputs and outputs can be separated into many classes, but for this study three were chosen: (1) digital data, (2) video data, and (3) electronic data convertible to or from digital.

4-9.1 Digital Data

Digital data are those data that are transmitted from one unit to another via landlines (TELCO), troposcatter, or microwave. The system of transmission involves primarily frequency shift keying (FSK) and dipole and frequency shift modulation (FSM). Although we discussed FSK and dipole in Chapter 3, review their forms by looking at Figure 4-27A and B. Each time that a binary 1 is transmitted or received in FSK, the circuits sense and process a change in frequency. Contrast the dipole data, where each binary 1 is represented by an *AC* pulse and a binary 0 is represented by a level. The FSM, not discussed previously but shown in Figure 4-27C, combines some of both systems in that frequencies are modulated—one representing a binary 1 and one representing a binary zero. In all three cases timing is related, since the speed of sampling of the pulses corresponds to the data content.

Adjustments performed upon circuits using these systems of data transfer use both pots and variable capacitors. The pots primarily control amplitude and pulse width. The capacitors affect frequency amplitude and phase control. Adjustment routines require the use of measuring devices, frequency counters, and oscilloscopes. Some of the common names applied to these input–output units are:

1. Message processors.
2. Modems.
3. Modulators–demodulators.
4. Input/output units.
5. Transmitters or receivers.
6. Decoders or encoders.

4-9.2 Video Data

As discussed earlier, radar and SIF may be provided in many forms, from raw to digitized. Radar sets, of course, receive a *very* small pulse return, and the amplifiers within the set boost them considerably. If the return digitized within the radar set, all target returns are presented to the data-processing unit at a standard pulse width and amplitude. The data-processor input unit might then have amplitude pots as controls, but not much more. However, if the data are selectable by personnel using the data

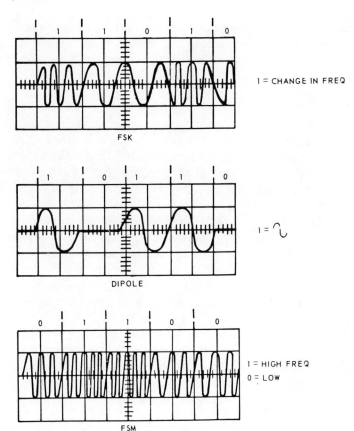

Fig. 4-27. Digital-Data Forms in Audio Frequencies

processor where digitized raw or processed radar enters the input circuitry, extensive use is made of variable components. Capacitors are incorporated to provide gain control for high-frequency pulses, and potentiometers are used for low-frequency (dc) pulse control, pulse-width control, duty-cycle control, and bias control. Some of the common names applied to these units are:

1. Quantizers.
2. Video amplifier units.
3. SIF processors or beacon processors.

4-9.3 *Electronic Data Convertible to or from Digital*

Units providing data to input/output units in this category are:

1. Punch-card readers.
2. Teletype.
3. Printers.
4. Video printers.
5. Paper-tape machines.
6. Keyboards.

Many of these units have adjustment controls installed in their circuitry which eliminate the need for the data processor or computer to have adjustable components in their input/output circuits. For instance, a certain card reader has two controls, one for pulse-width adjustment and the other for timing of a strobe pulse generated by a saturable reactor. There is a selection control within another unit, with a variable amplitude control for each level. Some printers and keyboards have variable mechanical and electrical controls, so input/output units do not use them. These are examples of adjustments being provided on I/O equipment feeding to or being fed from data processors or computers, or communication equipment. The data codes used by these devices differ from both the digital input data and video in that frequently the data are converted to current pulses, are fed in parallel, travel at a higher rate of speed, may be completely digital at prescribed logic levels, or are converted to digital from relays and switches.

TEST QUESTIONS

1. What are the two types of variable capacitors?

2. What are the principles of the variable capacitor and the rheostat?

3. What is the difference between a potentiometer and a rheostat?

4. Are provisions made during manufacture of pots which tell the technician that he is at the turning end of the pot?

5. While performing the balancing adjustment on a meter movement, how much current is used?

6. What is the principle of a differential meter?

7. Why is it common to adjust the potentiometer within an ohmmeter when changing scales?

8. What is the purpose of the pot shown in Figure 4-15? Does it affect the input circuitry or the output circuitry?

9. Can you correctly match the following terms with the type of control?

   a. Capacitors   1. Affects the low frequency of a signal
   b. Potentiometers   more than the high frequency.

                               2. Affects the high frequency of a signal
                                  more than the low frequency.

                               3. Pulse amplitude and width control.

                               4. Phase control.

5

Alignment

The bringing together of individual elements to provide an overall function is the primary concept in alignment.

Operational performance checks were identified and analyzed in Chapter 3. These checks were made almost entirely on functional circuits which provided a specific output necessary for the entire equipment to perform. Some checks took into consideration only small segments of the equipment, such as video amplitude validation. Others checked the entire unit, as in the case of a printer.

From the study, in Chapter 4 we analyzed the variable components used to make the individual adjustments. The analysis brought out that adjustments involve individual circuit elements as well as interconnecting and interrelating circuits and often other functions.

5-1 Alignment Concept

Combining the objective of these Chapter 3 and 4 aids in acceptance of the concept that for alignment to be meaningful and effective, complete understanding of the overall function of the circuits within the alignment is essential. The principal objectives and selected applications are identified, explained, and analyzed in the paragraphs that follow.

5-2 Principal Objectives of Alignment

Look at the man in Figure 5-1. Does he resemble someone you have seen during the period of time you have been in the work environment? He is well equipped. He has his alignment technical manual, test equipment, plenty of leads, and a job order. He is going to align a complex piece of computer equipment. Do you know that he will do a good job? In all probability, he will do an excellent job. The reason he will is that the instructions written within the alignment routines are clear and specific, and the standards are specified.

This man received praise for doing an efficient job on the alignment, but two hours later the equipment broke down. He returned to it only to find out that he did not know what had caused the failure.

We all know that a failure can occur at any time, but consider the close time interval between the completion of the alignment and the failure. Is one act the cause of the other? Is there more to performing an alignment than accomplishing the steps of a given routine? What could some of these

Fig. 5-1. Workman with Tools

answers be, and how could they relate to improving an individual's worth? How could answers to these questions be used to improve the man's understanding? Let's see if we can break down the task of performing alignments into significant elements.

5-2.1 Identify the Basic Objectives of the Alignment

Our man learned to perform the steps in the alignment. Did he understand the objective? Probably. He possibly knew what it was from the title of the alignment routine, but did he realize only that the title identified a particular area, function, or subfunction of the equipment?

To identify the basic objective of an alignment routine requires more study than reading the title. It involves an in-depth study of all the related circuits, components, electronic principles, and work techniques combined. Figure 5-2 illustrates that there are five major subdivisions to a complete understanding of alignment. First we have the alignment title and the objective of the alignment. Second is identification of circuits included in the alignment. The third element identifies the need to study interrelated functions which have a bearing on the objective. The fourth element is a study of all circuits and functions for priorities. Finally, the alignment of the objective element completes the study. The first of these is determining the objective. Expanding part of Figure 5-2 into Figure 5-3, we identify two elements necessary to obtaining a clear definition of the objective. The study must include first an examination of the specific alignment and the related technical references. In doing so, we must determine:

1. Various segments of the technical orders which would aid in understanding the objective.
2. The data or signal-flow paths that may be altered by the alignment.
3. Specifications and limitations of the various steps involved in the alignment instructions.
4. The theory of operation of the unit to be aligned.

The second element identified in Figure 5-3 as being necessary to obtain a clear definition of the objective involves certain electronic principles. As an example, if integrated circuits are included in the system, their capability must be thoroughly understood. Their physical makeup must be identified. The maximum and minimum variations possible with variable controls must be studied. If, as we pointed out in Chapter 4, a pot can only alter a circuit output by 10 percent and the measurements of the actual output vary by 20 percent, no apparent alignment can be

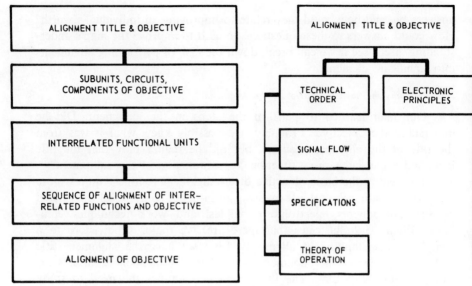

Fig. 5-2. Alignment   **Fig. 5-3.** Alignment Title and Objective

made. But is the circuit containing the variable control isolated, or is it interrelated? If it is isolated, then a local problem exists, and correction is required. If, on the other hand, the circuit is interrelated with another control circuit, the possibility exists that the other circuit is causing the wide variation from the specification.

Combining the two elements of the study to determine the objective of an alignment establishes the primary purpose for the alignment. This purpose must be established in clear, specific terms and must convey a specific meaning. It must identify either a major or a minor function which the machine must do. It must relate to the theory of the operation of the equipment. Finally, it must lead to development of an in-depth study. The next logical step, as indicated in Figure 5-2, is the identification of subunits or circuits that affect the main objective.

5-2.2 Identify Subunits or Circuits that Affect the Main Objective

Almost without exception a function of a computer system is made of multiple circuits. Some functions have no adjustment controls; others have one; and some have many. If the circuits within the function contain only one control, understanding the way the control operates is easy, as is verification of the control's functional operation. Complete understanding of the function, however, is no less important. This is so because any circuit, either preceding or following the circuit containing the variable component, may have one or more of its parameters changed, owing to physical breakdown of elements within the structures. For instance, heat affects all parts of components and causes changes in resistance and capacitance or thermal runaway of semiconductor devices. Changes in current, caused by the structural changes in components, alter conduction parameters of these components and their related circuits. The variable control is primarily designed to overcome these factors, and it will compensate for some of them.

Figure 5-4 illustrates that when functions are broken into subunits (individual circuits), data about the function must include the items listed. In computers and processing machines, manufacturers have built circuits on printed circuit cards and then interconnected the circuits with wire or cable. To identify these circuits you merely extract the circuits included in the function by:

1. Identifying the alphanumeric in the alignments.
2. Identifying circuit titles, parameters, and purposes.
3. Locating these elements in the circuit and diagram manual.
4. Placing the circuits, if not on the same pages, into a straight line (sequence) on a work pad, to show initialization, processing, and utilization.

If, for instance, circuitry within a function contains an oscillator circuit and a flip-flop frequency divider, identify the oscillator as one block and the frequency divider as another block. If the function contains switching networks, amplifiers, and buffers, make a block for each circuit: one for the switching networks, one for the amplifiers, and one for the buffers. Label each block. The separation aids in understanding relationships of circuits within functions. It also allows for listing selected necessary parameters of the individual circuits.

Because of the wide variety of circuit design and application, we cannot cover parameters in this book. However, in-depth understanding of them is essential to the understanding of the operation and alignment. Do not be misled by the comment that changing a printed circuit board (PCB) is always the solution to problems. This fallacy allows for restoration of equipment for operational purposes, but it does not permit

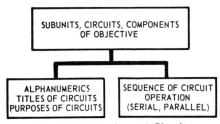

Fig. 5-4. Subunits and Circuits

identification of the causes of equipment failure. It does not answer questions about why the variable component in a function could not bring the function into line.

As an example, consider that transistors are classed according to frequency-passing capability (i.e., audio, RF, VHF, etc.) as well as current-handling capability. We know that two space regions exist in each transistor: one between the emitter and the base, and the other between the collector and the base. Under normal operating conditions of a given circuit using transistors, these regions are the controlling elements. The amount of forward and reverse bias determines operation. We also know that transistor amplifiers have interelectrode capacitance, and the capacitance existing between these regions affects their operation. Therefore, interelectrode capacitances may change under varying conditions, and when they do, they offer more or less reactance to the input frequency. This can cause a change in output frequency or amplitude.

Let's relate one more factor to this example. Most of the processing circuits develop rectangular waveforms, and we know that these are made from a basic frequency and infinite odd harmonics of the basic. If a partial breakdown occurs within the regions identified above and reactance changes, some of these harmonics will be attenuated by the amplifier, and the output waveform becomes distorted. It may become integrated, differentiated, or begin to ring. It may increase or decrease in amplitude. It may frequency-shift, causing a delay in time.

This example typifies the need to analyze an alignment to identify the elements. It furthers the need for basic electronic understanding of circuit design and interconnection. And it brings another significant element of alignment into view.

5-2.3   *Identify Interrelationships of the Function with Other Circuits or Functions*

This element, illustrated in Figure 5-2 and amplified in Figure 5-5, brings into focus the concept that very often functions other than the one being aligned must provide a discrete, specific output. An example, as shown, might be the timing unit that supplies time-share pulses at particular pulse widths and pulse recurring times (PRT) to a display unit.

Some system must be used in an alignment routine to identify external requirements. It may be subunits in the first stages of the alignment and may require verification of the externally controllable pulses. It may be a general statement stipulating the prerequisite that certain pulses be present in accordance with specifications. Or it may be sequencing of alignments within scheduling that provides the method for

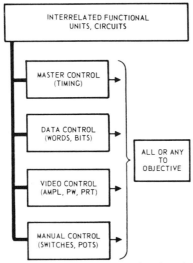

Fig. 5-5. Interrelated Functional Units

determining that all necessary controlled pulses are present in accordance with specifications.

Whichever system is used, the significant idea is that someone know that preliminary steps must be accomplished. These people also know and understood the entire unit operation. Therefore they were able to sequence the necessary steps. They knew from research exactly which functional units or circuits provided inputs to the functional being aligned. As shown in Figure 5-5, any or all of the areas may play a significant part in allowing the circuits to perform. If these people knew the system, you need to know the system. Therefore, identification of each interrelated function must be made. Its title, purpose, and significant data input to the function under alignment must be listed. Using a separate block for each interrelated function allows for quick, sure identification of its influence. Also include notations within the block about any and all controllable variables, such as pots, capacitors, and data.

For an example of the concept stated above, refer to Figure 5-6. The figure, shown in Military Standard 806B symbology, represents a functional alignment with other functions having a bearing upon its

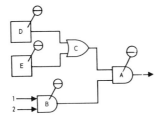

Fig. 5-6. Functional Elements

function. Function *A* is the function to be aligned. Notice, though, that function *B* must provide an output, and to do so, both signals 1 and 2 must be present at its input. Further, *B* is a functional unit which is in itself aligned. Notice that function *C* allows for the processing of either generator *D* or *E,* and both *D* and *E* are aligned.

We now have a situation in which *A*'s function is dependent upon its own internal circuits, parameters, and components, and also either *D* processed by *C* and *B* or *E* processed by *C* and *B*.

Consequently, the output of *A* could not be brought into proper specifications unless alignment of *D, E,* and *B* preceded A's alignment.

To point up this discussion, you need to analyze each alignment using the technical references to determine the complete picture. You must identify if any interrelationship of function exists, what it is, and how it affects the function being aligned. This brings us to the next element of the objective, as indicated in Figure 5-2.

5-2.4   Determine the Sequence of Occurrence of Interrelated Functional Units and the Objective Alignment

For overall success to be guaranteed, the broadest knowledge of processing must be thoroughly understood. This means that the theoretical knowledge of unit and subunit functions must be focused upon the question of which part should be aligned first, second, and so on.

This element is concerned with identification of sequencing alignments between interrelated functions and units but not within the functional unit being aligned. Let's use Figure 5-6 again. In order for *A* to be aligned, we see that it must have two inputs. Therefore, *B* in Figure 5-6 must be aligned prior to *A*. Also *D* and *E* must be aligned prior to *A,* because either *D* or *E* provides the other requirements to *A*. Therefore, *B, D,* and *E* must be aligned before *A,* but since *D* and *E* can provide a separate input to *A,* either can be aligned without regard to sequence. On the other hand, *B* may have an input on either of the two input lines which may be from an aligned circuit.

Should this be the case, *B*'s input must be proper. Therefore, the alignment of the circuit supplying the input must precede *B*'s alignment.

To recap the sequence: *D* or *E* can be aligned first. *B* can be aligned if its inputs are not coming from an aligned circuit. If either input does come from an aligned circuit, that circuit alignment must precede *B*'s alignment. Finally, *A* circuits can be aligned.

This discussion has illustrated in a very simplified manner our previous question of which part should be aligned first, second, and so on. A detailed study of your equipment can identify what interrelationships are dependent upon determining the data listed in Figure 5-7.

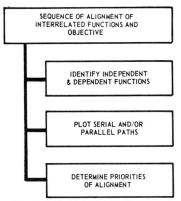

Fig. 5-7. Sequence of Alignments

INDEPENDENT/DEPENDENT. You must, after identifying the interrelated functions and their associated circuitry, determine if the function is independent or dependent. If the function is independent, then it is a generator of some sort which is designed and manufactured to provide discrete outputs. Except for power requirements, it functions by itself. A unit of this type usually contains an oscillator. It may include frequency dividers, phase shifters, discriminators, quadrature networks, multipliers, and other assorted circuitry. These internal circuits only prepare the discrete output which is necessary for the objective alignment. Detailed information for your study of the objective alignment need not include all aspects of the independent related function, but they must include enough to know what and when the generator outputs are, what generates them, and what circuits alter them.

If the interrelated function is dependent, you must identify its dependency. You must identify the major elements which cause it to be dependent. While doing this, determine whether or not the inputs to these elements are from other independent or dependent functional circuits. If independent, your study (as in the case of the generator) can be concluded. If dependent, you must examine further and identify all the relationships. This may require a search for the origin of the signals. After all functions have been identified and listed, data related to generation, distribution, and processing can be listed. They can then be related to the objective alignment as minor to the objective or major to the objective. This may sound like considerable effort, but experience has shown that dependency seldom exceeds three or four functions.

SERIAL/PARALLEL. The next step in this phase of the analysis is determining whether the interrelationships are serial, parallel, or both.

This means that you must identify by some method how the functional unit's output is relevant to the objective alignment; how it interacts and when it occurs. You must identify simultaneous occurrences, time sequences, delayed sequences, automatic and manual control sequences, and off-line test/on-line test sequences.

Refer again to Figure 5-6. This simple diagram clearly shows that the sequence of actions is combined serial and parallel. Most frequently, the elements common to complexing the definition of sequencing are the timing and control units. The wide distribution of these signals necessitates careful study. These control signals play an extremely significant role. In the past, the circuits containing timing and control units have been the ones aligned first. This trend must of necessity remain high on the list for starters. Other circuits, using any inputs from the timing and control units, could not be aligned without proper receipt of timing pulses.

PRIORITIES. Since interdependency is so significant even though the study may reveal that the relationship is minor, some consideration must be placed on the third element in the Figure 5-7 priorities. Each complex waveform may play an interrelating role with others, and because it may, it causes priorities to be established. Most often, though, the priorities you encounter are prerequisites of the alignment to be performed. They may be such items as determining that a specific dc voltage level is or is not present. Priorities also have to do with identification and verification of major signal inputs and voltage requirements. A final thought on priorities is that of the function being aligned. The function may provide multiple outputs at various times. It may be possible to use it in different modes. It may have test parameters other than the normal operating parameters. If any of these conditions exists, the priority to function validation through alignment may cause the alignment routine to specify particular sequences, comparison of results with alternate sequences, or serial validation while sequencing.

Determining the sequence of units to be aligned is the fourth in a list of elements discussing the principles of alignment. To this point we have identified the objective, listed the subunits affected, identified any interrelationship that the function to be aligned has with other functions, and, finally, determined the sequence in which the units or functions must be aligned. Now we must determine within a function where to start the alignment, the points to measure, and the intermediate and final adjustments.

ALIGN THE OBJECTIVE. The fifth element (indicated in Figure 5-2) within the study of alignments develops the information necessary for

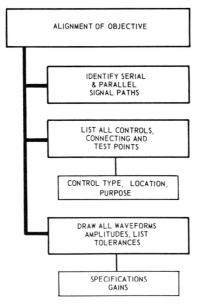

Fig. 5-8. Alignment of Objective

the understanding of the function to be aligned. Figure 5-8 shows that there are three main subelements that must be included to develop a complete picture. These are: (1) identify serial and parallel signal paths; (2) list controls, connections, and test points; and (3) draw waveforms and list tolerances. The second element in this entire study identified the requirement to list all *subunits, circuits,* and *components* of the *objective.* This fifth element requires the use of the data accumulated in the second element and the three subelements shown in Figure 5-8.

Before studying each subelement, let's examine a point. The functional unit being aligned may have as few as 1 to 3 circuits or as many as 20 to 30. It becomes reasonable to assume that in a function containing one or two adjustments a study reveals that if the:

1. Controls are independent and parallel, either may be done first.
2. Controls are interdependent and serial, the one preceding the other must be adjusted first.
3. One control is dependent upon the other, the independent control must be properly set before the dependent control can be set.

If the function contains numerous controls, an analysis of each of their purposes and functions is necessary. The study must reveal the same information as a function having one or two controls. It must also reveal sequences and priorities.

SERIAL/PARALLEL PATHS. The block diagram being developed for the study of the function must be arranged in serial and parallel order as shown in Figure 5-6. Connecting lines should be used but held to a minimum to avoid confusion. Include only significant lines which provide major or minor control data to the circuit.

CONTROLS, CONNECTING POINTS, AND TEST POINTS. List all controls by name, type, and symbol in the block on the drawing where they occur. This information is obtained from the alignment itself. Include alphanumerics on the controls and locations of the test points. Draw the symbol for the control. Standard symbols are shown in Figure 5-9. Figure 5-9a represents a control including a knob, 5-9b a screwdriver adjustment, 5-9c a potentiometer or rheostat control, 5-9d a variable capacitor, and 5-9e a tunable coil. For filling in your block diagram, you must choose any of these symbols or combine them. Finally, Figure 5-9f shows a typical test-point symbol.

WAVEFORM, SPECIFICATIONS. Up to this point in your analysis, you should have almost a complete picture and understanding of the alignment. You have the:

1. Objective.
2. Subunits within the function identified.
3. Interrelationships of other functional units noted.
4. The sequence of adjustments to be made.
5. The test points used for checking the accuracy of the individual adjustment and the intermediate functional stops.
6. Final output test point.

From the technical references you can obtain the final data needed for your study. These are the exact waveforms, voltage levels, and current amplitude. Place these waveforms as close to their point of occurrence as possible (i.e., input and output waveforms located at their respective

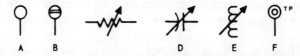

Fig. 5-9. Adjustment Control Symbols

test points). Record exact voltage amplitude and allowable deviation specifications. Identify, along with the alphanumeric code of each control, its purpose and limitations. For instance, if it is a pot, list its maximum and minimum gain in volts or current, and so on. If it is a capacitor, list it as trimmer for overshoot/undershoot, frequency compensation, or gain, and specify its maximum and minimum effect. Know or list in notes on the sheet where the adjustable component is located in a given circuit (i.e., input, output, base, emitter, collector, grid, cathode, plate coupling, or filtering).

There it is—all the requirements for an understanding of what it takes to make an alignment meaningful. Of course, you realize as well as we do that the actual performance of the alignment takes considerably less understanding than we have presented here. You might even be thinking, "I don't need to know all this information just to turn a pot and get the unit back into tolerance during an alignment." You don't, providing every pot you turn accomplishes (within the specified limits) its intended function. However, what are you going to do if that pot doesn't accomplish its intended function? You're the technician. You're the one who will have to find out why that pot didn't perform its function. You're the man who will have to do the troubleshooting and correct the problem. Don't you think that your job of correcting the problem will be much easier if you are equipped with the knowledge of the functions and interactions of the circuits within the particular alignment?

5-3 Block-Diagram Overview

To be sure that you have a complete picture, let's put the whole program together in block-diagram form with proper sequence. Let's also identify each element of the study as a step. Figure 5-10 illustrates each phase of the study and lists for us the pertinent data needed for that phase of the study. As you can see, no phase can be omitted from the study. In the final study, certain phases may not be present because they do not have a bearing on the alignment. However, the phase must be examined to determine its nonexistence. Finally, step 5 must complete the picture that step 2 started, and steps 3 and 4 must include information in the depth necessary for understanding.

In the next four sections, we discuss general areas in which alignments are most frequently performed. They are displays, electromechanical assemblies, memory units, and message processors. In each of these studies, except memory, there is an example study of an alignment as detailed in this section. Preceding the study is an explanation of the type

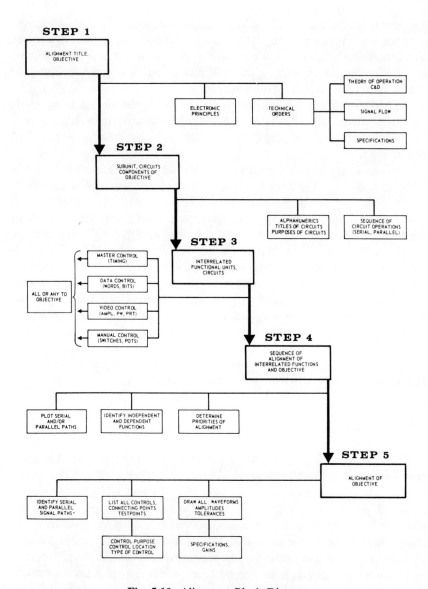

Fig. 5-10. Alignment Block Diagram

of unit (e.g., display) on which the alignment is to be performed and
an identification of the limitation of the scope of the alignment. Your
objective is to read and study each section carefully in order to:

1. Gain understanding in areas related to your job requirements.

2. Broaden your knowledge of related areas.
3. Gain knowledge of new areas.
4. Make comparisons and correlation to the equipment you work on.
5. Identify with the concept of alignment in order to improve your worth to your unit through expertise.

5-4 Displays

Let's review what was already covered in a previous chapter about displays. Our analysis identified four logical functions in almost all display units. They are:

1. Timing.
2. Intensity.
3. Vertical deflection.
4. Horizontal deflection.

Associated with these areas are alignments, and as we will see in the example study, the identification and comprehension of interrelationships are performed in all the units.

5-4.1 Timing

Alignment of timing affects all units in the display; consequently, it is usually aligned first. Some of the most significant subfunctions in the display functional areas using timing are:

1. Sweep-time generation.
2. Sweep and symbol modes' time sharing.
3. Intensity unblanking and blanking.
4. Data or video control.
5. Expansion factoring.

Special pulses for special display features are impressed on vertical, horizontal, or intensity units.

5-4.2 Intensity

The alignment of the intensity unit affects the control of the CRT display. This unit provides control for the cathode and control grid, which effects emission in the CRT. Alignments are performed for:

1. Intensity of the different types of display, as, for example, normal and expanded modes.
2. Unblanking and blanking of the CRT. The unblanking provides a display period, and the blanking provides a retrace period.
3. Video selection or symbology processing of data, which requires amplification, clamping, limiting, inversion, and shifting.
4. High-voltage power supplies, which provide the voltage for coupling, focus, astigmatism, aquadag, and acceleration.

5-4.3   Deflection

Display presentations most often use composite waveforms for generation of the display. Vertical and horizontal deflection units generally use the same sweep generators, have time-sharing symbol-generating capability, and develop sweep signal inputs. For instance, range marks and radar data are often combined and processed simultaneously. Concurrently, through deflection, symbols may be presented on the scope screen. Alignment, therefore, requires at a minimum a clear understanding of where the displayed signals are coming from. However, an in-depth understanding of the alignment provides, in addition to a clear picture, a knowledge of each element of the display, its origin, and its use.

5-4.4   Principles of Statistical Display

The purpose of the development of statistical information displays (SIDS) is to provide visual, graphical presentation of digital information for command personnel to monitor and evaluate. Most often the display can be classified as being used for tactical control of air space within the environment, for use of air defense of the environment, or to provide data readout, as in the case of bank accounts.

The presentation includes vector diagrams, numerical notations, and symbology designating classification. Alphabetical and numerical listings are presented for identification in the case of aircraft headings, speed, armament, altitude, time to target or base, weather conditions, plus other data pertinent to evaluation. They may also include geographical outlines of terrain boundaries or show line grids. Each element of the display requires circuitry for its generation and insertion into the display.

5-4.5   Requirements for Circuits

Foremost in circuits required for display is the symbol generator. Since lines, curves, and dots are used extensively to create patterns on the display, symbol generators are built for these uses. One technique of activating these generators is to have a digital input cause an output. For example, a symbol is assigned to a particular type of aircraft. A generator is provided to create the symbol when the operator elects to use it. He initiates console action, which creates a digital word. If the word has the four bits 1101 in it, for example, a detection circuit as shown in Figure 5-11 activates the generator. Examination of the vector gate in Figure 5-11 shows that the four-bit word must be 1101. The generator output is processed through the intensity channel (Z axis) or deflection circuits for presentation on the CRT face.

Vector generators are another requirement for these types of displays. The generators usually require two locations for storage of the coordinates of the vector. Assume that a vector is to be drawn on the face of the CRT as shown in Figure 5-12. The vector is in the first quadrant; therefore, positive values of X and Y are used. The signs of the values are positive. The origin of all vectors is the center scope. The least significant digit (LSD) of each bit is 8 miles. The contents of the register must have binary values of 24 for start Y and 80 for stop Y; 16 for start X

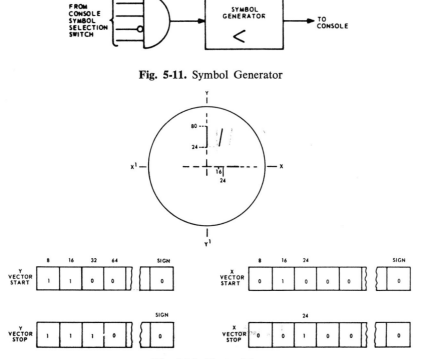

Fig. 5-11. Symbol Generator

Fig. 5-12. Vector Line

and 24 for stop X. These values are added to the normal X and Y registers during sweep generation and deflection to cause intensification of the vector line. Vector lines can be drawn in any direction, but there are two limitations:

1. The total number of lines that can be drawn is based on the number of storage locations allocated to memory.
2. The length of each vector is restricted to the number of bits per register in storage and the bit value of the LSD.

5-4.6 Requirements for Digital Information Displays

Digital information displays (DIDs) are similar to SIDs. Generators are activated by an operator through selection of switches. Characters and symbols are displayed on small CRTs. Various types of CRTs and circuits are used. One type is the charactron tube shown in Figure 5-13. The CRT incorporates two sets of deflection units: plates for character selection and coils for character positioning. Three-bit binary words are converted into deflection voltage for selection, as shown in Figure 5-13.

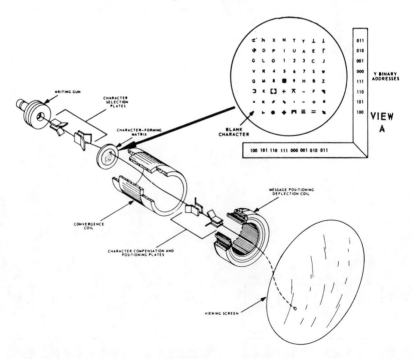

Fig. 5-13. Charactron Tube

Compare the charactron tube with the typotron tube. The basic difference is the use of plates for character instead of coils. This is shown in Figure 5-14. In each of these systems the sweep-positioning voltages allow for a horizontal and vertical positioning of characters and symbols to form words and statistical data and have a classification as DIDs. A newer device, shown in Chart 1, used as a DID, uses integrated circuits with programmed memories. Binary values are used to address the memory and select the characters. The unit uses a standard CRT, and the character is painted on the screen in a series of dots through the grid circuits. Deflection voltages are developed from binary counts converted to analog voltages. The vertical position counter is advanced each time the horizontal counter resets. The generated voltages from the D/A converters position the character on the screen of the CRT. A review of the requirements for circuits on these types of displays leads to:

1. Type of CRT.
2. Types of circuits used for generation of deflection voltages.
3. Circuits for conversion of digital to analog.

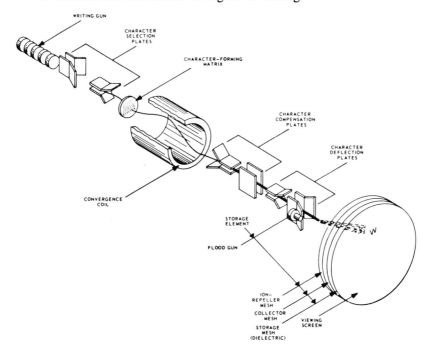

Fig. 5-14. Typotron Tube

138

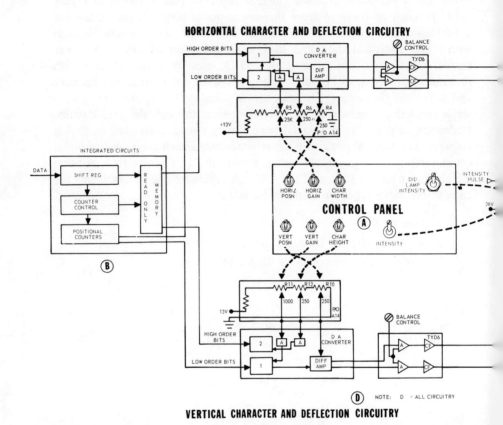

HORIZONTAL CHARACTER AND DEFLECTION CIRCUITRY

VERTICAL CHARACTER AND DEFLECTION CIRCUITRY

Chart 1

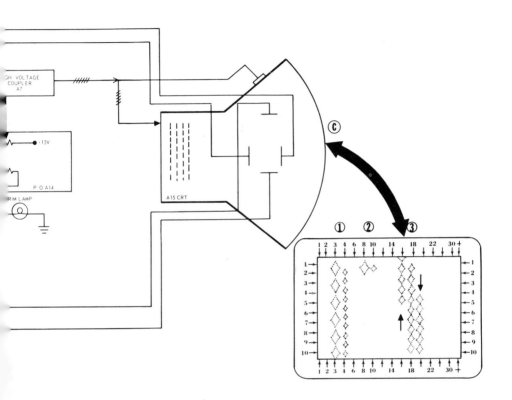

4. Symbol generators.

5. Input selection and decoding circuits.

6. Vector generators.

7. Vector coordinate registers.

8. Panels containing controls (pots, coils, capacitors) for aligning the systems.

5-4.7 Types of Display Programming

Although we have mentioned some of the types of programming for SIDs and DIDs in the discussion above, let us study a few now.

TIME SHARING. Time sharing is one of the most extensively used methods for display programming. Figure 5-15 shows clearly that only when the CRT is unblanked by timing control does the intensification of the signal cause a character formation. In the formation of the letter A, times 1 through 5 are painted; then the CRT is blanked for one time period while the symbol generators are idle. The CRT unblanks again for times 6 through 11 and the vertical amplifier output reverses its polarity to prepare for the painting of the horizontal bar. At the same time, the horizontal amplifier output also reverses its polarity to allow for a sweep from right to left during time periods 12 through 14. At the end of time period 14, the CRT is blanked and stays blanked until the next character-intensification period.

HARD-WIRED MATRIX. In two of the DIDs mentioned above, stencil plates called matrices were used, and the flow of electrons through the character stamped in the plate created the shape of the character on the CRT screen. In the other DIDs examined, an integrated memory unit was used with each character as a permanent data entry. Addressing of a memory location allowed D/A conversion of the character storage to take place and a display on the CRT screen to occur through the grids of the CRT.

PROGRAMMED DATA. Many displays contain forced display data. These are data which are usually hard-wired and available all the time. The display may contain information by which analysis can identify and verify the operation of the:

1. Generators.

2. Circuits processing symbols and characters.

3. CRT circuits.

The programmed or polar-cordinated data may also be hand-wired (by patch panel) to provide a display. For example, we have:

1. Grid or polar coordinates.
2. Site relationship.
3. Maps of states, countries, and so on.
4. Maps of densely populated areas.
5. Elevation, contour maps, and so on.
6. Maps of air fields.

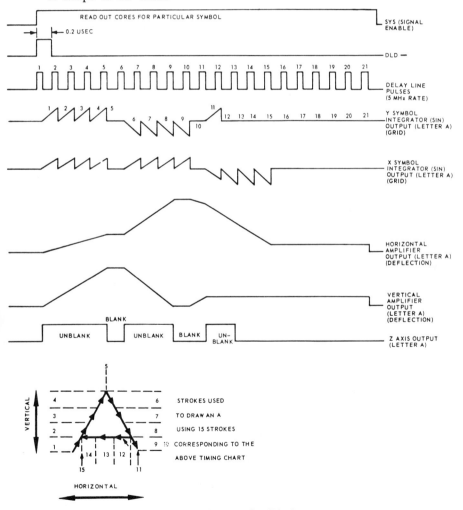

Fig. 5-15. Time-Sharing Display

7. Satellite positional data.

The hand wiring allows for easy change when conditions warrant. It also allows for individual site configuration, thereby adding versatility to equipment and inceasing its capability.

CALL-UP METHODS. Numerous methods are used to perform programming of the display. The most usual methods employ:

1. Switches.
2. Tag symbols.
3. Omniball or wheels attached to A/D converters.
4. Light guns.
5. Keyboard to memory program.

Each of these items provides an input of correlation which the processor can compare and react to. The input may be directly sensed as binary or may be transmitted by gray code. It may be an analog input or photoelectric input through sensors.

5-4.8 Principles of Radar Displays

Radar displays are usually associated with displaying radar returns. The two types of displays usually developed are the *search display* and *height-finder display*. The purpose of search radar display is to present all flying target positions on a CRT relative to the site location. We discussed this type of radar in Chapter 3. We also discussed radar antenna rotation and beacon returns. Each of these elements is necessary for a video display of air surveillance. Each flying object's position is assigned an azimuth heading relative to the site's position. It is also identified as to *type* of aircraft, by *beacon* code, by *aircraft flight plans,* or by scheduled-airlines routing. The purpose of height-finder displays is to determine the altitude of aircraft within range of the radar. To accomplish this the operator or computer controls the azimuth position and the height nod. Most height-finder radars are able also to locate an aircraft through a jamming situation. This operation is called *search-lighting.*

5-4.9 Requirements for Circuits

In addition to the basic complement of circuits that are normally used in displays, both types display certain characteristics of their radar. Search radar displays, as shown in Figure 5-16, have sweep and intensity coincident with the azimuth position of the radar. Height displays, also shown in Figure 5-16, have sweep coincident with the nod angle of the antenna. Since each display uses the position of the radar in its display, the voltage received from radar servos is processed by the display equipment and used for sweep or nod voltage in the display. In search displays, quite often the sweep generator is an integral part of the converter/ processor unit. It is a free-running generator that provides continuously changing sweep voltages for all search display consoles on the site. The principle used is quite simple. As the generator operates, detection circuits cause two independent outputs: one for vertical, and one for horizontal. A sawtooth of varying amplitude and inverse capability is generated for each deflection. When algebraically combined in deflection circuits the intensity is shown as the instantaneous value of each. Figure 5-17 shows how the operation can be performed. With two positive-going sweep ramps (Figure 5-17a) the displayed sweep is shown between north and east. The magnitude of the horizontal sweep is minimum at 0 degrees and maximum at 90 degrees, and the magnitude of the vertical sweep is opposite. This clearly shows that at any instant in time the combined values of sweep voltages provide a deflection between 0 and 90 degrees. In Figure 5-17b, horizontal sweep voltage decreases, and vertical sweep

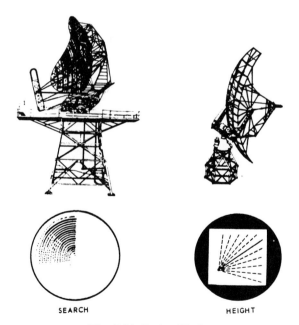

SEARCH   HEIGHT

Fig. 5-16. Radar Displays

voltage reverses polarity and increases in magnitude from minimum to maximum. In Figure 5-17c and d the two other requirements for a full 360° sweep are established.

The antenna rotates, and the sweep on the display shows rotation. The two must be synchronized. A method frequently used for synchronization is called *error-sensing correction*. A differential principle is incorporated whereby a feedback signal from the antenna servo is matched against the generator signal that is produced in the display equipment. If no difference is detected, the circuit is said to be null. If the antenna error

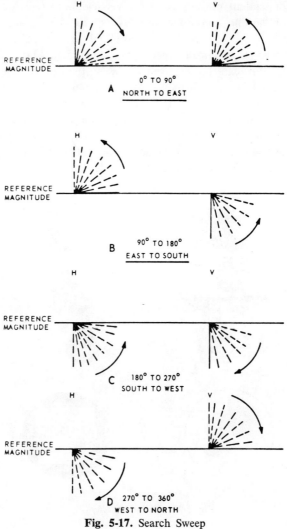

Fig. 5-17. Search Sweep

voltage is greater or less than the generator output, a *difference* voltage is generated by the differential circuit. This difference, called error or *correction* voltage, is fed to the generator to bring the sweep generators into synchronization by speeding up the operation or slowing down the operation.

In height-finder displays, two sets of generators (servos) are often used. One is for nod generation and the other for azimuth change. These generators function along with height-finder radar. Feedback voltages from antenna servos are used like search feedback voltages for control of internal generators. A significant difference in the operation of this display is that the sweep in azimuth is only done on command, whereas search is continuous. In addition, the nod origin is usually located in the lower left corner of the display. Nod voltages are shown in Figure 5-18. If the antenna is stopped at 0 elevation, the horizontal deflection voltage shown in Figure 5-18a is maximum, and vertical is minimum. A nodding antenna contains all angles of nod between 0 and 30°, as shown in Figure 5-18b. The horizontal sweep voltage decreases with increases in elevation, and the vertical sweep voltages increase from null with increases in antenna nod. The relative magnitude of horizontal and vertical sweep voltages for 0 to −2 degrees nod is shown in Figure 5-18c.

In addition to the requirements for sweep generators, servos, and differential circuits, range mark circuits are required. These circuits must provide a signal for each 10 mi of range. Each range mile is 12.36 μs. Therefore, for each 123.6 μs the circuits must produce an output. The

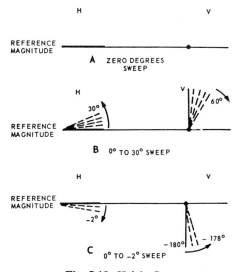

Fig. 5-18. Height Sweep

pulse width of the 50-, 100-, 150-, and 200-mi range marks must be stretched by blocking oscillator, delay line, or monostable flip-flop to allow a longer time for intensity. Finally, video processing circuits such as quantizers and video amplifiers are used to process radar returns and make these returns acceptable for display equipment.

5-4.10 Types of Display Programming

Programming in these types of displays include programming of:

1. Numerous kinds of search radar video.
2. Beacon video.
3. Height-finder video.
4. Limited displays through control functions.
5. Range marks.
6. Angle marks.
7. Video mapping.
8. Antijamming control functions.
9. Target identification.

DATA SELECTION. Each of the videos used by these display systems incorporates a specific limitation of the original video received by the radar set. For example, clouds are usually eliminated from the display by use of moving-target indicator circuits. Jamming is reduced by anticlutter circuitry. Echoes are reduced by use of main-lobe indicator circuits, with suppression of side lobes. Digitizing video returns allow for uniform intensity of all tracks regardless of the original track-intensity signal being received. Further limitation of display data is accomplished by circuits that limit the display to:

1. Specific height groups (e.g., 40–60 ft or 20–40 ft).
2. Initial tracks.
3. Old tracks.
4. Tracks with ID.
5. Tracks with beacon.
6. Hostiles.
7. Weapons.

Almost all the circuits, either generating the displays or limiting the displays, are controlled by switch actions at the console. Each switch is wired to the program through circuits in the processor. It either arms or disarms the processing circuits, which detect the data under their control. These switches seldom inhibit the accumulation of data.

TIME SHARING. Time sharing is an essential method used with these types of displays. It has the same weight as it did with statistical displays.

PROGRAMMED DATA. Video mapping is usually accomplished through a program of a video mapper. The display is fed, along with other data and range marks, into the CRT and displayed. Video mapping usually provides a map of geographical boundaries; however, it is not limited to just geographical maps. Coordinates, data content, and other data are programmed.

CALL-UP METHODS. As has been mentioned, switches are the primary call-up method. In addition to switches, light guns and omniballs are used as call-up methods.

5-5 Typical Alignment Requirements for Sweep Circuits

Generally the sweep alignments fall into two broad categories. One is the sweep generator, and the other is the centering. The sweep-generator alignment is performed to bring sweep-voltage amplitudes to specification. It may also prescribe specifications for pulse duration, slope angle, and proper phasing. Alignments usually will require isolation of basic sweep generators during a phase of the alignment. Prerequisites usually require verification of timing waveforms because an improper pulse width affects the duty cycle of the sweep generator. After alignment of the sweep generator, alignment of the combining or controlling circuits usually follows. Frequently, capacitors (trimmers) are used in the controlling circuits to compensate for variables in the operation of these circuits. This allows for a proper overall display.

The centering alignments usually require the use of meters and isolation of the sweep driver circuits. Voltages, sometimes dc, sometimes ac, are read simultaneously while individual adjustments are performed. When all meters read the specified voltages within tolerable allowances, centering is complete. Consideration may have to be given to the front panel horizontal and vertical positions of these controls. If they are included while centering is performed, their positions must be at the 50 percent point within the control. This allows for operator positioning of the sweep in all possible directions equally. In addition to sweep and centering alignments, intensity and high-voltage alignments are performed.

5-6 Typical Alignment of Intensity/Unblanking and High Voltage

Intensity and unblanking circuits contain pots and trimmers. The pots usually control amplitudes of different gate outputs which cause more or less intensification on the CRT. Each gate amplitude ultimately results in bias control for succeeding circuits and the CRT. Video and data are usually imposed atop the intensity gate. Therefore, the gate amplitude must be sufficiently high for proper intensification but low enough for the video data to cause further intensification of this display.

Trimmer capacitors, used in aligning these circuits, provide two functions: (1) they allow for squaring of gate waveforms, and (2) they allow for amplitude control of high-frequency (short-pulse-width) data and video pulses. Generally, considerable variations in amplitude are possible when using these trimmers.

Specifications must be followed, especially when aligning gate amplitudes. Assume that the maximum signal into a high-voltage coupler (HVC) is 15 V and the CRT turn-on voltage is 7 V. If an adjustment within the alignment were performed and the gate level were incorrectly set at 12 V, the conduction of electron flow within the CRT would be almost maximum (extremely high intensity). Add data or video to the top of the gate (amplitude 5 V) and clipping within the high-voltage coupler occurs. (12 V + 5 V = 17 V, 2 V clipped.)

The video or data displayed would be hard to see because of the clipping action. However, with proper alignment, a 5-V gate and a 5-V data or video pulse can pass through the HVC to the CRT without clipping and cause a display with a good contrast (signal-to-noise) ratio.

High voltage, focus, and other controls mainly consist of pots. These may, however, be alignment controls on circuits using the high voltage

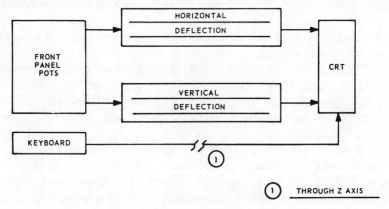

Fig. 5-19. Elements of Display

which compensate for ripple and amplitude. Others are in the focus-compensation circuits and they correct the focus at extreme edges of the CRT.

To recap, alignment of intensity/unblanking and high voltage includes the following:

1. Pulse-width (duty-cycle) control.
2. Pulse-shaping (squaring) control.
3. Amplitude (gate, levels, and data) controls.
4. Focus controls.
5. High-voltage controls.

5-7   Perform a Display Character Position Alignment Study

TITLE: Character Position Adjustment
OBJECTIVE: Align deflection units to provide characters of the proper size and placement.

The objective of this alignment is clear. Both horizontal and vertical deflection units are affected. Since these units are parallel, as previously defined, an interaction (interrelationship) exists. The interrelationship is *not* between units but *within* the CRT. Each unit is self-contained and has no interconnection with the other unit. However, a simultaneous combining of the two outputs is required within the CRT to produce a complete display (all other functions being present). Either one missing results in a lack of height or width (a straight line).

5-7.1   *Elements*

Viewing Figure 5-19 we see that a parallel exists. We also identify that front-panel controls are connected to the units. The CRT uses the output of each unit, and, finally, an input character generator (keyboard) provides data through the Z axis (intensity) to the CRT grids. In this alignment, selected characters provide the visual element needed for adjustment of the deflection units. Also, note that the front-panel control for height alters circuit operation of the horizontal deflection unit. The same is true for vertical control.

5-7.2   *Prerequisites and Interrelationship*

From the study of operation and elements, interrelationships exist and prerequisites are formed. In the order of their general priority the prerequisites are as follows:

1. Power adjustments.
2. Raster adjustments (front-panel intensity).
3. Front-panel height and vertical position adjustments.
4. Character intensity.

Character intensity consists of:

1. Z-axis adjustments.
2. Beam-current adjustments.
3. Focus adjustments.
4. Character input from the keyboard.

Verification of these prerequisites is required prior to performance of the deflection alignment.

Let's move along to Figure 5-20. In this figure the interrelated units are identified. They are:

1. Intensity circuitry.
2. Beam current.
3. High voltage.
4. Front-control panels.
5. Keyboard.

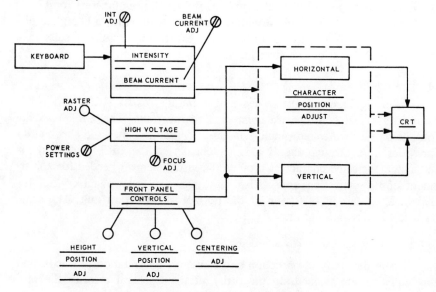

Fig. 5-20. Interrelated Functions

Notice that in each unit except the keyboard (which is not an integral part of the display), variable controls are included. They are:

1. Intensity control.
2. Beam-current control.
3. Raster and focus control.
4. Power-setting controls.
5. Front-panel controls.

Carefully note that focus and beam current have interaction. Therefore, one control effects the other circuitry.

5-7.3   Align the Deflection Units

Moving into the final phase of the study, we use Figure 5-21. Included are the three controls on the horizontal deflection unit and the three controls on the vertical unit. Looking closely at the *zero reference* (vert) pot

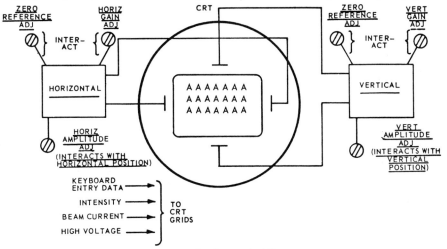

Fig. 5-21. Deflection-Unit Alignments

and *vert gain* pot, we see that these two controls interact. We also see that the *vert amplitude* pot interacts with the *vert* (front-panel) *pos* control. The same interactions of controls exist in the horizontal deflection unit.

This arrangement of controls requires a delicate touch while adjustments are made. Proper sequence of positioning these controls results in an accurate alignment.

The technical reference that listed the information for this study established the sequence, *not* in precise instruction, but in its format.

Finally, the *character position adjustment* routine was followed by a series of routines which refined other elements of the display unit.

5-8 Electromechanical Devices

Only two examples are provided of alignment on electromechanical devices: aligning a servo unit and aligning part of a printer. The principles of understanding alignment in this area are unique in that in addition to normal electronics, some mechanical changes occur. Electronic pulses (voltages or currents) are converted into mechanical actions (or work), or mechanical actions are converted into electronic data (voltage or current). One sample examines the alignment of a servo unit which converts two positional data messages into a vector-voltage magnitude. The vector voltage causes actions further on in two forms: (1) the electronic displacement of sweep voltages to a display unit, and (2) the conversion to mechanical readout unit through a chopper unit. The other example presents a representative selection of alignment of a mechanical element in a printer. This alignment is restricted to one small segment for presentation of the concepts outlined in the first section of this chapter. Research identified that electronic control is provided for the mechanical actions, and so it becomes part of the analysis. Keyboards, card readers, punches, tape units, and printers fall into a classification with electromechanical devices. So the discussion on the printer alignment can also provide an example for analysis of alignments on these other devices. The interaction of mechanical and electrical assemblies is closely related in all units. When you perform research on your equipment, apply the principles shown here on the printers to those electromechanical units in your equipment.

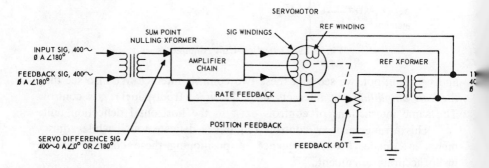

Fig. 5-22. Servo Unit

Selected requirements for understanding alignment of electrome-chanical devices relate to:

1. Understanding processing the immediate circuit or mechanical element.
2. Identification of specifications and tolerance.
3. Proper selection of circumstances to activate and control the element under alignment.
4. Visual recognition of mechanical assemblies from illustrations.

5-9   Perform Servo-Unit Alignment Study

TITLE: Align the Range Servo Unit

OBJECTIVE: The purpose of this alignment is to measure and adjust individual controls to specifications to allow for generation of voltages through coupling by mechanical means for positioning the displays on a console.

The above information provides an answer to the procedure that was detailed in the beginning of the chapter. The title and objective are clearly defined. The purpose clearly states that all adjustments must be aligned to specifications to provide an overall alignment of the servo unit. It also indicates that mechanical coupling is involved in the servo unit. This identifies that feedback positioning, although measured in voltage form, is accomplished by mechanical means. The title indicates that range data (X and Y) are involved. Therefore, feedback voltages from resolvers are to be included in the analysis.

Before going into step 2, a review of servo units, their purpose, and their operation is provided. Figure 5-22 shows a simplified block diagram of a servo unit. It shows an input unit, an amplifier chain, a servo motor unit, a feedback pickoff device (which can be electrically or mechanically linked), a nulling device or point, a rate feedback, and a power source. In the example that we discuss, the feedback is primarily electrical, through mechanical coupling from the drive motor.

5-9.1   Nulling

Servo loops operate on the principle of positioning a feedback pick-off device so that the feedback voltage can be summed with the input signal to produce a null. The difference between the input and feedback signals is fed through a chain of amplifiers to the "signal windings" of a two-phase, 400-Hz motor. The motor also contains a "reference winding," which is connected to a constant power source. For motor operation, both sets of windings must receive power, and the direction of rotation is a function of the phase relationships between the two sets of windings. Typical feedback pickoff devices are potentiometers, synchros, and resolvers. When the motor is correctly positioned, the feedback will null the input signal, leaving no further drive power to the motor signal windings. The drive motor will stop at the desired point.

5-9.2 Rate Feedback

A refinement is present in the form of a negative rate feedback, one whose amplitude is a function of motor rate of rotation. Without this feedback, the motor would have a tendency to "coast" beyond the actual null point and would receive an acceleration in the reverse direction. This could, in turn, cause an overshoot in the reverse direction, followed by another reversal, and so on, which would set up a continuing oscillation. The rate feedback tends to reduce drive power as the motor picks up speed but gives virtually no opposition at very low speeds, such as in the immediate vicinity of the null. Therefore, it helps to eliminate oscillation or hunting without destroying null accuracy.

5-9.3 Direction of Rotation

In the two-phase ac motor, the direction of rotation is a function of the phase relationship between the signal and reference windings. A reversal of current direction (phase) in either, but not both, will reverse motor direction.

When the input signal changes (which should drive the servo to a new position), the difference between input and feedback signals will result in a signal either in phase or 180° out of phase with the reference signal, and this will determine the direction of rotation.

It should be noted that a reversal of connections on either, but not both, sets of motor windings will reverse the current direction and, consequently, the motor direction. If these phase relationships are incorrect, the servo will drive away from the null position instead of toward it.

Using this information and Figure 5-22 we see that a voltage input signal into the resolver provides a signal to the amplifier chain. The phase and amplitude of the signal cause the servo motor to rotate. The feedback is coupled to the null point. A difference value to the amplifier chain causes the motor to rotate in a direction which reduces the voltage into the amplifier chain. This action continues until the signal into the amplifier chain is reduced to null.

Step 2 requires the identification of the subelements, circuits, and components of the unit to be aligned. Figure 5-23 illustrates these elements. In the sequence of their respective placing, they are, left to right:

1. The *input transformer,* which provides a method for coupling any difference between the input signal and feedback signal into the secondary of the transformer. If no signal is coupled, it may be assumed that the feedback voltage equals the input voltage.

2. The *amplifier chain,* which converts the single voltage input into push–pull outputs by inverting the input to one leg of the output. Two gain pots are used, one for each line. Noninverting amplifiers provide amplification of the signal to motor windings.

3. The *drive motor,* which reacts to the amplifier inputs based upon the amplitude of the signal, one signal wire being in phase and the other being 180° out of phase with the reference winding. The motor rotates, and its shaft rotates the wiper arms on three pots.

4. The *three pots: Er,* the ac pot, provides a feedback voltage for servo null and provides an ac range voltage to the console through the line driver board. *Vr* is a dc pot which is mechanically linked to the motor shaft and provides a dc range voltage through an amplifier board. Finally, the *Az gain* pot provides a rate control

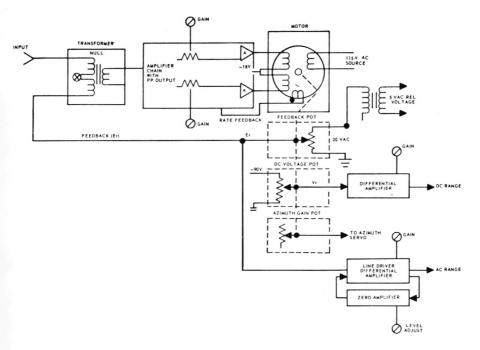

Fig. 5-23. Servo Subelements

to the azimuth servo loop by regulating the change depending upon the range of target data.

5. *Reference voltages,* which are provided for the motor and for pick-off voltages for the pots.

6. The *GAMI* and *LDRI* boards, which provide adjustable outputs to other functions.

Before proceeding with step 3, let's review the extent of work involved.

a. All controls are pots, therefore measurable on meters as ac and dc and on oscilloscopes.

b. Two gain amplifier controls are included in the amplifier chain.

c. Each output circuit has a gain control.

d. A level control is also included in both output circuits.

e. Potentiometer controls on the assembly are mechanically positioned by the shaft of the motor.

Step 3 instructs us to identify interrelationship of other functions to the basic functions. Therefore, we must establish where the data inputs are coming from and how they are derived.

Range voltage, as an input to the servo, is a product of D/A conversion. It is composed of two distinct and separate sources which are electronically combined in a servo unit. This brings into the analysis these points:

1. Generation of X and Y data.

2. Range data (X and Y coordinate).

3. D/A conversion.

4. Resolver action to combine the coordinates into one range value.

Taking the reverse method of identifying the interrelated functions shows that (refer to Figure 5-24) the resolver feeds the range voltage to the servo unit. The resolver has two inputs: an X-coordinate range voltage and a Y-coordinate range voltage. These voltages (ac) are developed from the amplifier chain and D/A converter circuits from X and Y digital range data.

Review of the text on this circuitry identifies the following specifications about the interrelated functions:

1. X and Y data can be programmed by a selected off-line test mode

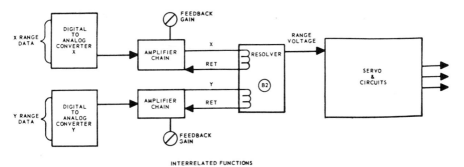

INTERRELATED FUNCTIONS

Fig. 5-24. Servo Amplifier Controls

of operation, and a range coordinate of 64 mi is equal to the reference voltage of 5 V ac.

2. The feedback pot of the amplifier chain is 10 Ω in series with 100 Ω and is thereby limited to 10 percent. Further, since the signal is in ac in the range of 5 V ac, a 10 percent or less change is not measurable on an oscilloscope; an rms (ac meter) is required.

From examination of these items, definite interrelationships of functions exist. The following prerequisites, which now have meaning, are identified:

1. The alignment is performed on an off-line test mode.
2. Selected switch settings are used to provide X and Y range data to the D/A converters.
3. Gain ratios of related functional amplifier chains are to be unity.
4. Resolver B2 (part of azimuth servo) must be properly oriented.

These four prerequisites definitely establish a sequence of operations which must be properly verified prior to alignment of the servo unit. At this point we are substituting the complete pictorial of the servo and interrelated functions in Chart 2. We do this now so that you can grasp the full significance of this discussion.

The fourth step requires that a sequence of alignment be established with reference to interrelated functions. Refer to Chart 2 and locate the test chart between the D/A converters. This chart shows test 4 with 64 mi in an X coordinate and test 5 with 64 mi in a Y coordinate.

The next phase is that of determining the sequence of interrelated functions. Obviously, the D/A converter and amplifier chain preceding the servo unit must be aligned properly if there is to be accurate alignment of the servo. Since there are two paths, one for X and one for Y, we have a parallel situation. Either one may be aligned first. Verification of range data in binary form as inputs to the D/A converter is a prerequisite. Verification of the 5-V ac reference voltage is a prerequisite. Operation of the azimuth servo unit (since resolver B2 is a part of this unit) is a prerequisite.

5-9.4   Prerequisite Verification

Step 1: Verify digital data. Step 2: Verify unity gain from amplifier chain for X and Y measured at AZA4XA7-6 and XA8-6 of driver boards, respectively. Step 3: Verify that output from R3 measured at A2A2XA8-4 is equal to output from amplifier chain. This completes the verification of interrelated functions. One factor not identified, but significant, is that for verification of R3 output to equal 64 mi either disabling of X while measuring Y, or disabling of Y while measuring X, is paramount. A combination of X and Y results in a coordinate range other than 90 or 180°.

5-9.5   Align the Servo Unit

The fifth step requires the alignment of the servo unit. Two points are examined. First, a new unit is to be installed and aligned. Second, an existing unit is aligned.

1. Prior to installation, the gain adjustments of pots Er, Vr, and Az must be positioned (see Foldout 2). Using an ohmmeter, set all three pots for very close to a short: for Er pins 2 and 3, for Vr pins 7 and 8, and for Az gain pins 10 and 9. After installation and power check, alignment is performed on zero amplifier boards A2A5XA7 and XA3, which are shown on the right lower portion of the drawing.

2. The remainder of the alignment is the same for either a new installation or realignment of an existing unit. Use a pure 64-mi X or Y into the servo. Er must measure 5 V ac. With proper operation of the transformer verified (null), measured voltages at both test points in the servo amplifier chain are set. The output of the line-driver-board-processing Er signal is set to a gain of unity. Finally, the GAMI board gain is set to the value 17.24 V dc with the entire test problem 4 inserted (X and Y, reference chart).

The alignment is now complete. All internal subunits operate properly. All interrelated functions have been identified and verified or aligned.

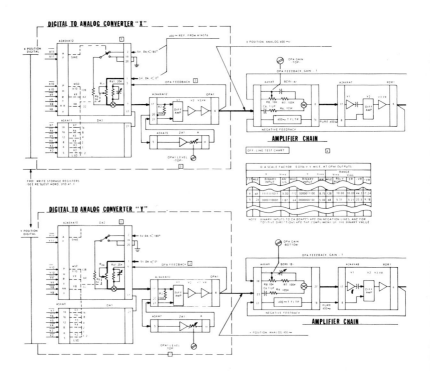

Chart 2

160

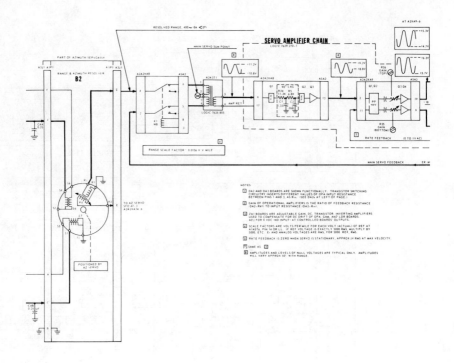

Chart 2 (contd)

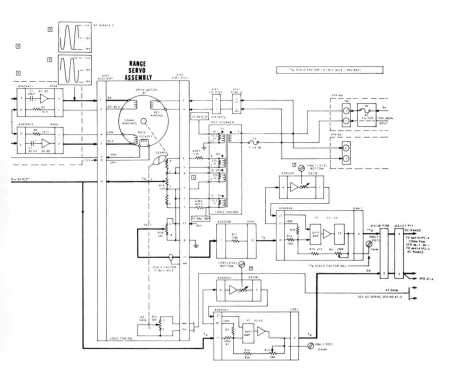

A complete picture of the unit is presented, and an understanding of its operation, purpose, and function is clear.

5-10 Perform Keyboard–Printer–Panel Space Alignment Study

TITLE: Space Magnet, Space-Pawl Stop Plate, and Space-Pawl Clearance

OBJECTIVE: The purpose of this alignment is threefold. The first requirement is to adjust the clearance between the space pawl and carriage rack teeth when the armature is energized. The second requirement is to position the space magnet and armature when the armature is energized. The third requirement is to adjust the clearance between the stop plate and the space pawl when the armature is energized.

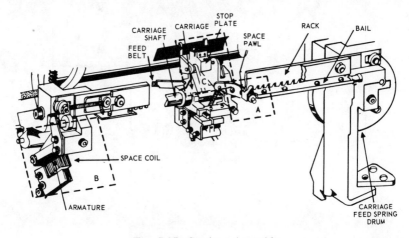

Fig. 5-25. Carriage Assembly

The previously identified alignment may be completely foreign to many computer technicians because it involves mechanical alignment. Therefore, we provide this brief review of the printer. In the operation of this impact printer, two characters are activated within a specific time interval (print cycle). The characters are printed on the paper by hammers. After printing the characters, the carriage is moved to the left, and the operation is repeated. A space between words is treated by the machine as a character. A rather complex mechanical assembly (Figure 5-25), controlled electronically, is incorporated into the printer. The logic package provides decoding, which releases a pawl for spacing and allows a spring to pull the carriage to the next position. It is in this carriage that the alignment must be performed.

5-10.1   Spacing Theory

An explanation of the spacing theory follows.

1. The spacing mechanism (Figure 5-26) consists of a magnet (coil), armature, bail, rack, pawl, and carriage-feed spring. The carriage-feed spring exerts a constant pull to the right on the carriage. The carriage is kept from moving by the engagement of the pawl in the rack. The pawl is mounted on the carriage in a way that allows it to engage the spacing rack. When the circuit emits a space impulse, the magnet energizes, causing the armature to move down. As it does, the bail rotates counterclockwise when viewed from the left side. The bail contacts the bottom of the spacing pawl, causing the pawl to move down and out of engagement with the rack.

2. The magnet is held energized for approximately 4–6 ms. This is just enough time to get the pawl out of engagement and allow the carriage feed spring to pull the carriage a short distance to the right. When the magnet deenergizes, the mechanism is reset by the bail spring and the pawl spring.

3. The rack is spring-loaded to the left. When the pawl leaves engagement with it, the rack spring causes it to move toward the left. As the pawl reengages, the rack will move slightly. This slight movement is enough to absorb the energy that the carriage has built up. The rack stops against a small rubber bushing, which cushions the bounce.

5-10.2   Two Methods of Spacing

Two methods provide ground to the space coil and thereby activate the space mechanism. These are shown in Figure 5-26. The first method is that of depressing the *space bar* on the keyboard. This action results in bail latches closing and generating a binary code of 0000010. This code is detected in printer logic in the *function detection* and is sent through the *function register* to the manual input of the *space circuit*. The second method is automatic sensing of the end of the print cycle. Since time is allocated for printing two characters before spacing, the print cycle ends with detection of both hammers fired. This action sets the automatic detection gates in the space circuitry, and a ground is provided to the coil.

5-10.3   Align the Printer Space Elements

The second element of Figure 5-8 requires identification of subunits of the function to be aligned; to do this, refer again to Figure 5-25. This

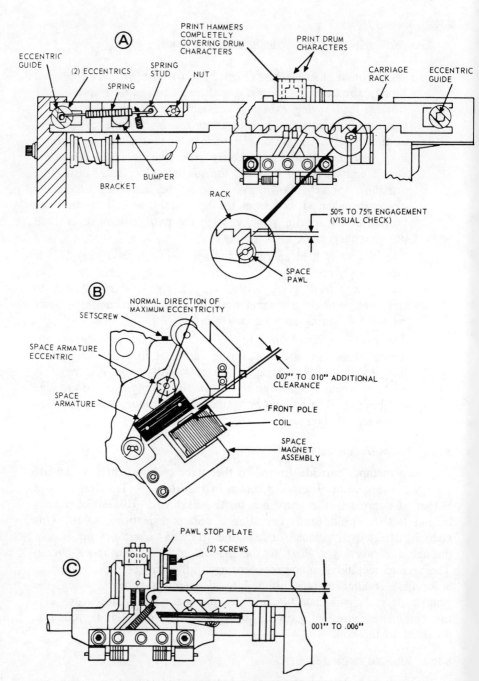

Fig. 5-26. Space Mechanism

figure is a view of the carriage assembly and shows each of the elements of the space mechanism. To repeat them and identify each as shown, there are the:

1. Magnet (labelled space coil), lower left.
2. Armature, lower left.
3. Bail, upper right.
4. Rack, upper right.
5. Pawl, upper center.
6. Carriage-feed spring, lower right.
7. Stop plate, upper center.

The three objectives of this alignment are shown in the blocked-in areas. *A* is for space pawl and carriage clearance. Blocked-in area *B* is for space magnet and armature, and blocked-in *C* is for the space pawl and stop plate. Each of these blocked areas is expanded for discussion in Figure 5-26. When studying it, combine the use of Figure 5-25 and those identified in the last element. Specific tolerances of individual adjustments are not included now but are listed in the final element.

Step 3 (Figure 5-8) requires identification of interrelationship with other functions and Chart 3 shows these. In Chart 3 mechanical and electronic assemblies are shown in block-diagram form, the mechanical in dashed blocks and the electronic in solid blocks.

The interrelationships in the serial and parallel sequence as required by step 4 are as follows (see Chart 3). Prior to the alignment of space pawl clearance, space magnet, and space pawl/stop plate adjustment, the space pawl rack clearance is accomplished. Prior to this alignment, the space bail is positioned. Prior to these two alignments, space armature and shaft-end-play adjustments are made. This then identifies that four elements are prerequisite to the alignment in this analysis in the mechanical area.

In each case of this alignment, the coil must be energized. Therefore, an electrical path is obtained through ground to energize the coil. Already identified are the two paths for obtaining ground: manual and automatic. Note in Chart 3 that R4 of the space circuit is a control in the single-shot circuitry, and it provides a variable pulse width. Consideration must be given to this circuit output when operation of the printer spacing is performed. Too short a time interval may provide insufficient time for proper operation and mislead a technician into adjusting space clearance. The opposite is also possible where too long a time could cause a skip or double space and again lead the technician astray. Further back in

166

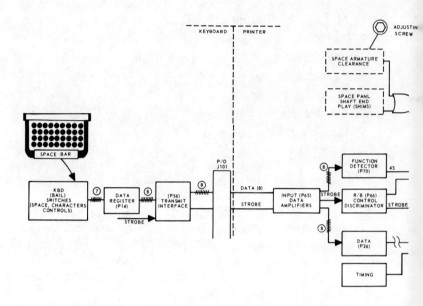

Chart 3

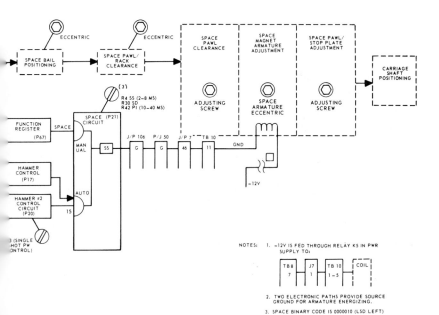

NOTES:
1. −12V IS FED THROUGH RELAY K5 IN PWR SUPPLY TO:

2. TWO ELECTRONIC PATHS PROVIDE SOURCE GROUND FOR ARMATURE ENERGIZING.

3. SPACE BINARY CODE IS 0000010 (LSD LEFT)

the circuitry, the hammer control circuits also have pulse-width controls, and improper adjustment of these may influence the spacing to cause improper selection of space timing. Finally, although this subject of troubleshooting is not included, a processing or decoding failure could lead the technician into realignment of these units where misalignment is actually not the cause.

For the final element, Figure 5-26 provides an exploded view of areas *A*, *B*, and *C*. In each case, specifications of tolerances are included for visual acknowledgment. The routine requires:

1. Verification of input data, completion of prerequisite spacing alignments, and power.
2. Alignment instructions which identify each screw to be turned, loosening and tightening, and the final securing of screws.

Completion of the task is relatively simple. Verification of mechanical prerequisites requires use of one of the systems outlined in the first part of the section. Verification of correct pulse width of the ground enable pulse is measurable on an oscilloscope. Complete understanding, verification of prerequisites, validation of entries, and accurate alignment of the steps listed in the routine ensure operational capability.

5-11   Memory Units

The coverage of memory devices presented in Chapter 4 defines in detail the many types currently in use. Various adjustments were discussed. Alignments of memory units require in many cases a repetition of the adjustment tasks: for example, *adjust a drum read/write head.* Normally one set of instructions establishes the procedure, and each head is adjusted the same way with the same instructions. Completing adjustment of all heads constitutes a complete alignment. The same situation exists for read/write amplifiers, tape heads, disc heads, and other memory devices. Consequently, this section does not present an alignment example. It does present significant data about the types of memories, principles, classification, and a comparison of the read/write cycles most frequently used.

5-11.1   Types of Memory Units

There are, at present, approximately 11 types of memory devices. Each is capable of providing data to a machine in language that the machine understands. However, not all can accept data from the machine for storage. For clarity we list the types according to two classes: (1)

those which can receive, store, and provide data, and (2) those that can provide data only.

Class 1: Receive, Store, and Provide	Class 2: Provide Data Only (Read Only)
Cores	Storage tube
Drums	Integrated (program memory) circuit
Disc	Capacitor read-only storage (CROS)
Delay line	Transformer read-only storage (TROS)
Thin film	Programs
Tape	

Similarities exist between the two classes in the sense that all require, at a minimum, each of the following functional areas:

1. Timing.
2. Addressing.
3. Interface circuits.
4. Read logic.
5. Memory device.

By contrast, class 1 devices require *write control logic* and *erase control.* The *read-only memories* do not.

5-11.2 Types of Access

The similarities of different memory devices can be further defined by the type of addressing media used. Currently, the two modes used most extensively are the *random-access mode* and the *sequential-access mode.* The two modes are well defined, and you have studied each. The random-access mode allows for rapid entry or recovery of data without limitations, whereas sequential access requires an address to await its turn in memory. The systems identified in classes 1 and 2 can be categorized once again into the address modes. Methods of access commonly used with the system are:

Random	Sequential	Combined Mode
Core	Drum	Disc
Storage tube	Delay line	Thin film
IC	Program	Program
TROS		Tape
CROS		

5-11.3 *Types of Memory Address Circuitry*

Four types of address circuits are widely used in computer systems. They are:

1. Registers.
2. Counters.
3. Decoders.
4. Matrices.

Each of these types may be composed of a variety of circuits. Most extensively used is the flip-flop. And it is used in the register, counter, and decoder. Combinations of flip-flops, transistors, and integrated circuits can be used to form ring counters or stepping counters. In addition, resistive ladders can be used in registers and decoders. Diodes, ICs, and transistors are used extensively with matrices and decoders.

5-11.4 *Types of Read/Write Cycles*

Two basic types of read/write cycles exist. They are the *destruct* (volatile) and *nondestruct* (nonvolatile). The destruct read/write cycles, which are most commonly employed in core memory units, require that a change in state (usually hysterisis) take place in order that there be current induction into the read logic circuits. Then the data are usually rewritten into the same location for future use. In the nondestruct read/write cycle, data from memory are sampled by various modes, with no change to the memory media. The representative examples of this type of memory are magnetic tapes, discs, drums, thin film, punch tapes, and delay line. Also included in the class of nondestruct read-out memory units are the read only memories. These units are fixed program elements activated by input control and sampled during read.

5-12 Message Processors

Message processors provide a distinct function for data processing. They accept input data and convert them to a language acceptable to the machine. They also prepare data for transmission media. Of necessity, one of the primary requirements for circuitry within the unit is modulation and demodulation.

5-12.1 *Requirements for Circuitry*

To achieve modulation or demodulation, many methods may be selected. Along with the variety of methods is a wide range of circuits.

Functionally, though, a limited number of requirements can exist. These requirements must be satisfied through design of circuits which are compatible with parameters of the system.

5-12.2 Serial-to-Parallel and Parallel-to-Serial Conversion

Almost without exception, messages are transmitted over a medium in serial form. Almost without exception, data are processed within Electronic Data Processing units in both parallel and serial form. EDPs are presently operating at rates up to 3 MHz, but serial transmission of data is at audio rates (1,300–2,400 Hz). Message processors therefore contain conversion circuits. The various types may be flip-flops, binary cores, and monolithic shift registers. These circuits are almost always operated with timing as the controlling factor. Two or more separate timing gates or pulses are frequently used.

Refer to Figure 5-27, which shows a shift register. Assume that the input (parallel data) is loaded at a megacycle rate. Only one timing pulse, of 1-μs duration, is needed to dump the data into storage. Assume that the data message which is dumped is properly formatted for serial transmission. Clocking of each stage of the register results in a shift. If the clock is 1,300 Hz, then bit by bit the data are shifted out. The same type of unit may be used to receive data. In this case serial data are received and shifted into the register. Upon receipt of the last bit, a megacycle timing pulse triggers a readout in parallel. So one functional requirement usually needed for message processing is an ability for serial-to-parallel or parallel-to-serial conversion. You might have also associated the speed times and their changes. Speed of data flow is a functional consideration.

5-12.3 Speed Reduction/Increase

While receiving or transmitting, data messages are caused to change

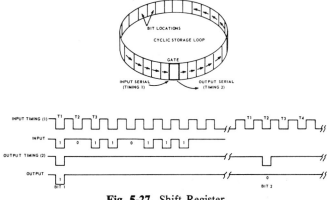

Fig. 5-27. Shift Register

their rate of speed per bit. This element is called *frequency conversion.*
The primary condition to be maintained during frequency conversion is
the absolute accuracy of data content. To best accomplish this, many
media may be used. A frequency divider may be used where data stored
are shifted out at the rate of one each time the divider produces a pulse.
Data, for instance, may be loaded into a cyclic register (Figure 5-28).
Timing, coincident with the data bit following the previous transmitted
bit, causes succeeding bits to be selected during each cycle. The process
slows transmission. An example of this method is shown in Figure 5-28.
The cyclic storage loop leads data at a rapid rate, one bit per timing
bit (1). However, data bits are shifted out at a rate much slower. Notice
that timing (2) is set to occur once each cycle plus one bit. Therefore,
each time coincidence occurs at the gate, a succeeding bit of the message
is gated out.

This same cyclic loop may be used to input data messages into an
EDP. Received data can be loaded at the receive transmission rate. When
loaded, timing (1) initiates a high-speed shiftout. Timing also brings
into focus another functional consideration, *time sharing*, which is sometimes called *time division* or *multiplexing.*

5-12.4 Time Sharing

A message processor may be designed to transmit data to, or receive
data from, a number of different stations or devices. A system of priorities

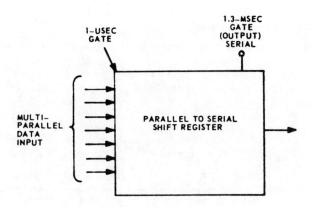

Fig. 5-28. Parallel/Serial Register

may be established to accommodate all stations. Sequencing on a recurring cycle basis may be used to allow all media to gain access. To accomplish this function, time sharing is incorporated, and various forms of circuits are available. Some of the typical circuits used are:

1. Switches.
2. Counters.
3. Switching networks.
4. Triggering.
5. Decoder units.
6. Encoder units.

Switches, triggering circuits, decoders, and encoders may use an assignment of numerics representing a specified priority system for the processing of multimedia data messages. Counters and switching networks often operate on a recycling principle. Through the priority circuits all channels may have equal time for access, or selected (high-value) channels may have more than one access period per cycle. With this brief understanding of message processor requirements, let's examine some of the different types of message input/output processors.

5-12.5 *Typical Message Input/Output Processing*

The objective to be obtained in the study made here is to identify the common goal of preparing messages for transmission to another media

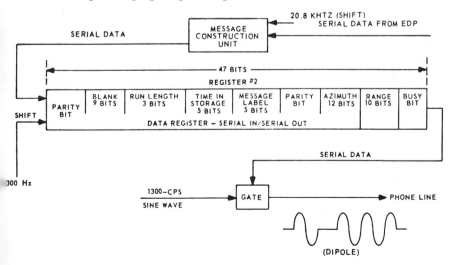

Fig. 5-29. Message Construction Unit

without real concern for message content. The study presents a few examples of conversion of digital messages into forms of voltage patterns that are acceptable to transmission media.

In Figure 5-29 data from the target-processing equipment are routed through the message construction unit, which slows the data bit rate (frequency converts). The data message is then shifted out serially with a 1,300-Hz shift pulse. It goes to an output gate, where each binary 1 produces one cycle of a 1,300-Hz sine wave and each a binary 0 produces a voltage level. In Figure 5-30, the digital message is composed in the unit preceding the message processor. You can see from the figure that this message contains many more bits of data; however, coming into the message processor, the similarity is close. The data sampler and control switch circuits consist of flip-flops. Each binary 1 causes a change in states. The output of the data sampler triggers the appropriate frequency generator (one of three), and the generator produces continuous outputs until the data sampler unit senses another binary 1. A change in the state of a flip-flop results in selection of another frequency generator, and the cycle repeats. The resultant output is frequency shift keying.

The third example, shown as Figure 5-31, represents a type of message that contains data other than machine-initiated data. This is the portion of the message labeled *operator-inserted data*. Using a keyboard, an operator types his message, and the machine converts it to digital (we discussed this under keyboards). Data bits which form the message are loaded into the output parallel-to-serial shift register, where they are serialized and modulated into a complex waveform. This waveform contains phase shifting and amplitude modulation of a basic carrier frequency. The data bit groups (8 bits) are converted into *tones* within the modem. The tone is dependent upon the 1s and 0s combination in each character and the transmit bit rate. The tone generators cause a composite phase shift equal to the sum of the detected data. The phase-shift signal is superheterodyned to the phone lines at a 0- to 3-kHz rate.

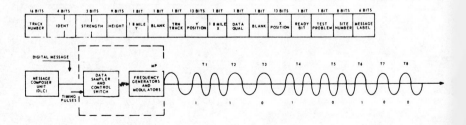

Fig. 5-30. Message Composer Unit

Alignment instructions, given in the technical reference, prescribe exact prerequisites for sequence.

5-13   Perform a Data-Detection-Circuit Alignment Study

TITLE: Signal Level Detector Alignment
OBJECTIVE: The purpose of this alignment is to adjust the receiver sensitivity to inhibit message processing of incoming data when the received signal level is too low.

This alignment is performed in a modem unit, and the circuit functions similar to the noise-cancellor circuit in a quantizer. If the receiver level of a transmitted data message drops below a specified decibel level, the data-to-noise ratio drops. Below a specified ratio, noise can be interpreted as data just as noise can be interpreted as radar video input to a quantizer. Therefore, this alignment is performed to ensure that only data received at the proper decibel level are processed, and that noise received at a low decibel level is inhibited.

5-13.1   Processor Theory

The demodulator section of this modem receives a frequency-shift-modulated (FSM) signal input from a 600-Ω balanced transmission line.

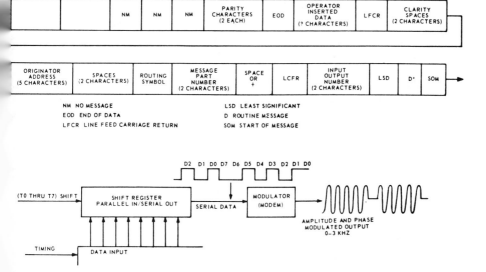

Fig. 5-31. Message Processor (Modem)

When no data are being received, the input to the demodulator consists of alternate 1s and 0s.

Upon receipt of incoming data, the front end of the unit references the data to modem ground, amplifies the signal, and detects the data. It also causes the data to be synchronized with the receiver timing.

An automatic gain circuit (AGC) is also incorporated into the front end and regulates gain of the amplifiers much like a radio. AGC circuit. This AGC circuit also influences the level-detection circuit operation.

The normal flow of data shown on Figure 5-32 is indicated by the heavy line passing through the blocks. The signals pass through:

1. Bandpass filters.
2. Equalizers.
3. Shaping circuits.
4. Phase-shift networks.
5. Discrimination circuits.

5-13.2 Align the Level-Detection Unit

Step 2 (Figure 5-8) requires identification of the circuits within the alignment. To facilitate illustrations and unify the text, the heavy blocked-in area containing the level detector is included with the interrelated circuits. This is normally a function of step 3 (Figure 5-8).

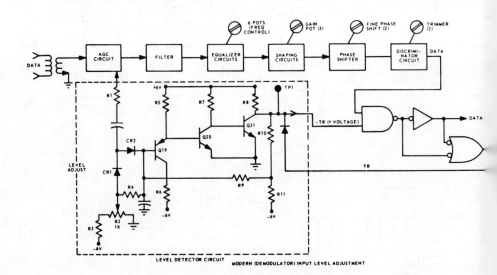

Fig. 5-32. Input Message Processor

Interrelationship of the level-detector circuit to other functions shows (in Figure 5-32) that it is almost like a generator. It is almost independent, and all other circuits are dependent upon its operation. The TR pulse is a feedback pulse and is generated as a result of all circuits functioning. The TR pulse provides a dc level plus pulse to the AND gate, which is processing data. Should it be an improper level, no data are processed.

This alignment presents us with a situation slightly different from those previously examined. The level-detector circuit is an input control device and causes all other control devices, further in the processing, to be dependent upon its setting. In this analysis, looking ahead is required to find that understanding. Interruption of data is directly related to the operation of this circuit. Verification, then, of data, valid data, or no data may be directly related to positioning of the level-detector pot.

For the alignment to be performed, substitution of input-decibel-level signals is made by use of a signal generator, electronic counter, ac voltmeter, and multimeter. Reference to the level-detector circuit in Figure 5-32.

Input to the level detector should be approximately +3 V. If the adjustment has been done correctly, Q19 is held at cutoff, and Q20 conducts while Q21 is held at cutoff. This provides +5-V level and enables the data to be processed. Should the input drop below this acceptable level, Q19 conducts, Q20 cuts off, and, with Q20 cut off, a positive voltage is felt on the base of Q21, causing it to conduct. Since Q21 is conducting, its output goes to a low logic level and prevents the data from passing through the inhibit gate.

Establishing the proper operating level of the detector circuit requires that a 6- to 24-mV rms input signal provide a 0-V dc level output. This indicates that 100 percent of the noise is inhibited with a magnitude input of 5 mV rms or less. This also indicates that weak data and strong noise with magnitude between 5 and 6 mV rms cause the detector output to be 5 V dc, and above 6 mV rms, the output provides a 5-V dc level. The TR level arms the data gate.

The conclusion to arrive at based upon information presented in this section clearly identifies that *for alignment to be meaningful*:

1. Incoming and outgoing data conversion must be understood.
2. A unit usually processes data in serial fashion, and later in processing converts the data to parallel.
3. Time sharing input source data with use of message processors to coding or decoding individual messages.
4. Alignment routines generally require extensive use of ac (rms)

meters, frequency and electronic counters, signal generators, and oscilloscopes.

5. Steps in alignments which are usually sequenced to allow for proper processing procedures.

6. Prerequisites are usually identified.

TEST QUESTIONS

1. What are the five steps necessary for a study of alignment? Describe them in detail.

2. In what way can there be interrelationships among functions that may affect an alignment?

3. Can priorities be established that have bearing on alignment routines? Explain.

4. Where does the interrelationship of circuits within a display become visual?

5. What are the commonly used types of display programming?

6. Where are data usually fed in a display unit?

7. What causes the servo motor in a servo assembly to rotate?

8. Which types of memories have mechanical alignment routines? Which types have electrical routines?

9. In a message processor, how does conversion of data from one form to another often require alignment?

6

Advanced Concepts in Performance of Checks, Adjustments, and Alignments

Reliability and maintainability of operational systems require responsible maintenance programs which efficiently and effectively keep the equipment at peak operational readiness. Responsibility for success of the program is identified in industry by numerous programs. All levels of management from the apprentice to the superintendent are involved. The technician in the work center has a unique position. He is the most qualified to work on the system. He also has a vital interest in the system. He has a feeling for the sensitivity of the equipment, and he takes personal pride in working on the equipment.

The supervisiory tasks required of the technician in the electronic-computer-system work center, coupled with the maintenance tasks identified, discussed, and studied in this and subsequent chapters, indicate clearly that the experienced technician is really a *technical manager*.

For the manager to be effective, one of his primary responsibilities is knowing, understanding, and using reliability and maintenance programs. These programs establish the maintenance principles and responsibilities for each computer system. Various sections of these programs define the terms of maintenance and provide guidelines in establishing maintenance objectives. Some of their major objectives are to:

1. Define the extent of maintenance.
2. Require maintenance to support the role and mission of the command and the system.
3. Minimize interruption of operational use of the system.
4. Perform repairs only as units fail and at the minimum level that best fits the situation (has least impact on operation).

Reliability is defined as "the probability that a system will perform a required function under specified conditions for a specified period of time or at a given point in time." Maintainability is defined as "a characteristic of design and installation expressed as the probability that an item will be retained in, or restored to, a specified condition within a given period of time when the maintenance is performed according to prescribed procedures and resources." Various aspects of these programs identify that the overall effectiveness of a system is a prime requisite, and human-reliability factors usually are included in studies conducted. The results of these studies are incorporated into the design and development of systems.

To increase the reliability of operational-systems programs:

1. Review and analyze the current reliability of the operational system.
2. Analyze the printouts (MDS and other) to identify areas of low reliability.
3. Recommend corrective action.

At the unit level (work center) these objectives are clearly a part of the technical manager's responsibility. Through monitoring of the system and analyzing reports obtained from the systems, areas may be identified that require reliability improvements. Actions taken by managers frequently result in simplification of equipment maintenance procedures.

With these brief definitions and an understanding of the scope of responsibility, this chapter develops for the technical manager a study of performance checks, alignments, and adjustments from three points of view:

1. Maintainability and reliability pertaining to checks and alignment of a system.
2. The use of resources required to perform operational servicing.
3. Analyzing the efficiency of a developed system through checks and alignments of that system.

6-1   Maintainability and Reliability Pertaining to Checks and Alignment of a System

The technical manager should always make it known that each person in a work center has the responsibility for maintenance of the system, but the prime responsibility and authority for its maintenance rests with himself. The responsibility to become a technical manager focuses on the training for the job. This is part of your training. In this section the study identifies and relates elements of knowledge necessary for career development in the specific area of performance checks, alignments, and adjustments. The study is developed under the following titles: capabilities and limitations, parts of the system that require performance checks and alignments, evaluation of systems from performance of adjustments, and visual symptoms used to determine alignment requirements versus scheduled routines.

6-1.1   *Capabilities and Limitations*

How can these help prepare you? Generally, the list of capabilities and limitations for a system are included in the first chapter of the technical reference manual. The list may be in text form or in table form. Specifically, the listings identify the operating parameters of the equipment and frequently contain data relevant to the subject of this chapter. For example, input/output minimum and maximum amplitude levels are included, and voltage, current, and frequency characteristics are listed. Rise and fall times for signals are given and, most significant, the percentage of deviation for signals is included. These frequently may be indicated as 5 to 10 percent overshoot or undershoot, or 10 percent depression.

The chapter in the service manual often provides the remainder of the significant capabilities and limitations as charts, tables, and may include illustrations of parameters. The charts and tables list voltage requirements with plus or minus deviations, resistance values, and frequency output signals with plus or minus percentages of error. The illustrations show most of the significant waveforms used throughout the system or within the equipment group.

Other maintenance data related to this subject, also included in the maintenance chapter, are:

1. Criteria for percentage of distortion.
2. Stability parameters.
3. Termination requirements.
4. Operational tests.
5. Resistance tests.

How does this information relate to performance checks, alignments, and adjustments? A technician cannot memorize all parameters of complex circuitry within his environment. Therefore, he must know where to obtain the data. He must be able to recognize that data or signal interruptions are caused by numerous conditions. If a subordinate performs a preventive maintenance action but does not identify the correct indications, only a technician who is knowledgeable in the system can correlate the fault with external causes. Solutions to this type of problem frequently require extensive knowledge of the capabilities and limitations of the system assembly and component.

Maintenance documentation frequently reveals a high component rate, especially where replacement with substitute items is used and where variable controls are used. The lifespans of variable controls are established, but this information is seldom available. Research may be in order, especially if your reports indicate a high failure rate. Now, let's move into the second area of consideration in the study of developing advanced concepts.

6-1.2 Parts of the System That Require Performance Checks and Alignments

What can be gained by studying performance requirements by area? For this study the system is broken into four segments—input/output, displays, central processors, and power.

INPUT/OUTPUT. Primary consideration must be focused on the change in the form of data. Data in many forms enter the equipment from a variety of sources. The data may be from tapes, punches, TELCO lines, microwave, radar, beacon, keyboards, or telegraph. They pass through interface units called demodulators or modulators. These units may be termed modems, message processors, multiplexers, and others. The usual purpose assigned to these units is to:

1. Change the data from analog to digital or digital to analog.
2. Change the data from electromechanical voltage to digital or analog.
3. Establish or reestablish logic levels.

Performance checks must contain clear instructions about the parameters of the data entry and exit, as well as internal modification of data (restoring logic levels, pulse width, timing). Alignment of circuits in I/O equipment must be accomplished in accordance with shop performance standards and equipment specifications. Finally, performance checks on electromechanical assemblies and components which have definite life cycles must be given close attention to detect breakdown indications.

DISPLAYS. Studies in display areas show that three considerations require careful, conscientious maintenance practices. They are *visual indications, electromechanical assemblies,* and *power.* Checks and alignment requirements on these units are most easily identified. Any distortion of visual indications, such as the absence of a portion of a display, are readily identifiable. Selection of the correct method of maintenance (adjustment, alignment, removal, and replacement) can often be accomplished by exercising the display equipment. Use of the electromechanical assemblies (relays, switches, servos, and photocells) quickly identifies the status of these elements. In many cases, deterioration of the assembly is discernible through visual check or by observing the mechanical operation. Because of these visual aspects of display, small errors become apparent, and minor corrections, through adjustment and alignment, rectify the problems. However, operational reliability may decrease as the equipment becomes older. This may be due to wear and tear of the equipment because of operator usage. A clear sign of this may be obtained from examining reports for failure-rate increases in a portion of a display or an entire display.

CENTRAL PROCESSOR. Computers, digital data processors, or communications equipment provide a challenge when applying the concepts developing advanced concepts of maintenance. Failure rate, intermittent problems, and environmental conditions complicate the problems of performance checks and alignments. The variables in these machines are not as easily identified as in I/O and displays. However, through proper testing of the unit's development of or refinement of existing tests, the reliability of the machine can be accurately obtained. These tests may be software program diagnostics or hard-wired tests. However, each test must be examined for the:

1. Reliability of the test itself.
2. Its detection criteria (capability).
3. Its validity (detection versus number of runs).
4. The interval of testing versus failure rate of the system being checked.

The more reliable the test, the greater the existence of high maintainability. Translated, this means that the test will *accurately* define a fault to a specific location, and the maintenance action taken will clear the fault.

POWER. Performance checks on power units generally sample only a few characteristics of the unit. They are the output voltage and/or current and the ripple signal on the output. The reason for this is that these are the useful product (voltage or current) and the problem area (ripple). If either is incorrect, the machine using the power does not operate correctly. Although most power supplies are stable and trouble-free, maintainability is a problem that always confronts the maintenance man. Infrequent work on these units results in lack of skill and knowledge of them. Performance checks must be thoroughly understood and extremely reliable.

Objectives of performance checks usually provide the bulk. of information needed to determine where and when alignments are to be performed. This brings us to the third part of the study.

6-1.3   Evaluation of Systems from Performance of Adjustments

How can system status be predicated from performance documentation? The following concepts are presented to provide you with a background for your training as a technical manager. With the application of these concepts, you can evaluate system status from routine performances.

TIME AND MATERIAL VERSUS CORRECTIVE ACTIONS. This element takes into account two aspects—time and material—and compares their expenditure against the corrective actions accomplished. Each performance check or alignment or adjustment results in a cost. The cost may be purely time, or it may include the replacement of parts during alignment. By weighing these factors against the number of times the actions are performed you can identify (1) deterioration of a system's reliability and (2) excessive time spent for very infrequent repair or alignment actions. By combining your studies of equipment capabilities and limitations, deficiency reports, and local quality-control inspection reports you can substantiate that excessive time and material are expended for very little corrective action.

OPERATIONAL TIME LOSS VERSUS PERFORMANCE AND ADJUSTMENT REQUIREMENTS. This element focuses on evaluating the methods of performing checks and relating them to operational time lost. Performance checks and adjustment requirements are performed by two methods—one with equipment on-line, the other with equipment off-line. In performing a study of this element, determine the checks and adjustments that can be accomplished on-line and off-line. Find out which ones interfere with system operation and which do not. Check to find those that examine only parts of machine operation, and determine their interference. If the system is checked on-line (time-shared), it provides less impact and interference with mission requirements. If, though, the check or adjustment impedes the operation, does the check provide reliable data in a minimum time and of a quality sufficient to allow high maintainability of the system or assembly? Consider also the frequency of performing the check with the number of failures it finds and weigh its worth.

NUMBER OF ACTUAL ADJUSTMENTS PERFORMED VERSUS TOTAL NUM-BER OF POSSIBLE ADJUSTMENTS PER ALIGNMENT. This final area of the evaluation of system status from performance checks and adjustments relates to complex alignment routines requiring extensive preliminary adjustment and internal adjustments. The requirement to perform an adjustment is determined by performing a check. The check of reliability should identify where the adjustment must be performed. For example, during the performance check of a read/write amplifier failure the test should clearly identify which read/write amplifier has failed. Corrective action (adjustment, removal, replacement, and adjustment) should be directed to this local area. The alignment routines of read/write amplifiers may provide repetitive instructions, a set for each amplifier. Complete alignment for the whole unit decreases maintainability of the system when only one small segment has a malfunction.

Another concept under this heading is that of identifying the adjustments which are actually performed during each scheduled routine and those adjustments not performed but indicated in the text. Determine if each adjustable component requires adjusting each scheduled period, every other scheduled period, or only when remove-and-replace action occurs. Does it only require adjusting when interrelated with other variable components that are being adjusted? Answers to these questions relate to reliability of routines, maintainability of system, and efficient use of materials with minimum impact to operational time loss.

6-1.4 *Visual Systems Used to Determine Alignment Requirements versus Scheduled Routines*

The fourth part of developing advanced concepts should ask the question, Is a visual indication reliable or is only a scheduled routine reliable? The first part of this chapter stated that a continuing requirement for the technical manager is to increase the reliability and maintainability of the system. This does not mean that he has a choice of performing or not performing scheduled routines. However, it does indicate that studies conducted by managers and data reported by them are often primary means by which system reliability and maintainability are enhanced. Include in any study you perform the answers to the following concepts.

PERCENT ERROR MEASURED VERSUS PERCENT ALLOWABLE ERROR. Two points must be considered: (1) the amount of signal drift that is tolerated in equipment as viewed from displays, meters, dials, and so on, based upon known capabilities, limitations, and standards before unscheduled corrective alignment or adjustment is required; and (2) the actual measurement of the drift of discrete signals from one scheduled period to the next. Each of these points provides data on the status of a system with direct relationship to its reliability. By analyzing documentation taken from measurements while performing routines, changes in routines can be recommended. Documentation of circuitry that required correction as well as circuitry that did not require correction should be included and cataloged. Since percentage of change in circuit, assembly, or unit operation can be attributed to many causes, try to correlate the reason for drift with some of the causes listed below. Was the cause of the drift:

1. Operator handling of controls?
2. Lifespan of components reaching maximum age?
3. Climatic variations upon components that caused thermal change?
4. Excessive handling by maintenance personnel?
5. Wear and tear of moving elements?

If, during a study, the percentage of error measured never varies out of tolerance, it may be assumed that the reliability of the circuit or function exceeds established standards. Decreasing the frequency of phase testing may prove effective and may increase operational time.

INTERPRETATION OF SYSTEM INTEGRITY BY VISUAL MEANS. Foremost in this area of study, the confidence panel should provide a solid indication of system integrity. Its reliability is good provided the circuits that supply voltage to the indicators are functioning. If faulty maintenance is used, the confidence panel will not identify correct system status and a false integrity will result. Performance checks when accomplished must validate system integrity by providing data (test points, waveshapes, voltage levels) where confidence panels do not show them. Integrity can also be determined by visually examining:

1. Displays.
2. Printer outputs.
3. Keyboard outputs.
4. Motors measuring voltage, current, and signal strength.
5. Passing or processing of data from unit to unit.

Data gathered by visual means must be cataloged. Visual means of determining system integrity must be coupled with precise knowledge of system capabilities, limitations, and performance standards.

DETERMINING THE VALIDITY OF PHASE-SCHEDULED ROUTINES. The validity of a phase-scheduled routine can be determined by use of data available within the work environment. The daily maintenance reports identify the areas in which adjustments were performed. These data should be recorded separately from the performance check. If scheduled routines include adjustment instructions and the scope of equipment coverage is limited, the report has the same degree of validity as separate repair actions. If repeated performance of a check fails to reveal a decrease in reliability (need for correction), one of two possibilities exists—the phase schedule may be too frequent, or the checks do not sample the equipment at the proper locations under the most adverse conditions. If either condition prevails, the reports should identify these elements, and the validity of the routine should be challenged.

Another element that may be used to determine the validity of performance checks and alignments is reliability data. These data, often called *engineering data,* may be readily available for original equipment but not for *suitable substitutes* installed during repair actions. Suitable substitutes theoretically provide the same characteristics as original equipment. But if failure rates tend to increase when these items are used, engineering data on them should be obtained for determining the validity of using them as part of your system.

Finally, system integrity through performance checks must be reaffirmed after a modification. Examination of the modification and the understanding of its changes in operation must be correlated with the performance checks. Validity tests using existing or modified performance routines should be made. The results should be documented so that any recommendation for change be substantiated.

All these elements prepare the manager to expend and control his resources. The concept he develops must be related to material actions. Further, these actions must be dedicated to specific task objectives. To best accomplish this, you must identify what the resources are, how they have been used in the past, and how they are currently being used.

6-2   Resources Required to Service, Check, and Align Systems

What resources do we have, and which do we use? The tools for maintenance vary from system to system. More significantly, though, is the variation or degree of use of a specific tool. The most important tool is *man* and the next is *time.* Man becomes the most valuable tool because of his brain and physical characteristics. He is the capability by which all other tools can be effectively controlled. Time is the critical element in contest with man. This element is the threat, or the achiever, depending upon the skill of man. To relate these two elements to a study recently conducted, three systems were identified according to their age (years of development). The use of man and time to maintain the systems started with many men on site and volumes of work. Maintenance of early systems required many hours of time. With the development of the intermediate system, fewer men and less time were used in its maintenance. Its reliability and maintainability were both improved. The latest system requires still fewer men and less time than its predecessors to achieve greater reliability and maintainability. Let us not forget that we are restricting our study to performance checks, alignments, and adjustments. Resources used (excluding man and time) are examined from three points of view:

1. Selection of the most applicable checking device to use to validate system integrity.
2. Selection of the most applicable technique to use to prepare the system for peak operation.
3. Selection of the proper resources and techniques to determine the need for alignment, to include sequencing of alignments and rate of repetition.

6-2.1   Selection of the Most Applicable Checking Device
To Validate System Integrity

The devices most often used for the task of validating system integrity are:

1. Various types of meters (dc, ac, frequency, etc.).
2. Oscilloscopes.
3. Special AGE (test equipment, e.g., card checkers).
4. Printouts.
5. Lamps and alarms.
6. Display equipment (DIDs, SIDs, RAPPI, RHI).

These six groups of devices were sampled against a list of units of equipment, and the units were cataloged under areas of equipment. The catalog listing looked as follows:

Area   I   *Input/output Units*
                 Interface
                 Modulator, demodulator
                 Message processor
                 Printer, keyboard

Area II   *Peripheral Units*
                  Tape
                  Punch
                  Reader
                  Communication (telecon)

Area III   *Display Units*
                  Digital information display (DID)
                  Situation information display (SID)
                  Confidence indicator display
                  Converter

Area IV   *Processor Units*
                  Data processor
                  Central computer
                  Memory

Area V   *Ancillary Units*
                  Power (low)
                  Power (high)
                  Power (commercial)
                  Category II test equipment

Three systems were chosen to provide input data. They were chosen for specific reasons. First, each system was developed and began operation in a different time period. System I was developed in the late 1950s and began operation in the early 1960s. The equipment was primarily of the tube type. The second system was developed in the early 1960s and began operation in the mid-1960s. The equipment was primarily of the solid-state type. The third system was developed in the mid-1960s and began operation in the early 1970s. The equipment was primarily of the integrated-circuit type. These selections illustrate the trends in system development over a period of 12 to 15 years.

The second consideration in the selection of systems is system makeup. Each system contains a variety of equipment and can cross-tell. Each system has:

1. A central computer.
2. Input/output equipment.
3. Displays.
4. Peripheral equipment.
5. Data-processing equipment.
6. Some type of control memory.

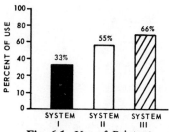

Fig. 6-1. Use of Printout

With the elements of the study compiled, a sampling of personnel skilled (technician or supervisory) in each system was used to identify which device was used most frequently to validate system integrity. The following sections explain trends in the use of these devices.

6-2.2 Printouts

A most significant element is identified in Figure 6-1. The percentage of use of the printout as a device to validate system integrity has increased remarkably. The increased reliance on printouts is well founded because of tremendous advances in the software. Programming technology has advanced to a point where diagnostic testing is a part of an operational program. By means of time sharing, fault location and isolation are a matter of routine.

Another aspect that makes the printout more significant is the construction of the newer system. The introduction of integrated circuits has caused a great many circuits to be included on one printed circuit card. As many as 20 to 25 circuits per printed circuit card is not unusual. Under this concept an entire function may be contained on one card, whereas earlier systems required 10, 15, even 20 or more printed circuit cards to perform the same function.

6-2.3 Lamps and Alarms

Figure 6-2 shows that the reliance on lamps and alarms remains consistently high even in the newest system. The value of this device in determining system integrity can be relied upon, provided certain factors are considered. The lamps and their circuits must be operable before the validity of the circuits or functions they represent can be determined. The lamps or alarms must be of sufficient numbers and strategically located in order to sample groupings of assemblies. Maintenance tasks that use lamps and alarms as status verification (i.e., performance checks, alignments, adjustments) can provide accurate data if the maintenance man properly associates the lamp with the function it samples.

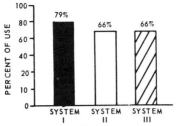
Fig. 6-2. Use of Lamps and Alarms

6-2.4 Oscilloscopes

Reliance on the oscilloscope as a device for determining system integrity, as shown in Figure 6-3, has decreased remarkably, from intensive use on systems I and II to 22 percent for system III. The use of integrated circuits, printouts, and lamps accounts for the decreased use in system III.

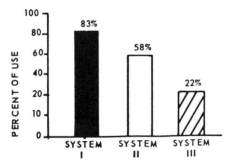
Fig. 6-3. Use of Oscilloscopes

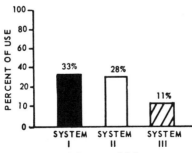
Fig. 6-4. Use of Meters

6-2.5 Meters

Figure 6-4 illustrates decreased emphasis on the use of meters as devices used to determine system integrity. The percentages of use for each system as a whole hide the fact that meters are used extensively in power supplies, displays, and I/O units. In each area the percentage of use is high:

	I/O	Display	Ancillary
System I	50	100	100
System II	20	50	100
System III	10	0	100

6-2.6   Special AGE

Figure 6-5 illustrates that a greater emphasis on the use of special-purpose AGE was made on the second system in this study. The concept was that a large assembly could be manufactured and tested as an entity, then a substituted item (operable) could be installed in its place. As the graph shows, the latest system (through the use of integrated circuits) lessened this trend. The small percentages shown in systems I and III are accounted for by equipment such as card and power-supply checkers. Card and power-supply checkers account for about the same percentage of system II.

6-2.7   CRT Display Equipment

Figure 6-6 illustrates the relative importance of the CRT display as a device for validating system integrity. Both systems I and III make use of the device because of its availability at all levels of configuration within the system. However, system II only has a limited number of locations which have display equipment capable of determining system integrity. This accounts for its extremely limited use.

6-2.8   Overview

Figure 6-7 shows a fairly clear trend. Determination of system integrity now definitely requires greater use of printouts and lamps and alarms. Reliance upon the other devices for this purpose is on the wane. However, the use of meters in the power supply, display, and I/O units is still substantial. The chart shows, by system, distribution by percent of use of each device. The total percentage of all devices (by system) equals 100 percent. From this graph some concrete, significant concepts can be derived and may be useful to the manager. Let's analyze a few.

DEVICE MOST HEAVILY RELIED UPON BY SYSTEM. In system I the oscilloscope, lamps and alarms, and CRT display equipment are used 71 percent of the time to validate system integrity. In system II, printouts, oscillo-

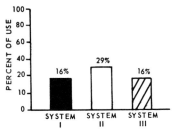

Fig. 6-5. Use of Special AGE

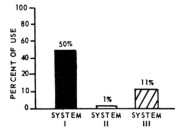

Fig. 6-6. Use of CRT Display Equipment

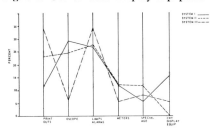

Fig. 6-7. Use of Devices

scopes, and lamps and alarms are used 75 percent of the time as devices for validating system integrity. In system III, printouts and lamps and alarms are used 68 percent of the time to validate system integrity. Clearly a comprehensive knowledge of system data flow is essential for systems II and III. Performance checks must be designed to specifically examine the equipment and provide results in terms of printout and lamp indications. In contrast, system I relies most heavily upon the oscilloscope, with almost equal weight on lamps and alarms. Performance checks on system I can be expected to require measurements of waveforms and validation of specific data operations (test problems, data).

PROFICIENCY. From analysis of this chart, proficiency in the use of each device varies according to its use. When a device is heavily relied upon, as are lamps and alarms, proficiency remains high. However, loss of proficiency results in seldom-used devices. The graph indicates that proficiency in using the oscilloscope to work on system III equipment may deteriorate. The use of meters, special AGE, and CRT display equipment as indicated on the graph shows that for most of the systems their use (percentagewise) is infrequent. This may result in personnel becoming nonproficient (rusty, as we sometimes say).

In the study of the use of resources, the selection of the device to best validate system integrity is significantly important. But, suppose you coupled a specific technique with the selection of a device? Would you then have a firmer basis for validating system integrity? Consider the following discussion of the techniques used for bringing the system to peak operation.

6-3 Selection of the Most Applicable Technique for Bringing a System to Peak Operation

Primarily, the techniques involve the interpretation of numerous sources of data. Selective interpretation of data produces specific indications of system deterioration, quality, performance standards, and specifications validation. The techniques are:

1. Reading of printouts.
2. Performing of checks.
3. Comparing special-test-equipment indications against standards.
4. Measuring of noise levels.
5. Interpreting general-test-equipment indications.
6. Interpreting lamps and alarms.
7. Viewing display-equipment indications.
8. Determining required adjustments.
9. Determining required alignments.

These techniques were sampled using the same criteria and unit designations as were used with the sampling of devices. Selected techniques were used more frequently in certain areas than others, and after the analysis of the nine graphs we will identify these special conditions.

The same three systems were used to compare the use of the techniques. To review them, they are the early-1960s system, the middle-1960s system, and the early-1970s system.

6-3.1 *Reading Printouts*

The graph shown in Figure 6-8 indicates that the interpretation of the printout as a technique for validating or peaking a system carries about the same weight from system to system. There is a distortion in this graph, though, because system I does not have the variety of peripheral equipment the other two systems do. Second, the printout produced by system I is generally restricted to the central computer area and not to displays or general data processing. A distortion also exists in the graph when analyzing system II. The printout is extensively used by intermediate stations.

6-3.2 *Performing Checks*

The graph is Figure 6-9 shows how extensively the performance check is used to determine peak operation of systems. Although a span of 15 years is included in the development of the three systems, this technique remains consistently high. Therefore, the elements of this technique must be thoroughly understood and applied.

6-3.3 *Comparing Special-Test-Equipment Indications Against Standards*

Figure 6-10 shows that a heavy reliance for determining system peak operation was used by system II, but because of advances in techniques of software and circuit development, the newer system places decreased emphasis on special AGE.

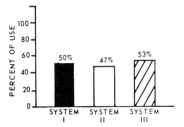

Fig. 6-8. Reading a Printout

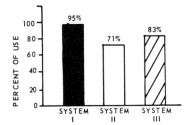

Fig. 6-9. Performing a Check

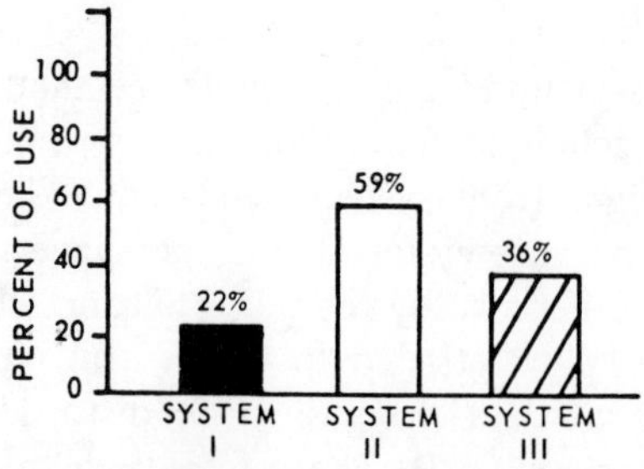

Fig. 6-10. Comparing Special-Test-Equipment Indications Against Standards

6-3.4   *Measuring Noise-level Indications*

The graph in Figure 6-11 shows a marked increase in the use of noise-level indications as a technique for determining peak operation of system III. Many of these measurements are made on cross-tell data, power, and analog signals in display areas.

6-3.5   *Interpreting General-Test-Equipment Indications*

The graph in Figure 6-12 shows a deemphasis on the use of general test equipment from system I through system III. The low percentage for system II is accounted for in part by the use of special AGE. Meters, oscilloscopes, counters, and generators are used in all three systems.

6-3.6   *Interpreting Lamp and Alarm Indications*

The graph in Figure 6-13 shows the extensive use of this technique throughout the years for determining peak operation. Except for those lamps used to show counter operation and data flow, the indicators usually provide a go–no go condition. Even so, they are reliable for use as a technique.

6-3.7   *Viewing Display-Equipment Indications*

The graph in Figure 6-14 shows that, as a whole, many data can be obtained from visual observations of displays which can be interpreted to determine system integrity. Operating this equipment causes exercising of numerous areas of equipment, including central processors and computers, converters, tape units, interface, and others. The indications presented on the CRT, readout indicators, and dials can readily identify quality of data flow and circuit operation.

6-3.8   *Determining Required Adjustments*

A marked drop in the reliance of determining required adjustments as a technique for determination of system operation is showɹ in Figure 6-15. The earliest system used extensive adjustment routines to peak its

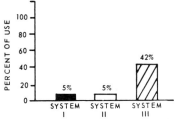

Fig. 6-11. Measuring of Noise-Level Indications

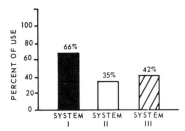

Fig. 6-12. Interpreting General-Test-Equipment Indications

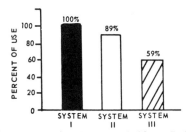

Fig. 6-13. Interpreting Lamp and Alarm Indications

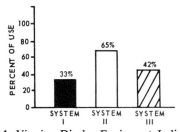

Fig. 6-14. Viewing Display-Equipment Indications

operation. Intervals of 30 days between performance of the task were common. Generally a high percentage of circuits was operating outside the specified parameters at the end of 30 days. With simplified circuitry and lower power requirements, the circuits in the newer systems remain within specifications for longer periods of time. Thus we can interpret the graph

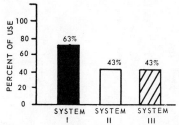

Fig. 6-15. Determining Required Adjustments

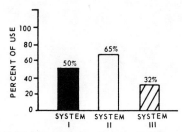

Fig. 6-16. Determining Required Alignments

and account for the drop in use as a technique for determining peak operation.

6-3.9 *Determining Required Alignments*

The distinction between adjustments and alignments was brought out in Chapter 4 and is repeated here as a reminder. "Alignment involves bringing a series of happenings into a straight line (order)" (e.g., a sweep circuit function). "Adjustment is the individual action of altering a single component or part" (e.g., potentiometer, capacitor).

Figure 6-16 contains a graph which shows that each system makes extensive use of alignment as a means or technique for determining system operation. The fact that a broader scope is usually involved when alignment is required definitely aids a technician. This aid is understandable and accounts for increased use of alignments, as compared with adjustments in both systems II and III.

6-3.10 *Overview*

Of the nine techniques used to determine peak operation in the different systems, interpretations of performance checks, and lamps and alarms, are the two most often used. Printouts, alignments, adjustments, and display indications are the next most frequently used techniques. Special and general AGE are used about equally, and noise-level inter-

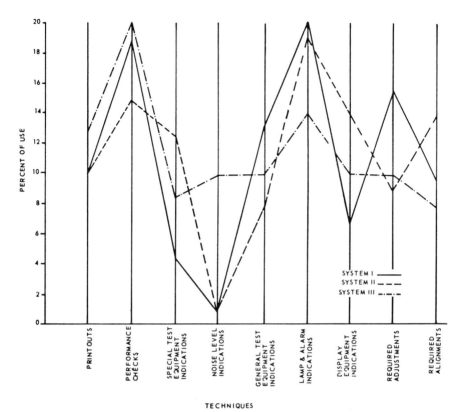

TECHNIQUES

Fig. 6-17. Uses of Techniques

pretation is the least frequently used technique. The graph in Figure 6-17 shows these relationships.

From the data in the graph and your knowledge of the present system, you should be able to correlate the various techniques.

If you work on system I-type equipment, performance checks using general AGE and lamps will be extensive.

If you work on system II-type equipment, performance checks using lamps, special AGE, printouts, alignments, and display-equipment indications will be extensive.

If you work on one of the newer systems, performance checks using lamps, printouts, and display equipment indications will be extensive.

Other statistics can be derived from the graph relating to combined use of techniques for performance of alignments or adjustments. And if you combine the statistics shown about devices in Figure 6-7 with those of Figure 6-17, a specific study about efficiency can result.

6-4 Study of the Efficiency of a Maintenance Work Center

So far, study of the tasks related to performance checks, alignments, and adjustments for the technical manager has pointed to the efficient use of his resources to identify that the system is operating correctly or is not. To accomplish this end, the study provided discussion about the use of all the resources available. It also identified typical types of devices and techniques which are used to maintain general areas of equipment. Placing all aspects of the study into one cohesive plan clearly identifies two goals.

1. A comprehensive system knowledge must be coupled with technical experience.
2. The manager's job is to quickly and accurately assess the situation and dispatch repairmen and the proper tools to the task area.

At this time you may or may not have had experience on more than one system. If you have worked on only one and are proficient in the tasks of performance checks, alignments, and adjustments, it may mean you have an extensive knowledge of the equipment. Since you have entered technician training you have a few years' experience in equipment maintenance. With both conditions present the study presented in this chapter may have put into words your thoughts about the system. The study may have stimulated some new thoughts.

By combining data in Figures 6-7 and 6-17, specific devices coupled with techniques can result in efficient maintenance practices, especially while performing performance checks, alignments, and adjustments. The performance check (Figure 6-17) requiring use of printouts, oscilloscope lamps, and alarms or meters will prove extremely effective in validating system integrity. Research of the content of the checks in the technical reference, coupled with the identification of the devices' capabilities, should provide a comprehensive knowledge of:

1. Overall coverage of the equipment.
2. Parts of the equipment only briefly tested.
3. Parts of the equipment tested in only one mode.
4. When more than one mode of operation exists.
5. Parts of the system that are not tested at all.
6. Parts of the system that are tested repeatedly but in which no failures exist.
7. Parts of the system that are tested repeatedly but in which failures are discovered infrequently or seldom as a result of the test.

The second goal may be improved from your point of view by studying Figures 6-7 and 6-17. First identify with a system. Remember the relative age of each:

System I: late 1950s, early 1960s.
System II: early 1960s, mid-1960s.
System III: mid-1960s, early 1970s.

These figures show what techniques and devices effectively and efficiently determine system integrity and make maximum use of available resources. You can make a statistical analysis of your specific system as was done for this chapter. Your results may differ slightly or may be the same as one of these systems. If you desire, in place of general categories of devices, you can list specific devices. Then you can, with a high degree of accuracy, assess your equipment operation by the technique that provides the highest degree of reliability. Upon your assessment, you can dispatch repairmen to a specific area with instructions as to which devices to use and which checks or alignments to perform.

This second goal probably has the greatest impact on the efficiency of a developed system. It demands the correct on-the-spot selection of resources and assignment to tasks based upon very slight to catastrophic situations. It requires great sensitivity to the system being maintained, to the personnel assigned, to the exact moment of occurrence, and to the impact upon the mission in progress. For example, a technician walking through a console room observes each console and detects a deflection error of a few degrees in all consoles. A mission is started. What should be done? Well, the situation could be critical, and obviously the problem is not in each console. Research of alignments for the system (previously studied) indicates that only two adjustments can be made to correct the problem. Another factor is the fact that the unit controlling deflection is in the data-processing room. Based upon the decision of the supervisors (operations and maintenance) a correction can be made without interruption to the system provided qualified personnel perform the task. Equipment is connected, the adjustment is made, correction is effected, and the mission is completed without interruption. This typical example shows that visual techniques coupled with video displays, an in-depth knowledge of the circuits and their alignment, and the proper selection of resources unite in efficient, effective maintenance even under the most adverse conditions.

You can see by this one example that a study of a system and its checks, adjustments, and alignments can:

1. Minimize the impact to a system while performing maintenance.

2. Minimize the impact to an operational mission when correcting a misalignment.
3. Be effective in maintaining equipment through research of the checks and alignments.
4. Obtain results by selection of the correct resources for repair of a system.
5. Ensure results of efficient repair from minor variation to catastrophic failures.

We could provide numerous examples similar to the one just completed, and in all probability you would identify with one or more. However, as a future technical manager it is most important to develop concepts that have been proved through use. Further, these concepts must be such that they have flexibility. The degree of flexibility will be governed by:

1. Change in mission requirements.
2. Change in competence of assigned personnel.
3. Change in equipment configuration.

And the most challenging demand to a concept occurs with a change to a new system.

Figures 6-7 and 6-17 clearly identify that, within the individual systems, the tasks associated with performance checking, aligning, and adjusting require combinations of techniques and devices. Through the careful study of the capabilities, limitations, and characteristics of a system, accurate predictions and evaluations can be made. With the specific knowledge of a function, capabilities of a routine, exercising of the machine, and research of data documented by various means, dispatching of repairmen to a local area results in efficient use of resources.

The degree of error discovered through performance checking necessarily dictates who should be selected to do the repair work. How much time is available will influence the selection of men. Supplying the proper device to the man is partly accomplished by identification of the appropriate maintenance action.

In preparing a study of your current system and developing the concepts, guides, and the records you initiate, keep the following four ideas foremost:

1. Ensure that your actions, assignments, and decisions result in minimal impact to the system and maximum restoration.

2. Determine that any action taken or projected will not impede an active operation.
3. Research the routines and instructions about checks, alignments, and adjustments to determine their specific goals.
4. Finally, select the checking device and technique that will provide the most reliable results in the least time.

TEST QUESTIONS

1. What purpose can be made of a system's capabilities and limitations while studying performance check routines?

2. In studying the requirements for performance checks, what is a primary consideration of the:
   a. Input/output unit?
   b. Display unit?
   c. Central processor?
   d. Power?

3. What benefits can a manager obtain from a time-and-material study versus a corrective-action study?

4. What data about equipment reliability can be determined from a study of the number of actual adjustments performed versus the total number of possible adjustments in an alignment?

5. What are five reasons for signal drift in circuit operations?

6. What development in the software of computers has caused the printout to become a method to validate system integrity?

7. What are the techniques most frequently used with each of the three systems identified in this chapter?

7

Equipment Identification

This chapter presents information that advances knowledge related to locating components in a system. The task is frequently combined with tasks in equipment modification and troubleshooting. Because of the vast number of components that may be located in numerous assemblies signal tracing is often difficult. Tracing signals through rack jacks, logic sheets, and wiring diagrams is usually difficult. Even the best technicians sometimes lose their way and reverse themselves while tracing a signal. They find themselves right back at the start of their examination.

7-1 Understanding the Component Number

The full nomenclature of a component is dependent upon the extent and complexity of the equipment. In a radio it might be assigned a printed circuit number plus its own classification. For example, resistor 17 in the IF circuit might look like A2R17, A2 being the IF printed circuit and R17 being the 17th resistor in the circuit.

Notice that this example when written out placed the assembly first and the resistor last. This is always the case. When a full component location is developed, the first part of the number will identify the largest part of the system containing the component. These parts may include a *unit* or *cabinet.*

Figure 7-1 shows two units. Each component has its own distinctive location number. They look like these:

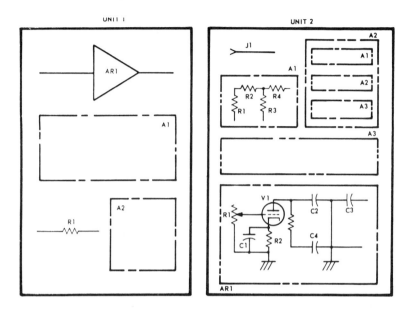

Fig. 7-1. Unit Layouts

UNIT 1:

1AR1—triangle.
1A1—rectangle in the center.
1R1—resistor affixed to the unit.
1A2—square next to the resistor.

UNIT 2:

AJ1—jack 1.
2A1R1, R2, R3, R4—board with four resistors.
2A3—assembly A3.
2Ar1—assembly Ar1 with
    2AR1R1—resistor R1.
    2AR1V1—tube V1.
    2AR1C1—capacitor C1.
    2AR1R2—resistor R2.
    2AR1C2—capacitor C2.
    2AR1C3—capacitor C3.

2AR1C4—capacitor C4.
2A2A1—board A2 with assembly A1.
2A2A2—board A2 with assembly A2.
2A2A3—board A2 with assembly A3.

Another important characteristic in component numbering is that of the number of digits assigned a component. If there are, for example, 100 components or more, but less than 1,000 within an assembly, every component must have three digits. The lowest assigned component has a number of 001 and the highest may have 999.

With these few ground rules examined we now can begin the task of making wiring lists for locating a specific component in a specific assembly. Either of two methods may be employed. They are called the *vertical* listing method and the *horizontal* listing method. Rather than explain each now, examples are provided which show their development and use.

7-2 Interpret Wiring Diagrams and Correlate the Diagrams with Connectors, Interconnecting Cabinets, and Remote Equipment

Interpreting wiring diagrams is an extremely important task of any qualified maintenance technician. This is especially so when you realize that your equipment is often made by different contractors and is linked together through cables. Each unit, operational amplifier (OA) group, assembly, or subassembly has some form of interconnecting wiring. Each unit contains interconnecting cables within the unit. It therefore follows that a complete understanding of the data flow between units and within units and a comprehensive knowledge of the techniques employed by contractors to interconnect components is essential for you. You have been through school and have learned to read logic. You probably received some explanation on rack-jack signal tracing. You may have heard of the *main distribution frame, filter panel,* or *junction box.* This section presents a study of (1) the equipment and terms of systems, (2) technical references, and (3) vertical and horizontal methods used to form lists of data and voltage signal distribution routes.

7-3 Elements

In Chapter 1 we analyzed connectors and learned exactly what a jack is, what a plug is, and what a fixed connector is. These subjects are brought into focus in this chapter. Each one is directly related to the discussion on interpreting wiring diagrams. They must be identified and understood in the layout of the equipment in order to effectively trace data or voltage through cabinets and units. The following list of terms will aid you in understanding this study.

Terms	Description
Bays or racks	1. Assemblies usually reaching from the floor to the ceiling within a cabinet. 2. They may be fixed or hinged. 3. They usually contain chassis, drawers, and subassemblies. 4. They generally have a distinctive identifying location number. 5. They generally provide a major function for the overall system.
Cabinets	1. A unit or OA group consisting of a functional group of assemblies designed for a specific purpose. 2. Examples: console, printer, data processor, memory unit, input device.
Cable	1. A length of wire, either single or multiple leads, usually covered with a protective outer weather-resistant coating. 2. Generally the cable is labeled with a "W" and a number, identifying it. 3. The label often contains the length of the cable and the connecting units to which it is attached.
Chassis	1. Assemblies or subassemblies within a unit designed as a logical assembly which normally provide a function for the unit.
Drawer	1. Similar to a chassis but designed to be rapidly removed and replaced.
Filter panel	1. Usually an assembly panel affixed to the outer shell of a unit for the purpose of filtering data leaving the cabinet. 2. A filter panel may be remote from the unit, but it still provides the same function.
Jack	1. The more fixed connector of a mating pair. 2. Designated by the letter "J" or "X."
Main distribution frame	1. A common focal point where cables from units and assemblies are joined to elements within the frame in order to allow passage of signals between units. 2. This unit reduces the need for extensive cabling and permits greater distribution of signals and greater variety of equipment configuration.

	3. This term is not to be confused with the definition of a main frame used in computer terminology.
Plug	1. The most movable connector of a mating pair.
	2. Identified by the letter "P."
Terminal board	1. A rectangular unit consisting of multiple connectors, usually the screw type.
	2. Designed to connect two or more lines to a specific source.
	3. Quite often found in high-voltage couplers, filter panels, main frames, and circuit-breaker boxes. Usually designated "TB."
Unit	1. A major assembly. It may be a cabinet or an AN item; it may be an OA group; in any event, it is a numbered item.

7-4　Technical Reference

The service manual usually provides the technical data for installation of equipment in the second chapter. This chapter defines:

1. Installation layout.
2. Requirements for power and environment.
3. Site consideration.
4. Inspections of installations.

In the descriptions and tables in this manual, the data needed to interpret wiring diagrams are:

1. Cable identification, cable number.
2. Routing data.
3. Termination.
4. Jack and plug pin lettering and wire color coding.
5. Component-part number.

The circuit diagram manual provides the technical data for point-to-point signal tracing of data. This may be accomplished in various forms. It may be in the form of a wiring table, or it may be in the form of a plug and jack layout. This manual also provides data on cable numbers between units, between units and main distribution frames, and between units and filter panels. Quite frequently the J number on the unit or component is shown on a block diagram along with the W wire number. We will examine some of the methods most commonly employed and you must determine which methods are used in your system and where they are used.

In the following paragraphs you participate in the identification of connection points of signals in a problem-solving type of presentation. After the titles Data Signal Flow 1, Data Signal Flow II, and Data Signal Flow III, carefully study the italicized objective of each problem; then follow its analysis to formation of a signal wire list.

7-5 Data Signal Flow I

Identify the interconnecting connectors of a data signal from its origin to its point of use. This situation presents one signal that is routed through components, jacks, cabinets, and cables so that you can visually trace the signal as it proceeds from point to point. The objective here is to identify each connecting point and, by forming the alphanumeric code, relate the number to a real place in the equipment. By proper full alphanumeric formulation and sequential listing of the numbers, you will easily know when you have exited a chassis, rack, bay, or cabinet.

Before making a wiring list, follow along and see how the range marks are routed. Refer to Figure 7-2B and locate module XA22 in Cab 45. This is the origin of the range marks. Follow the connecting lines through XA13, 12, and 14, out of the rack jack J2, out of the cabinet jack J17, through cable W6060 into connector panel A14, jack J2 cabinet 46;

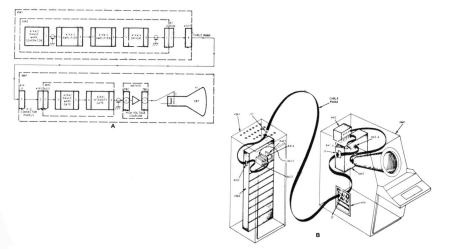

Fig. 7-2. Range-Mark Routing (Courtesy of General Electric Co.)

through rack pack J2, into module XA2, then to module X2 1, to the high-voltage coupler, out of the coupler into the rear of the CRT, and to the displayed range marks on the CRT face. When you, as the man who has to identify these routing data, compile them as shown in Figure 7-2a, they are complete. However, when you physically try to locate those points and the signal is routed, as you can see, from chassis to racks to cabinets to other cabinets, your wiring list takes on a physical dimension. You must translate these physical characteristics into knowledge and understanding of the nomenclature of the connectors as well as their physical placement.

Refer to Figure 7-2A. List, by using a full alphanumeric code and the vertical listing method, the assemblies, jacks, plugs, and cables in order from the range-mark generator to the CRT.

1. _____   9. _____
2. _____   10. _____
3. _____   11. _____
4. _____   12. _____
5. _____   13. _____
6. _____   14. _____
7. _____   15. _____
8. _____

List the jack/plug and terminal boards connectors for chassis and cabinets using the full alphanumeric code.

Chassis   Cabinet

1. _____   1. _____
2. _____   2. _____
3. _____
4. _____

The complete list called for above would look as follows:

1. 45A2a1XA22-7   9. 46A2A2J2/A1P3-G
2. 45A2A1XA13-16/4   10. 46A2A2XA2-16/6
3. 45A2A1XA12-17/6   11. 46A2A2XA1-8/6
4. 45A2A1XA14-19/6   12. 46A1A1OTB2-6
5. 45A2J2/A1P202/J   13. 46A1A10
6. 45A1J17-6   14. 46A1A1OTB1-1
7. W6060   15. V1-3
8. 46A1A14J2-6

The added list called for above should look as follows:

Chassis	Cabinet
1. 45A2J2/A1P202-J	1. 45A1A1J17-6
2. 46A2A2J2-G	2. 46A1A14J2-6
3. 46A1A1OTB2-3	
4. 46A1A1OTB1-1	

7-6 Data Signal Flow II

Identify and list the connecting points of a multiused signal using the chart and Figures 7-3 *and* 7-4. In this problem, data generated from module 611 are to be used in various portions of the fine-grain-data (FGD) equipment. It is routed to two remote units, the selective identification feature (SIF) unit and the SM-137 simulator. Again this circuitry must be studied with the approach that data transferred to other areas and

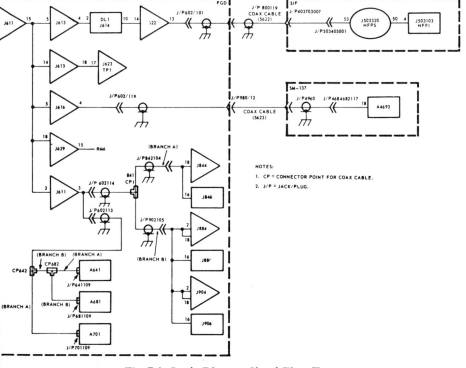

Fig. 7-3. Logic Diagram Signal Flow II

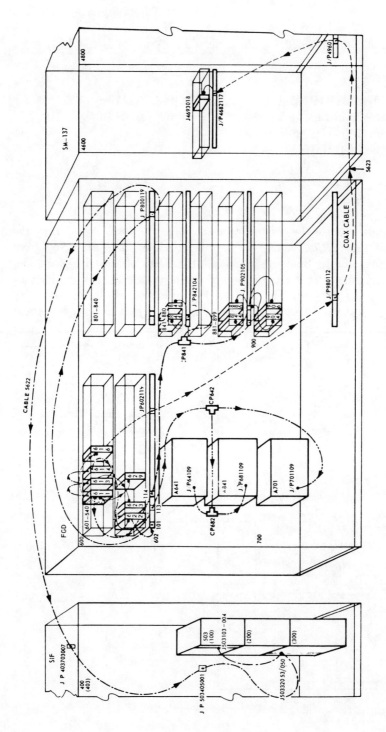

Fig. 7-4. Physical Layout Signal Flow II

212

units must be routed by cables through connectors and all the connecting points must be identified.

Refer briefly to Figure 7-3 and observe that the original generator 611 is distributing its output to five main paths. Three paths complete their action in the FGD cabinet and, of the other two, one goes to the SIF and one to the SM-137.

Now follow along and observe from the pictorial view in Figure 7-4 how the physical routing of the signal is accomplished. Find card location 611, *the darkened rectangle in the FGD cabinet bay 600,* subassembly 601-640:

1. Follow the solid line from 629 to 622. This is the termination of this leg which generates a new data signal (RM6).

2. Also from 611 to a pin on 613, the signal is fed through 613 to 623, where it generates another signal (TPI).

3. Follow again from 611 the line to 613 (pin 5) to 614, through 622, through jacks and plugs, to bay 800, through more jacks and plugs, out of the FGD cabinet, into the SIF cabinet, and more jacks and plugs in the top of bay 400, to drawer 503, and jacks and cards in rows 3 and 1 of drawer 503. This signal terminates in card 503103 of the SIF unit.

4. Again follow another output from 611 to 616 through the jack and plug 602119, out of bay 600 into the lower portion of bay 800/900 to location J/P980112. This signal exits bay 800 here and is routed by coax lead to lower rack jack 4960 to 4800. From here it goes to jack plug 4682117, and then into card 4693018. The signal is terminated at A4693 pin 018.

5. Locate 611 again and trace the line leading from it to J/P602113 and J/P602114. Note that two circuits on module 611 are used before the connection at 602113 is made. J/P602113 coax lead is fed to the three assemblies A641, A841, and A701. The CP connections are coax T connectors. The lead from J/P602114 goes to bay 800 and 900. In bay 800 it is tied at CP841 and one line is fed to J/P842104, which feeds two assemblies, 844 and 846, and the other branch of the tie is fed to J/P902105 and feeds four assemblies, 884, 886, 904, and 906.

Now, by using Figure 7-5 laid out by the horizontal method, all the points of connection can be listed in order. This is done by identifying the jacks, plugs, cables, and assemblies in each path. Identification of input and output pins on jacks are indicated at the rear of the jack number as

Wiring List for Signal _____ (Hor Technique)

1. Origin (RM6) ——— Terminating Jack

2. Origin (RM3 to TP1) ——— Terminating Jack

3. Origin (RM3 to SIF) ——— Terminating Jack ——→ Bay Jack/Plug ——— Bay Jack/Plug

4. Origin (RM3 to SM 137) ——— Terminating Jack ——→ Bay Jack ——— Bay Jack ——→ Cable ——— Rack Jack

   Cable ——— Cabinet Jack ——— Drawer Jack ——→ Terminating Jack

   Rack Jack ——— Terminating Jack

5. Origin (RM3 to Assemblies in Bay 600) ——— Bay Jack ——— Connector Pt

   Branch A ——— Jack/Plug ——— Terminating Assembly

   Branch B ——— Connecting Pt ——— A to Jack/Plug ——— Terminating Assembly

   B to Jack/Plug ——— Terminating Assembly

   Branch A ——— Branch A Jack/Plug

   Branch B ——— Branch B Jack/Plug

6. Origin (RM3 to Bay 800 - 900) ——— Bay Jack/Plug ——— Connector Pt ——— Branch A Jack/Plug ——— Branch B Jack/Plug

   Branch A ——— Terminating Jacks

   Branch B ——— Terminating Jacks

Fig. 7-5 Horizontal Layout Method

214

follows: $\begin{array}{cc} \text{in} & \text{out} \\ \text{J611014/018} \end{array}$ ·

The completed chart may look like this when completed:

1. RM 3 to SIF
   $\qquad\qquad$ in $\qquad$ out
   J611015 → J613014/018 → J614002/010 → J622014/013 →
   J/P602101 → J/P800119 → Cable 5622 → J/P403703007 →
   J/P503405001 → J/50332053/95 → J50310304 (HFF-1)

2. RM 3 to RM 6
   J611015 → J629018/015 → J622016

3. RM 3 to SM 137
   J611015 → J616005/004 → J/P602119 → Cable 5623 →
   J/P4960 → J/P4682 → J4693018

4. RM 3 to Assemblies in Bay 600
   J611015 → J611002/003 → J/P602113 → CP642 Branch A
   J/P701109 → A701; Branch B CP682, Branch A →
   J/P641109 → A641; Branch B J/P681109 → A681

5. RM 3 to Bay 800/900
   J611015 → J611002/003 → J/P602114 → CP841 Branch A
   J/P842104 → J844018 and J846016; Branch B J/P902105 →
   J884002 and 018, and J886016, and J904002 and 018, and
   J906016

6. RM 3 to TP1
   J611015 → J613014/018 → J623017

This exercise compiled individual lists of a multipath signal. In real application, possibly only one or two of the paths would have had to be checked. However, in this objective we had to prove that in interpreting wiring diagrams connectors are used to route data. The figure and completed lists have proved this. A signal that started in a card in a bay has been distributed to chassis, other bays, and other cabinets each time a connector, jack, or connecting point was used. This is the second interpretation of wiring diagrams and some very definite characteristics are becoming evident.

1. Originating signals are generally fed to a connecting point, such as a jack.

2. Multiple routing of a signal is accomplished with jacks and connectors.

3. Each point of a junction is identified by a location number.

4. The data for making a complete signal wire list may be extracted

from various reference manuals (such as the manuals on the FGD, SIF, and SM-137 equipment in this example) and, within the manuals, from selected chapters or sections providing connecting point listings (jack listings).

7-7   Data Signal Flow III

Use the wiring table to identify and locate interconnecting cables between the main distribution frame and units. In performing this task we will have to identify what a main distribution frame is and show its relative position in a system wiring scheme. It was defined earlier and if you observe Figure 7-6 you can see a pictorial representation of a typical frame. This analysis is based upon the use of a main frame, but the principles of usage are the same if a filter box or junction box is used instead of a frame. The frame is the most complex of the three, so it is selected for this analysis.

Refer again to Figure 7-6 and observe how this unit is made of rows and columns and tiers or planes. Each location is identifiable by a coordinate number consisting of a row, a column, and a plane number usually

Fig. 7-6. Main Distribution Frame

given a J prefix. Each pin connection on each jack further identifies the exact point connection. Generally, all connections from a unit are located within specific groups of rows and columns. The transfer of signals to another unit is usually accomplished by use of single-strand wire from point to point within the frame. In order to facilitate the installation and tracing of signal paths, tables are formed, with the main frame being the focal point of the table.

Refer to Figure 7-7. The table will very likely contain these columns and these data:

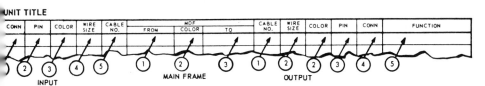

Fig. 7-7. Table Layout of Main Distribution Frame

Input

1. The connector point.
2. The pin number in the connector.
3. The color of the wire.
4. The size of the wire.
5. The cable number.

Main Frame Connectors

1. The point of connection of the input cable.
2. The color code of the wire.
3. The point of connection to the output cable.

Output

1. The output cable.
2. The size and color of the wire.
3. The pin number.
4. The connector number.
5. The functional requirement of the signal.

With this information we can begin to apply the analysis to a situation or problem. To do this we will use Figure 7-8. Our task, once again, is to use the table to identify and locate the interconnecting cables between the main frame and the units.

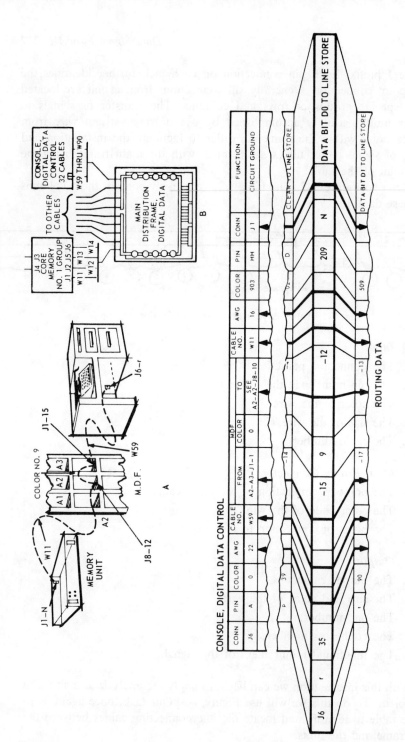

Fig. 7-8. Routing, Signal Data III

Follow along once again as we use Figure 7-8. Let's suppose we are required to determine where data bit DO was routed to understand a modification change or for some other reason. Look at the table and observe the darkened outlined area (Figure 7-8). The DO data signal is transferred from *J6* pin *r* of the console through cable *W59* to the main frame, where wire little *r* is connected to *A2-A3-J1-I5;* vertical row A2, horizontal row A3, first terminal row J1, and contact I5. From that point it is routed by a colored #9 wire to *A2-A2-J8-12*. Pin 12 has one lead from W11 with a colored #209 wire connected and the other end of the cable W11 wire color #209 is connected to J1 and pin N on the Line Store (memory unit) functional assembly. It is actually quite easy to perform this task once analysis is applied.

Situations A and B, which follow, are examined by using the vertical listing method, and by listing in order connector points, cables, jacks, and so on, of each signal path. Starting at the console in situation A and at the memory group in situation B, use Figure 7-9 to obtain the inputs to the vertical list. If necessary, refer back to Figure 7-8 for physical routing correlation.

Situations A and B preliminary Vertical List:

Situation A	Situation B
1. _____	1. _____
2. _____	2. _____
3. _____	3. _____
4. _____	4. _____
5. _____	5. _____
6. _____	6. _____
7. _____	7. _____
8. _____	8. _____

Situations A and B Completed Vertical Lists:

Situation A	Situation B
1. J6, Jack 6 at console	1. J5 at memory unit
2. Pin *r* in *J6*	2. Pin HH on J5
3. Cable W59	3. Cable W13
4. A2-A3-J3-9 (MDF)	4. A2-A2-J5-20 (MDF)
5. A2-A2-J6-19 (MDF)	5. A3-A3-J3-11 (MDF)
6. Cable W11	6. Cable 64
7. Pin W on J1	7. Pin A on J6
8. Jack J1 at memory unit	8. J6 at the console

CONSOLE, DIGITAL DATA CONTROL

CONN	PIN	COLOR	AWG	CABLE NO.	FROM	MDF COLOR	TO	CABLE NO.	PIN	COLOR	PIN	CONN	FUNCTION
J6	A	0	22	W59	A2-A3-J1-1	0	SEE A2-A2-J8-10	W11	16	903	HH	J	CIRCUIT GROUND
	B	900			-2	9	A6-A2-J1-1						
	DD	6			-7		-17			925	U		DATA BIT D6 TO LINE STORE
							-18			205	V		DATA BIT D5 TO LINE STORE
J6	FF	62	22	W59	A2-A3-J3-9	9	SEE A2-A2-J6-19	W11	22	...	W	J	DATA BIT D7 TO LINE STORE

SITUATION A

CORE MEMORY GROUP

CONN	PIN	COLOR	AWG	CABLE NO.	TO	MDF COLOR	FROM	CABLE NO.	AWG	COLOR	PIN	CONN	FUNCTION
J5	z	906	16	W13	A2-A2-J5-13		OPEN						
J5	AA	325	16	W13	A2-A2-J5-14		OPEN						
J5	BB	532	16	W13	A2-A2-J5-15		OPEN						
J5	CC	096	16	W13	A2-A2-J5-16		OPEN						
J5	DD	623	16	W13	SEE DWG 4580262		SEE DWG 4580262	W63	22	5	X	J6	CHASSIS GROUND LUG
J5	EE	326	16	W13	A2-A2-J5-18		SEE DWG 4580262	W64	22	5	X	J6	CHASSIS GROUND LUG
J5	FF	230	16	W13	A2-A2-J5-19		A3-A3-J1-1	W63	22	0	A	J6	CIRCUIT GROUND
							OPEN						
J6	HH	903	16	W13	A2-A2-J5-20	0	A3-A3-J3-11	W64	22	0	A	J6	CIRCUIT GROUND
J6	A	29	22	W14	A2-A2-J1-1	9	A3-A3-J7-6	W65		...	...		SEND COMPLETE FROM KEYBOARD Q6
J6	B	59			-2		A3-A3-J7-2						SEND PARTIAL
J6	C	6°			-3		A3-A3-J7-20						ADDRESS

SITUATION B

Fig. 7-9. Signal Routing Situations A and B

In this study we examined how the main distribution frame is used as a connecting point between units. It is easy to understand how useful this unit is because of its great flexibility. Tracing connectors and connector connections is simplified when the pictorial view is associated with the tables and the cable layout drawings. If a filter-box layout or distribution-box layout were used in the analysis just completed, the following data would have been needed:

1. Cable numbers for incoming and outgoing signals.
2. Jack and plug numbers.
3. Pin numbers on jacks.
4. Filter or terminal-board connector points.

Figure 7-10 shows a few examples of how jacks and plugs are laid out in logic and wiring diagrams. These symbols have been used in each of the situation analyses just completed.

We have analyzed some of the typical wiring situations found in data processors, where the task of interpreting wiring diagrams is employed. We have identified that all components must be listed so that a complete picture of the signal path can be obtained. Some terms were identified and explained. Remember that when using wiring diagrams and tables in forming a list or tracing a signal to find its connecting points, you sometimes may double back upon yourself. This means that while

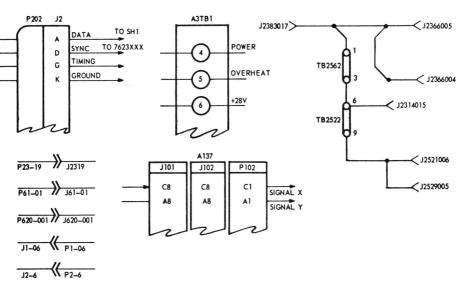

Fig. 7-10. Jacks

going from jack to jack and flipping pages of logic, you can reverse your direction and return to the starting point. To prevent this, a complete understanding of jack/plug nomenclature and a complete nomenclature of all connectors must be recorded in your list. These data will reveal any reversal trend. We have identified and used the vertical and horizontal listing techniques in the three situations. Adaptions of these techniques should be developed by you after a study of your equipment configuration so that you completely understand the signal routing.

Let's list once more the points this study has identified which will aid in interpreting wiring diagrams.

1. Cables are numbered with a W on both incoming and outgoing lines.

2. Jacks and plugs each have numbers prefixed with J or X or P.

3. Jacks are indicated at the *point* of the double arrow or the rectangle on schematics.

4. Plugs are indicated on the *back side* of the double arrow and on the rounded corner rectangle on schematics.

5. Each pin has a letter or number or both on jacks and plugs. All letters are used except I, O, and Q.

6. Capital and lowercase letters are used.

7. Terminal boards normally use numbers in preference to letters for connecting points.

8. Main distribution frames, filter boxes, and junction boxes provide the same basic functions, but the filter box also provides isolation by filtering.

9. You will need logic and wiring diagrams and wiring tables, cable listings, and rack-jack listings to perform this task.

TEST QUESTIONS

1. When a component is identified by its full equipment nomenclature, what does the first part of the number usually identify?

2. Why would a resistor have a location number with three digits when it is the first resistor in the circuit?

3. What does the term "bay" mean in a computer?

4. When a cable is identified by number, what alpha letter is usually used?

5. What important element can a vertical list of signal flow provide?

6. What, if any, different purposes can the horizontal signal flow list fulfill compared with the vertical listing method?

7. Why is a wiring table so convenient when tracing through a main distribution frame?

8. In a schematic or logic drawing, what symbol would designate the jack of a jack/plug connection?

8

Equipment Modification

This chapter presents concepts that technical managers of computer centers should be concerned with while planning and incorporating modifications in their equipment. Modifications require the expenditure of resources—time and materials. They also require scheduling for installation and checkout since most modifications cause an interruption in normal operations. Finally, bookkeeping chores must be performed, such as up-dating equipment records and up-dating (posting) changes in the technical reference materials of the computer.

The requirements of the computer system change constantly. To meet these changing requirements contractors are employed to produce systems or support systems that will satisfy the needs of the users. They may neutralize an enemy weapon or provide the United States with a weapon or control system which gives us a tactical advantage. They may be used for data processing in banks, laboratories, and schools. The process of taking a known need and developing it into a system is gigantic. In the beginning, problems seem almost insurmountable, yet systems are built and they work. However, since most of us have tremendous hindsight, we often analyze a system and find that there is a better way of doing something, and this is part of the job of maintenance men. We may see a hazard, or think of an innovation which we think is good for the system; or the operators of the system may need a capability not there presently. Equipment is usually modified by a plan with instructions for accomplishing a *one*-time change, including modification, inspection of equipment, or installation of new equipment. Probably no other single maintenance task is as broad in scope as a modification. In industry the term "engineering change" is often used to identify a modification. This text presents all phases of a program of modification so that you can appreciate how each element of industry and some of the military's maintenance organizations fit into the pattern. You will read how groups both inside and outside the organization work together to accomplish the task.

Before we start the analysis, it is important to know where you belong in the picture. As a technician you will participate to a great extent not only in the installation but in other phases of the task, such as reviewing the modification for its impact to the work center, estimating the complexity of the task, and determining how many units and squares will be modified, what tools and equipment will be necessary, and other aspects of the task. The list below provides a glimpse into the different parts of a complete program.

1. Responsibilities of maintenance organization personnel.
2. Originating a modification.
3. Identifying a modification.
4. Installing a modification.
5. Recording a modification.

8-1   Responsibilities of the Maintenance Organization

The chief of the maintenance organization has a full and varied job of controlling and directing his organization; therefore, his organization is broken into specific areas. He, as well as each person performing in the specific areas, has direct responsibility for specific phases of a modification. Listed below are the areas under control of the chief of maintenance and an explanation of the parts that each plays in the modification of the equipment.

8-1.1   *Chief of Maintenance and Maintenance Controller*

Briefly stated, the chief of maintenance has the primary responsibility, according to regulation, for all that pertains to his maintenance organization. In practice, the maintenance controller for the chief of maintenance assumes the chief's role in carrying out the functions ordered by the chief. In this respect he controls scheduling, supplying, inspecting, and performing of the installation, which involves other staff positions. Each of these other staff people has a particular part to perform in the task of modifying the equipment. Observe the flow chart, Figure 8-1, and try to obtain an overall concept of the processing a modification plan takes in a typical maintenance organization. Also understand the basic responsibilities of each of the staff members and the work centers, as explained below.

8-1.2　Quality-Control Inspection Staff

The quality-control (QC) inspectors receive the modification plan from the maintenance control section. They review it for applicability to site equipment. Upon determining applicability, they forward it to the records section for processing. During and after the actual installation, the QC inspectors make inspections of the installation, the records, and the technical reference files.

8-1.3　Records

Records-section personnel, upon receipt of the modification plan from QC, prepares necessary forms for recording the modification. If parts or kits are not needed, the section sends the plan to the work-load control for scheduling.

8-1.4　Supply Section (Material Control)

Upon receipt of the plan and record forms from the records section, the supply section of the maintenance organization reviews the plan for parts or kit requirements. It then orders the materials. When kits are received, supply denotes that the kits have been received and routes the notification to the scheduling section; then it stores the kits.

8-1.5　Scheduling Section

This section, upon receipt of the plan, programs the installation by scheduling it. This action often requires coordination from headquarters or users, since the installation of modifications frequently causes disruption in operation of the equipment. After receiving an approved time to install the modification, the scheduling is accomplished, and the plan is forwarded to the work center, which has responsibility for the installation.

8-1.6　Work Center

The work-center personnel do the installation. If spares are wanted, these are usually handled first. Where possible the modified spare equipment is installed in the operational equipment, thereby minimizing operational-equipment downtime. The work may be recorded as "on" or "off"

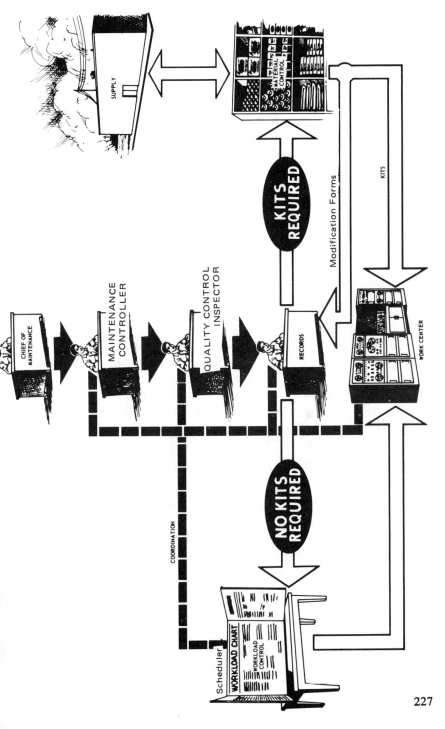

Fig. 8-1. Modification Procedural Processing

227

equipment work or a combination of each. The work may be so extensive that special teams perform the installation. Work-center personnel usually pick up kits, which may include special tools required to complete the installation, from the supply section. The installation-time special instructions, forms, and plan are received from scheduling.

This discussion has included the basic responsibilities of the sections in a maintenance organization, but this does not mean that the work center first sees the plan when it is ready to be installed. We shall analyze in the section of "Typical Steps Involved in an Installation" to what extent decisions about the installation have been accomplished prior to the installation itself.

Before we analyze these factors, it would be good to know how a modification plan comes into being. Where does the idea for it come from, who makes it, and what people and agencies are involved in its formation?

8-2   Origination of a Modification

The introduction to this chapter gave you some insight as to the need for modifications. They were, if you remember, to correct a hazard, to improve the capability, or to add a new capability to a system. These faults, factors, and ideas are accumulated by various means and are forwarded to the inventory manager, the system support manager, or the system control manager. The means of collection include unsatisfactory reports (UR), emergency URs, wire messages, and engineering change proposals.

It is important to understand URs and EURs. When a user submits a UR or EUR the data contained in the report are compared with URs and EURs submitted from other units having the same type of problem in the same type of equipment. Studies are then performed by the engineering section of the manufacturer of the equipment. These organizations determine what is causing the problem and what must be done to eliminate it. The speed with which the processing is done depends upon the urgency of the fault. The results of the study often create an interim engineering change authorization (IECA) to be prepared and sent to the field. This change is used to expedite the removal of the fault and restore the equipment to operational capability, or it is used to validate a change that will become a formal modification.

The engineering change proposal (ECP) is another method of accumulating information leading to a formal modification. This involves either site personnel (users) or manufacturers' technical representatives (tech reps) developing an improvement or better way of having a circuit or system function. Most often an ECP is proposed during category testing of a new system, but in the new system design they are not restricted to this early time period. An ECP can be submitted any time. Another time when an ECP design will usually be formed is when a new or modified operational capability is needed in a system. The operators or site managers secure engineering help in development of the ECP. The ECP is installed for study. Site personnel or special teams perform the installation. An IECA is used to authorize the installation.

The manager of a system prepares an equipment-change proposal in a systematic method. Some of the most significant steps in these methods are:

1. Analysis of EUR, UR, and ECP data.
2. Preparation of IECAs based upon results of engineering studies.
3. Conduction of prototype installation for validation.
4. Preparation of kits for each item to be modified.
5. Preparation of document and technical reference page changes.
6. Shipment of kits and change notices.
7. Recording of all completed installations by examining installation reports.
8. Termination or suspension of a modification plan upon complete installation of all units affected.

8-3 Identifying a Modification

Installing a modification requires knowledge of the various types of plans, the ability to recognize and understand each segment of a plan format, and the ability to determine applicability. This section presents an in-depth study of these phases of the task of identifying a modification.

8-3.1 Understanding the Format

Let us look into the elements of a typical plan. Refer to Figure 8-2 and observe that the general format presented here is basic. However, each paragraph will be broken down to include specifics for that modification. For instance, the data found in each paragraph may include:

1. Application. A listing of applicable items to receive the modification.
2. Purpose. The specific purpose for the modification.

```
┌─────────────────────────────────────────────────────────┐
│  HQ                                                       │
│  TITLE    _____        TO # _____               │
│           _____                                      │
│                             DATA CODE _____              │
│                                                           │
│                             DATE_____                │
│  TCTO                                                     │
│  TITLE    _____        Rescission Date___            │
│                                                           │
│   1.  Application                                         │
│                                                           │
│   2.  Purpose                                             │
│                                                           │
│   3.  When To Be Accomplished                             │
│                                                           │
│   4.  By Whom To Be Accomplished                          │
│                                                           │
│   5.  What Is Required                                    │
│                                                           │
│   6.  How Work Is Accomplished                            │
│                                                           │
│   7.  Supplemental Information                            │
│                                                           │
│   8.  Record                                              │
│                                                           │
│                                                           │
│   SIGNATURE BLOCK                                         │
│   APPROVING OFFICER                                       │
└─────────────────────────────────────────────────────────┘
```

Fig. 8-2. Modification-Plan Parts

3. When to be accomplished. This paragraph establishes the time for compliance data.

4. By whom to be accomplished. This paragraph designates the agency that will perform the modification. They may be on-site personnel or special teams.

5. What is required. This paragraph provides information about supply requirements, such as parts or kits to order; drawings required; cost of supplies; personnel requirements, which include the type of maintenance man and man-hours required; and special tools.

6. How work is accomplished. This paragraph gives step-by-step instructions for compliance of the modification installation.

7. Supplemental information. This paragraph may provide operational checkout requirements, technical manuals affected, and equipment marking (if not included in paragraph 5).

8. Records. This paragraph indicates what record action must be taken by the organization. Updating historical records and filing of

completed work reports will usually be indicated in this file. It also is possible that instruction will dictate that a separate form be prepared and forwarded to the senior project officer.

8-3.2 Determining Applicability

Although we briefly identified the subject applicability in the previous paragraph, it is important to examine it more closely so that we can be related to the impact upon the work center. Each plan has a listing of all items to be modified. Serial numbers are assigned to assist with the identification of equipment. These numbers are assigned to major units, assemblies, and often subassemblies. Very frequently selected units are designated for modification because of various reasons. Only the units listed by their serial number in the plan will be modified. This modification information is then made a part of the permanent history of that serial-numbered item. Should the modified unit be moved to a location that has an operational capability that does not use the modified version, the equipment would have to be reconfigured and the record annotated. On the other hand, if all units must be modified for one reason or another, the word "ALL" would be used in the serial number list. This would mean that all serial-numbered units would be modified.

If a modification plan is applicable, the time has come to study it to determine its impact on the system. What can be obtained by such a study? Can any work that will lessen the operational interruption be accomplished before the installation? Would examination of a typical step usually performed by a supervisor provide an insight to the problem? Let's see!

8-3.3 Typical Steps Involved in an Installation

By examining the sample format in this study or any other plan, you may have access to certain steps used in installation. These steps often are accomplished in such a manner that they may not be obvious. One person may accomplish them, but no matter how they are accomplished, it is important to know they exist and what they are.

PREINSTALLATION EXAMINATION. This first step can include:

1. Study of the plan.
2. Decisions about the plan relative to removal of units to make access to the area to be modified.
3. Determination of the complexity of the installation.

4. Development of checklists for replacement of removed items that must be reinstalled.

5. Determining operational capability losses.

SELECTING A CREW. The next step is selection of a crew. The modification plan identified the type of personnel to perform the installation. It is up to the supervisor to evaluate his personnel and designate who will install the modification. These people must, after being chosen, study the plan closely.

SECURING TOOLS, KITS AND PARTS, AND TIME. Unless special tools are needed, the required tools should be in the workmen's kits; however, an examination of the tool kit is often made by the supervisor. Supply personnel secure the parts of kits and advise the work center when they arrive. The work-center supervisor and/or the selected crew inventory the kit or parts for accuracy and quantity of parts. The scheduling section sets the work time for the crew. The supervisor can then make his decisions to ensure that the crew is rested before the installation begins and that the crew has enough people to accomplish the installation in the allotted time.

PERFORMING THE MODIFICATION. The selected crew will perform the modification according to the step-by-step instructions; this involves:

1. Careful checking off of each item completed.
2. Careful listing of any component or assembly removed to provide access.
3. Reinstallation of removed components.
4. Installation of new parts.
5. Lacing of wire runs, if applicable.
6. Marking of equipment that has been modified.

CHECKING THE INSTALLATION

1. Visual checking, point to point, by another member of the crew or supervisor.
2. Performing continuity checks.
3. Performing operational and functional checks.

QUALITY-CONTROL INSPECTION. The quality-control section will inspect the installation for:

1. Workmanship, including neatness, proper terminations, and labeling.
2. Accuracy of installation.
3. Operational readiness by use of dynamic checks.

Six basic steps have been listed which are used in an installation. It is easy to realize that these steps are necessary, that they are important, and that they are always done, but that they may not be evident to the average worker. Since you will be accomplishing an installation sometime, these factors will be part of your responsibility, too. To make the program complete, one final step must be accomplished, and that is recording the modification.

8-4 Recording a Modification

The recording of a modification requires careful accuracy of each entry on each form. Maintenance personnel may use quite a few different forms to record these data. Some of the broad categories requiring records are:

1. Receipt of a modification.
2. Receipt of kits.
3. Final installation of a modification.

8-4.1 History of Equipment

The dictionary defines history as "a systematic account of happenings, usually with an analysis and explanation" and "all recorded events of the past." The configuration of the equipment must be recorded and known. Historical data are accumulated by various means; however, most often a data entry is the result of a modification. After the modification is installed, the historical records are updated to show the new configuration. Historical data entries are valid until all the equipment in the inventory is modified and new technical manuals are published. After this period of time, the entries can be deleted from the record because the modified equipment is considered standard. This means that histories show limited historical data, and they are usually current. Each piece of equipment has some form of historical record. It may be very simple, such as an inspection label affixed to the instrument or a colored dot on the equipment case, or very lengthy, such as a completion of a record jacket containing many various forms and reports. Some of the reasons for compiling and maintaining historical data on a piece of equipment are:

1. Configuration control.
2. Standardization of inventory items.
3. Enables personnel to maintain equipment without specialized training when personnel are transferred from one location to another.
4. Minimizes logistical problems.

Now that you briefly understand that all equipment has historical records, let's examine what a historical record jacket may contain.

8-4.2 Record File Jacket

An individual jacket may be maintained on each complex equipment unit. The jacket may contain two sections: one for active records and one for inactive records. Refer to Figure 8-3 for a typical record jacket. Examples of material to be filed in the active section of the jacket are:

1. Work-installation (work-order) forms.
2. Historical record forms type 1.
3. Historical record, permanent.
4. Current mechanized status reports.

Fig. 8-3. Record Jacket

In the inactive record-jacket section:

1. Old work-installation forms.
2. Completed correspondence about the equipment.
3. Outdated record forms type 1.
4. Outdated historical record, permanent.

Who maintains the record jacket depends upon geographical conditions and official desires. Either the work center maintaining the equipment or the records sections may maintain the file. An example of a case for which the work center might maintain the file is when the equipment is installed at a remote unit such as a site or microwave station. If your work center maintains the record jacket, review its content and determine for yourself that this information is included in the file and also see if the file is divided between active and inactive.

8-5 The Program in Perspective

We have exposed a great amount of information about modification installations. To do this it was necessary to examine many aspects of the program. In examining the responsibilities of the staff of the chief of maintenance, we found out that almost all staff members are usually involved. The records section prepares the forms, the quality-control section inspects and determines applicability, the supply section orders parts and schedules the work, and the work center does the work.

Each modification plan has a beginning and we discovered that unsatisfactory reports, emergency unsatisfactory reports, engineering change proposals, and local documentation were all methods by which deficiencies are identified. From these entries engineers formulate a modification plan. Then a prototype modification is installed for validation purposes. After a validation period, kits are prepared and shipped, and all units are modified. When the organization and work center become involved, many factors that can cause problems enter the picture. Some of these are directly related to the urgency of the modification or the type of modification. *Impact* to the equipment operation is an important factor, as are *equipment downtime, number and kind of personnel* needed for the job, *extent* of the job, and *special requirements*.

Typical steps did evolve during this examination. They were:

1. Preinstallation examination.
2. Selecting a crew.
3. Securing tools and parts and time.
4. Performing the modification.
5. Checking the installation.
6. Quality-control inspection.
7. Examining how a record jacket was compiled; seeing that certain forms usually are found in the jacket.

The program is extensive and complex. Your part in it may be very limited; however, you can see that managers have considerable responsibility in the program.

TEST QUESTIONS

1. In what parts of an equipment modification do quality-control personnel participate?

2. What is an IECA?

3. Who originates an ECP?

4. What are four considerations that should be made during preinstallation examination of a modification plan?

5. What are the six steps that outline the processors that are usually part of a modification installation?

6. Under what condition(s) can historical entries on equipment records be deleted?

9

Programming and the Control Program

Electronic computer systems capable of processing enormous amounts of data at high speeds have become an established support element for industry and the military. The computer industry continues to make state-of-the-art improvements which enable users to incorporate computers as essential elements of defense, for industrial logistic operations and personnel, and for research and development for hospital users. However, the computer, being a machine, can do no more than its program permits. The development of computer programs is a task that is no less exacting than the design of the computer system itself.

Once engineers design these computer systems and the programmer writes the required programs, each system must be put through various phases of testing before it is accepted.

This chapter is partially concerned with the computer programmer's talents, that is, how he develops the program for a computer system. More importantly, it is concerned with providing you with an understanding of the variety of control programs and automatic programming techniques.

The term *control program,* as used here, is synonymous with *operational, active,* or *main control* programs. Control programs are written for the specific purpose of accomplishing the day-to-day mission of the computer system. The number of programs necessary is determined by the mission of the particular system.

The method of storing and filing these programs is normally up to the operating staff. In many computer systems, magnetic tape is used for program storage, and each tape contains a single program or several work-related programs. The task of revising these programs, once stored on magnetic tape, is accomplished by a *utility program,* which is normally part of the computer system's program library.

9-1　Phases in Developing Programs

Programming is a highly complicated art, and good programming cannot be performed efficiently by amateurs. Programming aids and conventions, known as automatic programming (to be discussed later), reduce the time and effort required to produce efficient programs. Using these aids, however, does not reduce the skill required; generally a much higher degree of knowledge is needed if they are to be used efficiently. Emphasis may be changed from coding to systems design, but the need for skill is still there.

By the nature of his work—although not necessarily by his training —the programmer is (1) a problem analyst, (2) an engineer, (3) a systems analyst, and (4) an interpreter, all in one. As a problem analyst, he must be able to visualize the problem as a whole, then reduce it to its component parts. As an engineer, he must understand not the circuitry but the logical working of the computer, its operating capabilities, and the use of all equipment involved in processing a problem. As a systems analyst, he must constantly be aware of the fastest and best method for producing accurate results. As interpreter, he must translate the logical steps of problem solution into computer language.

In summary, the programmer's job involves four basic phases of work:

1. Analysis—breaking the problem down into its component parts.
2. Application—combining problem solutions and computer capabilities to achieve computer solutions.
3. Flow charting—making further analysis of computing operations into basic steps by means of symbolic diagrams.
4. Coding—interpreting the flow chart into coded instructions which the computer understands.

The programmers and the systems analyst's jobs often overlap and must, of necessity, overlap to a degree sufficient to enable the programmer to understand, in complete detail, the area of the program in which he is working and where it fits into the system as a whole. The exact point of development where the systems man and the programmer start working together and the point where the programmer starts working alone will vary considerably with the individuals involved.

It is generally agreed that three levels of flow charting are required in designing a library of programs for a new electronic computer system. The first is called a *general system flow chart* and shows the flow of information throughout the entire system. The second flow chart, called a *logic chart,* shows the human logic of a particular computer run. The third flow chart, a *detailed programmer's flow chart,* shows the details of the program logic in computer logic detail. The general system flow chart is usually designed by the systems analyst, the logic chart by the systems analyst with the assistance of the programmer, and the detailed flow chart by the programmer, thus completing the design of the program. The last step is often carried out by coders rather than programmers.

9-1.1 Symbology Used

The examples of programming used in this chapter employ the standard, generally accepted flow-chart symbology. Figure 9-1 shows these symbols, and each one's purpose is explained below. The subparagraph letter correlates with the designating symbol on the figure.

    a. Direction of flow. The direction-of-flow indication is used to connect all symbols and indicate the direction of flow. It is not necessary to use the arrowheads if the direction of flow is in the normal path of left to right or top to bottom.

    b. Operations. This symbol is used for all operations not involving reading, writing, decisions, or modifications.

    c. Decisions. Either of these symbols can be used to indicate a point in an operation at which two or more courses of action are possible, depending on existing conditions. Many notations are used with the various decision symbols; for an example of the function of these notations, briefly look at Figure 9-3.

    d. Modifications. This symbol denotes an alternation in the address or operation part of an instruction. It may be used also to denote modifications that are essentially counting in nature.

    e. Comparisons. The comparison symbol is the same as for decisions, since some course of action must be taken regardless of the result of the comparison. We have shown it separately to illustrate the various signs that can be used to indicate a comparison and the possible results.

    f. Connector. This symbol is used to connect remote portions of a

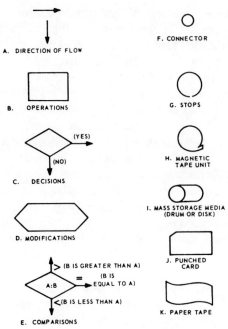

Fig. 9-1. Flow-Chart Symbols

flow chart with one another without the use of long or crossing lines. An *exit connector* terminates a flow line. It is normally labeled with a number or letter reference. The program will then continue at an associated *entry connector* symbol, which is labeled with the same number or letter reference.

g. Stops. All programmed halts are indicated by this symbol. The word HALT and the number of the halt are usually placed within the symbol.

h. Magnetic tape data entry symbol.

i. Drum storage or disc.

j. Punched card.

k. Paper tape.

9-1.2 *Analyzing the Problem*

The programmer must take the most basic logic chart and develop his program from it. To do this he must analyze the problem (the problem could be the system's mission) as a whole and at the same time view the whole as the sum of its parts. As he breaks the problem down into its component operations, he must not lose sight of the total picture. In preparing a problem for processing by the computer, the programmer must first ask, What is the problem? or What results are desired? He must, therefore, know the form and the contents of the results desired. Knowing this, he must then make sure the information needed to get these results is available. This is the input information. For example, in a payroll problem the computer works with the names, hours worked, rate of pay, and many other relevant items of information to develop a paycheck.

Processing of data by a computer is like a factory operation. Input is the raw material to be processed; output is the finished product. The programmer must determine what operations and processes are to be performed on the input to get the desired output. Naturally, he is interested in finding the best procedure to make optimum use of his equipment. An important consideration in any factory operation is the possibility of producing a useful by-product as a result of processing, with a minimum amount of added cost or effort. The programmer must seek the same results from his computer. He must evaluate the possibility of by-product information that may be useful at a later date and is easily obtainable without waste of time and money.

9-1.3 Consideration of the Computer System

When the programmer has arrived at a complete understanding of the problem, he next considers it in terms of the electronic computer system being used. His prime concern in planning the program is getting the greatest benefits from the system—benefits in the form of maximum savings in time and money by using the computer to its fullest capabilities. The programmer knows the system and the equipment available. He knows how to use it for the greatest speed and efficiency. Since every problem is different, special considerations may be involved; for instance, the problem may have enormous volumes of input information (such as long-range radar inputs), which must be sorted before it can be used.

9-1.4 Flow Charts and Coding Technique

Throughout his work, the programmer's chief concern is to maintain a logical working order in all phases of the process. In order to visualize the sequence of operations, a flow chart, which is a picture of the programmer's thinking for the computer, is used. Upon completion of this flow chart, the programmer knows what the computer is to do. Therefore, the next phase of programming is to translate the steps of the program solution into computer language, or coding. Once the program is coded, it is listed so that it can be desk-checked for obvious errors. It is then debugged on the computer by the use of sample data for which the answer is previously known. After this is done, it is advisable, if possible, to test the program with actual data before finally accepting it.

9-2 Problems Encountered in Planning the Details of a Program

To give you a feeling for some of the problems encountered in program preparation and the amount of detail and familiarity the programmer must have with the problem, the paragraphs that follow present examples of automated personnel-records updating. Keep in mind the following:

1. Personnel records are maintained on a magnetic tape master file.
2. The master file is updated from transaction cards received from the personnel office.
3. It is necessary to be certain that the data received from the personnel office are accurate before updating the master record.

9-2.1 *Time and Cost Considerations*

The chart shown in Figure 9-2 portrays the time investment for two systems, punched-card automatic machine (PCAM) and electronic computer system (ECS), and of validating these two items on 100,000 master records. As indicated, research and procedure time for the ECS is almost double that required for the PCAM sort-check procedure. However, the savings in machine time make the ECS man-hour investment worthwhile. Because of the volume and time involved, it is not practical to validate items as they are received from PCAM updating. The validation is done at the end of each month on the entire active file, and the scope of validation is considered greater than that of the PCAM operation.

To illustrate the work involved in updating personnel records, the following items are considered problems to solve: (1) validation of coded information in ECS source documents (punched cards) and (2) com-

PCAM		ECS	
RESEARCH AND PROCEDURE	27 MANHOURS	RESEARCH AND PROGRAMMING	48 MANHOURS
MACHINE TIME TO EXECUTE	13 HOURS 40 MINUTES	MACHINE TIME TO EXECUTE	9 MINUTES, 15 SECONDS
MACHINE TIME (12 MONTHS)	164 HOURS	MACHINE TIME (12 MONTHS)	1 HOUR 32 MINUTES

Fig. 9-2. Time and Cost Considerations

parison of validated data with related items already in the tape master record to assure compatibility of relationship before recording the changed item in the master record.

9-2.2 Correlation Considerations

Each item of recorded personnel data is represented in one of many tables of codes applicable to personnel while assigned to specific departments.

Certain coded items, although individually valid, cannot be accepted in records unless they are compatible with related or controlling items in the record. For example, a race/sex code of "A" (female, white) is valid by itself but could not be accepted for entry in a record if an existing code in the file identified the record as that of a male. Determination of item relationship, controlling factors, and specific limitations is developed by painstaking research.

In carrying our analysis further, there may be from 40 to 60 separate fields of information in the tape master record which must be validated when, or as, reported to the computer system. For example, the job-title-number prefix may be a limiting factor on a component, which, in turn, specifies the maximum term of service. In determining the compatibility of these items, the validity of coding for service-number prefix and component must be checked.

9-3 Automatic Programming

The job of writing a program can become rather tedious. Programmers and manufacturers soon recognized the problem of telling the computer what to do as one of the biggest obstacles in the effective use of ECS equipment. They have spent much time and money developing methods that may make the problem easier to deal with.

9-3.1 The Development of Automatic Programming

Automatic programming is defined as any technique whereby the computer itself is used to convert programs from a form that is easy for a human being to produce into a form that is efficient for the computer to carry out. One of the first developments, although not an automatic programming technique, for easing the burden of programming resulted from the observation that there are identical routines in many programs. For instance, an error routine telling the computer to print out a failure, or a routine to find the square root of a number, is encountered over and over by programmers. The repeated writing of these routines each time they are needed resulted in much duplication of effort and a waste of time and money. The solution to this problem is obvious. Write these routines once, debug them, and use them as often as needed, in not one but numerous programs. It becomes simply a matter of providing storage space for this routine in memory and then jumping to it when necessary, then jumping back to the main program when the routine has served its purpose. A routine such as this is called a *subroutine*. That is, it is substituted in the main routine when and as needed.

As the volume of ECS equipment increased, it became apparent that installations using like equipment had many of the same problems and had programmers writing like subroutines. This is one reason "users" organizations came into being. Through such organizations, operating installations standardized their approach to many problems. They soon were able to exchange not only subroutines but whole programs. Everyone benefits, in that better use of equipment is obtained.

The purpose and exact content of subroutines are variable, but common problems exist with respect to using a subroutine—any subroutine—in a main program. The basic problems common to all programs are:

1. How to get to the subroutine and then back to the correct place in the main program.
2. How to make available to the subroutine the factors to be used in computations.

The portion of a program used for getting to and from a subroutine is known as a *linkage*. The portion of the program used for informing the subroutine of the whereabouts of factors to be used in a computation is known as a *calling sequence*. Figure 9-3 is an illustration of a logic chart showing how subroutines are used and indicating the areas of linkage and calling sequence. Briefly stated, the problem is this: At a given point in the main routine a test is made to determine if the end of the main routine has been reached. If so, the program is halted. If not, a test is made to determine if there is an inquiry from a remote inquiry station. If there is no inquiry, control is returned to the main routine. If an inquiry has been made, it is recorded and an additional test made to determine if it is a valid inquiry. (Computers may be programmed so that they will accept only certain types of inquiries from specified inquiry stations.) If an invalid inquiry has been made, a reply to this effect is made, it is recorded, and control is returned to the main routine. If the inquiry was valid, the proper subroutine for satisfying this inquiry is selected and run, and then control is returned to the main program.

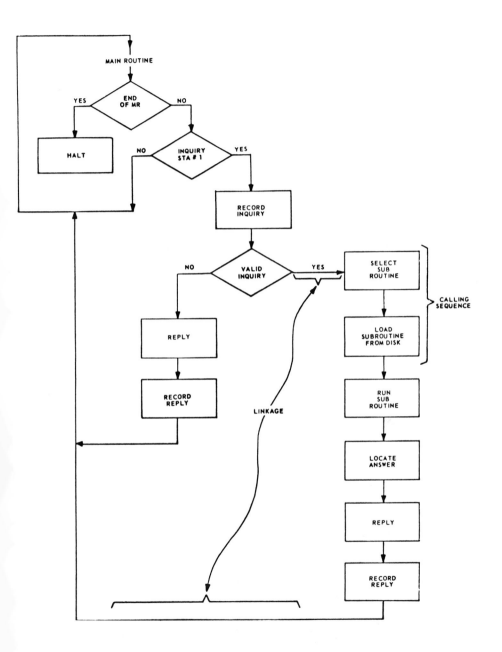

Fig. 9-3. Logic Flow Chart with Linkage

9-3.2 Relative Coding—Assembly Programs

Another problem that was difficult to handle from the outset was that of using exact or "absolute" addresses when writing programs. Consider the problem involved in changing the locations of several hundreds, or even thousands, of instructions should it become necessary to insert even a single instruction in a completed program. To avoid this problem, programs are broken down into smaller, more workable units and each group is given addresses relative to other groups. This technique is called *relative coding*.

After the program is completed, the relative addresses are converted to absolute addresses by a special program that assembles the individual sections into one program by assigning absolute sequential locations to each instruction. Such a program is called an *assembly program*. An assembly program could take one line of relative coding and convert it to an instruction in machine language. If it is desired later to insert new instructions in the middle of the program, it is a fairly simple task to do so, by using relative addresses, because the computer itself can again be used to assign new absolute instruction addresses.

9-3.3 Symbolic Coding

Symbolic coding is a technique whereby an arbitrary code may be used for programming convenience. Most computers operate on a numeric code, but for ease of programming it is sometimes desirable to assign a symbolic code to replace straight numeric operation codes. For example, if a given machine recognizes 111, 112, 113, and 114 as the operation codes for add, subtract, multiply, and divide, it would probably be easier for the programmer to arbitrarily assign the symbolic codes ADD, SUB, MPY, and DIV. The use of such symbolic codes is more meaningful and is easier to remember and work with than are numerous numerical codes.

Although a computer may not know what SUB or DIV means, an assembly program can be expanded to give it the ability to convert these symbolic codes to the proper machine-language code. Using this technique and relative coding, in conjunction with an assembly program, has done much to ease the burden of programming.

9-3.4 Compilers

The purpose of the compiler is to produce a complete machine-language program from a routine written in source language. This is accomplished by converting the relative addresses or the source program to absolute addresses and selecting appropriate subroutines from a subroutine library, as directed by the instructions or other symbols of the original routine. The compiler, in addition to its translating function, which is generally the same process as that used in an assembler, is able to replace certain instructions with a series of instructions, usually called *subroutines*. Thus, where an assembler translates item for item, and produces as an output the same number of instructions or constants that were put into it, a compiler will do more than this. The program that results from compiling is a translated and expanded version of the original.

Compiling may be accomplished by an auxiliary machine or by using the appropriate compiler program in conjunction with the computer itself. One of the first steps in automatic programming is to store the subroutines in their relative address form, and when the compiler assembles a program, have it select and incorporate the desired subroutine into the program. Thus it is possible to write a single instruction which will, in effect, call a subroutine of many instruction steps into the final program. Since this could occur many times in a single program, it becomes possible to produce, on the average, several instructions in a finished program for each instruction written by the programmer. Many compilers in use today can produce an average of four or five instructions for each instruction written by the programmer.

9-3.5 Generator Program

The generator program permits a computer to write other programs automatically. Generators are of two types:

1. The character-controlled generator, which operates like a compiler in that it takes entries from a library tape. It is unlike a simple compiler in that it examines control characters associated with each entry and alters instructions found in the library according to the directions contained in the control characters.
2. The pure generator, which is a program that writes another program. When associated with an assembler, a pure generator is usually a section of program that is called into storage by the assembler from a library tape and which then writes one or more entries in another program. Most assemblers are also compilers and generators. In this case the entire system is usually referred to as an *assembly system*.

Many times a given subroutine is not quite what is needed for a new program. As a result of this situation, subroutine libraries soon become clogged with many minor variations of the same basic subroutine. To eliminate this situation, a modified subroutine—one that is capable of doing a general type of job—is developed, but it is not capable of doing a complete job. Some "parameters" have been omitted and must be filled in before using it. A common example is a subroutine that sorts records on magnetic tape. The routine is almost complete but does not include, for example, the length of the records being sorted, the length and locations of the sort key, or whether ascending or descending sequence is desired. If these "parameters" are filled in, the routine is now complete and the program is capable of doing the sorting required. Thus it is possible to take a common, generalized routine, provide it with the necessary information, and obtain a completed routine tailored to the specific needs of an individual situation.

Generator programs that produce a sort program are called *sort generators;* those that can produce a desired report from a storage file are known as *report generators;* and so forth. When generator programs are included in compiler programs they make it possible to produce certain types of programs with a minimum of effort and programming.

9-4 Automatic Programming—Its Cost, Its Worth

Let us now analyze these developments and examine what the future holds to further ease the communications barrier between ECS equipment and man. At the beginning, programs were written in a very detailed machine code, but through the use of symbolic and relative coding techniques it became an easier task to talk to the computer. The increased use of subroutines, compilers, and generators actually took some of the burden of programming off the shoulders of the programmer and allowed him to use routines previously accomplished. More important, the computer itself began doing some of its own programming.

Aside from easing the programmer's tasks, there are other reasons for this trend toward automatic programming. Some of them are:

9-4.1 The High Cost of Programming

The time taken to write good programs may run into several man-years, and the programmers needed, if good programs are to be developed, often command salaries of over $10,000 per year. Thus the cost of programming a machine is quite high, in many cases an estimated $5 per instruction. Automatic coding is capable of cutting the cost of program production tremendously. Programming techniques presently available are said to be able to cut the cost of programming in half.

9-4.2 The Shortage of Programmers

The number of ECS installations is mushrooming at a phenomenal rate. The time needed to become familiar with a piece of hardware is not excessive, but the time required to become an experienced, high-quality programmer is often very lengthy. In many respects programming is an art, and the demand for good programmers is tremendous. By using automatic coding techniques, a fairly inexperienced programmer can often write a program that is just as good as that of the experienced programmer. Thus automatic coding techniques are a most important tool if new installations are to get the quality of programs needed to make their systems successful.

9-4.3 The Cost of Time to Write and Proof a Program

Because of the time required to write a program, a stated problem to be solved by a computer often changes several times between the time it is first presented and the time it actually gets into operation. The use of computers in many areas is not thought feasible, because of the time it takes to get a program written and in use. These problems are being overcome with the development of improved automatic programming techniques. The director who wanted a certain one-time report as soon as possible from a magnetic tape file used to have a long wait. Now, through the use of generators, compilers, and English-language techniques, these tasks are accomplished in a reasonable time period and at a reasonable cost. An electronic computer system should be as flexible as possible, and the development of automatic programming techniques is continually making the computer a more flexible tool. The less time it takes to tell a computer what to do, the more valuable it becomes.

9-4.4 The Language Barrier Between Different Computers

If an installation is doing a job identical to that of another installation but with a different computer, the program at the first installation is worthless to the other. If an installation is replacing an old computer with a new one, the old programs are likely to be completely worthless and will have to be rewritten in the language of the new computer.

One technique used to overcome the language barrier on a temporary basis during conversion from one computer system to another involves the use of an "interpreter" program. This is a program in the language of the new computer and is stored in the new computer along with the old program, which is written in the language of the old computer. The interpreter program in effect analyzes each instruction of the old program individually and interprets it into instruction understood by the new machine. This approach is similar to that of an interpreter interpreting a conversation between two people speaking different languages. One statement is made by the person speaking, analyzed by the interpreter, restated so that it can be understood by the person being spoken to, and so on. Obviously, the use of an interpreter program greatly reduces the effectiveness and speed of a computer program. If one were to converse with someone who speaks a language foreign to them for an extended period of time, it would be necessary to learn the language. Likewise, the use of interpreters is a stopgap measure in computer usage. Interpreters are valuable during conversion and also are of value in certain situations where it is desired to have the computer follow an instruction routine not provided in its instruction repertoire.

9-4.5   The Language Barrier Between Programmer and Manager

The more people involved in getting a job programmed and into production status, the greater the chance for misinterpretation and errors to occur. By the use of English-language programming, managers can read the sentences and understand the meaning of the program. Managers, in other words, can see exactly what procedures are being used by the computer and see if the prescribed actions are what they desire. By simplifying the language in which the computer is told what to do, to the point that it can virtually understand a written instruction, the computer is approaching the point where it can be given SOPs and so on and follow them. This, of course, is the goal toward which research in automatic programming is working. Then management personnel, systems personnel, maintenance personnel, and the computer system itself will be able to understand one another to a degree that misunderstanding of what is desired to be done can almost be eliminated.

It can be seen that while these automatic programming techniques were first developed as an aid for programmers, their advantages extend far beyond this original purpose. They cut the cost of programming, assist in alleviating the shortage of programmers, drastically reduce the time required to prepare a program, cross the language barriers, and enable management to better understand and use computers.

9-5   English-Language Programming

The next step in the development of automatic programming is currently being effected. Stating the problem in English-language sentences, and using the computer to convert these sentences into the desired coded program, is now a reality. Many program translator systems have been perfected that convert specific statements into the desired program code; two such translator systems are:

1. COBOL—COmmon Business-Oriented Language.
2. FORTRAN—FORmula TRANslation.

9-5.1 Common Business-Oriented Language

Much of the time and cost associated with control-program development could be eliminated if a common computer language existed for all systems. There are hundreds of government, business, and educational organizations using a wide variety of electronic computers in data-processing operations. Some of the major users have more than one type of computer applied to the same general application at different locations. The experience of these organizations to date indicates that a major problem in using computing equipment wisely and efficiently lies in stating the application in such a way that computer programs are developed and maintained with a minimum of time and programming effort.

A common business-oriented language, independent of any other make or model of computer, open-ended and stated in English, would do much to solve or reduce this problem. Such a language would also simplify and speed up the related problems of training personnel in the design of electronic computer systems and the development of their computer programs.

In May 1959 a meeting was called in the Pentagon for the purpose of considering both the desirability and the feasibility of establishing a common language for programming in business-type computer systems. Representatives from government installations, users, computer manufacturers, and other interested parties were present. As a result of this meeting, several committees or task forces were agreed upon to proceed with this project.

COBOL is a problem-oriented language that can be translated by a compiler into an object program to run on a specified computer. The language is a subset of normal English and is suitable for expressing the solution to business-computer-system problems. A source program of this type will contain three elements:

1. Procedure division, a set of procedures to specify how the data are to be processed.
2. Data division, a description of the data being processed.
3. Environmental division, a description of the equipment being used in the processing.

COBOL is divided into three divisions, one for each of the elements described above. Since differences in computers make it impossible to achieve *completely* a "common" business language, each division contains a decreasing amount of compatibility across different computers. Thus, the PROCEDURE DIVISION can be left virtually unchanged in moving the program from one computer to another, whereas the DATA DIVISION may or may not require revision. The ENVIRONMENTAL DIVISION contains information that is completely computer-dependent.

A COBOL *word* is composed of not more than 30 characters chosen from numerals (0–9), letters (A–Z), and the hyphen (-). A word cannot begin or end with a hyphen. The hyphen is used to represent a space between words. The placement of a space is critical, since it is used as the primary terminator for a word.

A COBOL *verb* is a single word and designates an action. Examples of COBOL verbs are:

ADD	SUBTRACT	MULTIPLY	DIVIDE
GO	ALTER	EXAMINE	READ
WRITE	ENTER	INCLUDE	STOP

A COBOL *noun* is a single word that acts as one of the following:

Data Name	Figurative Constant
Condition Name	Special Register Name
Procedure Name	Special Name
Literal	

A numeric *literal* is defined as a group of characters, chosen from numerals 0 through 9, a plus (+) or minus (−) sign, and a decimal point (.). Examples are:

359

+ 8185

− 46.3

Following are some examples of COBOL programming statements, the necessary instructions to accomplish them, and a brief explanation of the operation.

1. Add the number 261 to the number 456 and place the sum in the location containing the number 456.
   a. ADD: Two or more quantities are added and the sum is stored in *either* the last-named memory field or the specified one. To specify a field to accept the results of an ADD operation, a key word is GIVING.
   b. Instruction: ADD 261 and 456.
   c. Explanation: The 261 and 456 are added, giving a sum of

717. This sum is stored in the location containing the 456, since it is the last-named field and no other field has been specified.

2. Add the number 261 to the number 456 and place the sum in location 359.

    a. ADD: Same as 1a.

    b. Instruction: ADD 261 and 456, GIVING 359.

    c. Explanation: The 261 and 456 are added, giving a sum of 717. The sum is stored in location 359, since this is the location specified by the key word GIVING.

3. Add the number 1.23 to the number 4.56 and place the the sum in the salary-deductions field.

    a. ADD: Same as 1a.

    b. Instruction: ADD 1.23 and 4.56, GIVING deductions.

    c. Explanation: The 1.23 and 4.56 are added, giving a sum of 5.79. This sum is stored in the *deductions* field, since this is the location specified by the key word GIVING.

4. Add tax, FICA, and bond, and place the sum in the deductions field.

    a. ADD: Same as 1a.

    b. Instructions: ADD tax, FICA, and bond, GIVING deductions.

5. Jump from the main program to the square-root subroutine.

    a. GO: A departure is made from the normal sequence of procedures. Two options are provided. A jump may be made to one of the single subroutines, or a jump may be made to one of several subroutines. In either case, the key word TO must be used. If the second option is used, a second key word, DEPENDING, must be used in addition to a numerical data name.

    b. Instruction: GO TO root.

    c. Explanation: This is option 1. A jump is made from the main program to the square-root subroutine.

6. Jump from the main program to the square-root subroutine.

    a. GO: Same as 1a.

    b. Instruction: GO TO root, file, error DEPENDING 1.

    c. Explanation: This is option 2. A jump is made from the main program to the square-root subroutine, because the data name is "1" and the square-root subroutine is the first procedure given.

7. Jump from the main program to the end-of-file subroutine.

    a. GO: Same as 1a.

    b. Instruction: GO TO root, file, error DEPENDING 2.

c. Explanation: This, again, is option 2. A jump is made from the main program to the end-of-file subroutine, since the data name "2" is specified and this subroutine is the second procedure given.

8. Jump from the main program to the error subroutine.
   a. GO: Same as 1a.
   b. Instruction: GO TO root, file, error DEPENDING 3.
   c. Explanation: Option 3. A jump is made from the main program to the error subroutine because the data name "3" specifies the third procedure.

Note that in all the examples outlined in the preceding paragraphs, everything is in accordance with the rules of COBOL. That is:

1. Specified verbs have been used, indicating the action that is to take place.
2. Single-word nouns have been used, indicating data names or procedure names. Numeric literals have been used in some instances.
3. No word exceeds 30 characters.
4. Care has been used in the placement of spaces to properly indicate the termination of a word.

Numerous manufacturers are now developing machines that will interpret COBOL and convert it to the machine language peculiar to their equipment. The advantages of COBOL are obvious. Programs written at one installation can be automatically compiled for use at other installations, regardless of the system involved. When new equipment is acquired the old programs, if written in COBOL, can be immediately converted and put into use. In the future, equipment selection, studies, and even sample programs may be written and submitted to the manufacturers, who will compile, test, and give, for the first time, quantitative comparisons of the different equipment for a specific job.

9-5.2 *Formula Translation*

This translator system is very similar in concept to the COBOL system. The main difference is in the language the programmer uses to express his *source program* (a program written in a language designed for ease of expression). Where business English is used by COBOL, mathematical language is used with FORTRAN. The effect of the COBOL sentence *Add Dividends to Income* could be achieved by the Fortran statement *Income = Dividends + Income*. However, FORTRAN translators for some machines might insist that the words be abbreviated to something like *INCO = DIV + INCO*. The statement, in effect, tells the translator to insert the necessary instructions into the *object program* (the program that is the output of an automatic coding system) in order to make the INCOME data.

The computer is not merely instructed to find the value of INCOME, but it is also told where to put the result of the addition after it is performed. COBOL provided this same feature. If the original INCOME field (in storage) contained 10,000 and the DIVIDEND field contained 15, the original INCOME field would be replaced by 10,015 after the operation has been executed. If this result is not desired, the programmer could change the statement to INCOME1 = DIVIDENDS + INCOME. With this change, a new INCOME1 data field would be generated in storage, the result of the addition would be placed there, and the original INCOME field would remain unchanged.

The knowledge of how computer programs are developed, coupled with experience in using your system's programs, will enhance your ability to analyze computer-maintenance programs.

TEST QUESTIONS

1. What other names can be used in place of the title "control program"?

2. What are the four basic phases of work the programmer does when developing the program? Discuss each phase in detail.

3. Can you name (and draw) nine symbols used in flow charting?

4. In addition to the principal purpose for a program, what could a user demand from a programmer while the program is being developed?

5. What are the principles used in the automatic programming technique?

6. What is an example of a subroutine?

7. Can you define "relative coding"?

8. Can the word "ADD" be a form of symbolic coding?

9. What is a program capable of compiling another program called?

10. What are the three dimensions of a COBOL program?

10

Programming and the Maintenance Program

Because of the configurations of modern computer systems, the maintenance program is becoming extremely important. Recall from the study on advanced concepts in Chapter 5 how much more reliance for a system's verification of its operation was placed upon the printout of the test program. Many types of maintenance programs have been devised and used throughout the history of computers. This chapter examines some of their fundamental purposes. It also examines the type of program that could be effective in such areas of a computer system as memory testing and input/output testing.

Just what is a maintenance program? What is its function, and how does it perform its function? These are all fair questions that should be answered one at a time.

A maintenance program is any program designed to indicate whether or not the computer is capable of performing its intended function. When improper operation occurs, the program must specify the cause of the failure and, if possible, designate the corrective action to be taken by the repairman. From this you can see that the term "maintenance program" includes reliability, diagnostic, and confidence-diagnostic programs, as well as hard-wired (including the newer read-only storage hadware) programs. Many programs, such as the on-line (on-line as used here is synonymous with active, operational, and main control programs) and utility programs, may give some indications that an error is present within the hardware, but they provide very little aid to the immediate maintenance effort.

The primary function of a maintenance program is to ensure system integrity (i.e., locate any existent or impending failure). The maintenance program must attempt to treat all circuits in a manner that approximates the ultimate applications of the computer. This criterion can only be met by treating computer circuits as strenuously as possible.

A maintenance program is used as a maintenance tool much as oscilloscopes and screwdrivers are used. Therefore, it is necessary that you know the functions, capabilities, and limitations of the maintenance program just as you know the functions, capabilities, and limitations of the hand tools you use. Also, your ability to select and use the right hand tool for a particular job only comes through experience. This fact is also true with maintenance programs. Your ability to select and use the right program for a particular hardware failure will increase as you gain more experience on the job.

10-1 Maintenance-Program Considerations

There are two basic classes of automatic computers: (1) special purpose and (2) general purpose. Special-purpose computers are designed for a specific purpose and usually require only one program, which is permanently stored or wired in the computer. The term normally associated with this type of computer is *fixed-program*. General-purpose computers, on the other hand, are designed to be used for a variety of purposes. This type of computer is a stored-program computer which employs some type of electronic mass memory. The ease with which new programs can be loaded and changed in an electronic mass memory makes the stored-program computer more versatile than a fixed-program computer, in which the programs are normally loaded and changed manually.

Whether fixed or stored, the program directs the computer to perform a series of actions according to a specific plan. The computer automatically calls out each instruction in sequence, interprets it, and performs as it commands. The wired-in logic that controls these automatic functions is, in fact, a wired program, but it is classed as *system hardware* along with all nonlogic components of the computer. A stored program, whether stored in memory or other media inside or outside the computer, is classed as *system software*.

10-1.1 *Fundamentals of Maintenance Programs*

In performing its primary function of ensuring system integrity, the maintenance program performs two fundamental tasks: (1) fault detection and (2) fault isolation. Fault detection is the ability to recognize a malfunction; therefore, it is the most important task in a maintenance program. Fault isolation is the degree to which the malfunction can be isolated. To perform these tasks, maintenance programs are designed to exercise the hardware using programmed instructions, check the results through the use of known standards and/or programmed instructions, and alert maintenance personnel when errors are detected. This alerting can be accomplished through the use of machine printouts, indicator lights, CRT displays, programmed error halts, audible alarms, or combinations of these.

10-1.2 Failure Classification

The design of maintenance programs is based largely on the particular system's hardware, functions, and the type of failures that must be detected and isolated. System failures fall generally into one of three major categories:

1. Catastrophic. This type of failure is constantly present until it is repaired. It is normally easy to detect and isolate. The symptoms and fault indications of a catastrophic failure are very often clear enough, so that with proper selection of a maintenance program, it will search out the trouble from a limited group of circuits within a suspected area. At other times, you will have to run a group of programs on a major unit or even the entire system in order to isolate the failure.

2. Intermittent. Troubleshooting an intermittent failure can be frustrating. This type of failure is not continuously present but occurs only at random intervals. Because it appears and disappears at random, the intermittent failure presents an inconsistent set of symptoms and becomes extremely difficult to locate.

3. Machine state. These are failures present only under certain conditions, such as:
   a. After a certain sequence of instructions.
   b. After a specific instruction followed by a delay in time.
   c. At a particular pulse-repetition rate.

10-1.3 Maintenance Programming Techniques

There are many possible techniques that may be used to locate hardware failures. Five of the major techniques are listed and explained below. As you read through each technique try and relate it to the system-maintenance programs you may now use.

START SMALL. This technique, as the name implies, starts its operation by checking a small number of key circuits. These circuits are then used to check another small group of circuits. This process uses a continually expanding group of proved circuits to check out other groups until the total area within the scope of the particular maintenance program is checked out. The start-small process is thorough and well suited to diagnosing catastrophic failures and some types of intermittent and machine-state failures.

START BIG. Maintenance programs using the start-big technique are designed to test the computer while it is operating in a manner similar to its primary mission operation. Because many sections of the computer are operated simultaneously when the start-big technique is used, certain intermittent and machine-state failures, which would escape the attention of a start-small type of program, are identified.

MARGINAL CHECKING. As stated earlier, marginal checking is a must in many large-scale computer systems. Basically this technique is a method of prevention maintenance in which certain operating conditions are varied from their normal values in order to detect deteriorating components. The amount of variation necessary before a component malfunctions indicates its margin of reliability. Since component values normally change with age, the marginal check is a valid indication of how soon a component will need replacing. The most widely used methods of marginal checking found in many of our computer systems are variation of vacuum-tube filament voltages and variation of dc supply voltages. In the older computer systems, these voltage variations are applied automatically under the control of a maintenance program or manually by maintenance personnel. Many of the newer computer systems still use the marginal-checking ability; however, only manual dc voltage-supply variations are employed.

MULTIPLE-CLUE APPROACH. Once an error is detected, a program using the multiple-clue approach attempts to obtain the same error using varying sequences of instructions. If the error can be detected in a multiplicity of ways, it is only necessary to locate the common conditions in isolating the error.

PROCESS-OF-ELIMINATION APPROACH. Certain errors within a computer system are very difficult to analyze. However, it is possible for a maintenance program using the process-of-elimination technique to get solid clues about the error. In this technique, sets of programmed routines are employed to vindicate one area after another. By the process of elimination they infer the error to be in the remaining area.

10-1.4 Types of Maintenance Programs

The terminology associated with the various types of maintenance programs employed in computer systems may be different from those listed below, but from the explanation of each type you should be able to relate their functions with programs from the computer system's program library.

RELIABILITY PROGRAM. The basic task in this type of program is to verify that a specified portion, or logical area, of the system is functional. Therefore, the reliability program stresses fault detection and generally minimizes isolation. Theoretically, if this type of program runs successfully (without a failure indication), the circuits checked are in proper operating condition.

DIAGNOSTIC PROGRAM. The diagnostic type of program is constructed to isolate known failures. The emphasis is on pinpointing a failure in a restricted area and when possible to the component that has failed. Generally, a diagnostic program does not attempt to integrate large-scale operations or diagnose failures associated with the operation of widely divergent areas of the system. It may begin by checking a circuit and then include another small increment of circuitry for each successive test. This process is extended until all circuits included in the program have been checked. Modern-day computer software combines reliability and diagnostic programming into one program. Thus maintenance is enhanced since one program exercises the circuitry. The programming ability includes detecting and isolating errors.

OVERALL PROGRAM. An overall program is a system of reliability and diagnostic testing which is designed to completely check out a specific functional area or unit of a system. For example, the complete checkout of a drum system, disc system, or tape system can be accomplished through the use of the overall program.

CONFIDENCE-DIAGNOSTIC PROGRAM. This type of maintenance program is normally cycled in conjunction with the operational program. Basically, confidence-diagnostic programs provide the particular computer system with the ability to monitor the operation of on-line and backup (sometimes called standby) hardware. Confidence-diagnostic programs are capable of detecting and isolating failures within the on-line and backup hardware, as well as monitoring the status of this hardware.

10-2 Computer Test Program

A computer test program includes routines that check the logic circuits within the computer for correct operation, by performing various computer instructions with the use of selected data constants. The instructions performed by the computer are checked in a sequence which assures that each instruction has been checked before it is used in subsequent tests. Therefore, computer circuitry, whose correct operation has not been verified, is not used in checking other circuitry. Normally, each instruction tested is exercised only to the extent necessary for verifying the correct operation of the logic circuitry with which it is associated. It is not the purpose of these routines to exercise all possible variations of the instructions in the computer; the logic circuitry involved in these variations is checked through the use of other instructions, which use the same logic circuitry.

10-2.1 *Flow Chart (ADD)*

To better understand the operation of a computer test routine, your attention is directed to Figure 10-1. Here is a small portion of a typical flow chart for a computer test routine. The flow chart indicates that the addition (ADD) class instruction is to be checked. Recall that there are many programming methods of accomplishing this type of check. The method shown in Figure 10-1 performs the check as explained below. Each lettered paragraph corresponds to a lettered box in the flow chart.

   a. The number 4 connector indicates entry from the control portion of the maintenance program. Upon entry to this particular ADD class routine, the control program performs the required housekeeping routines, such as loading required constants to be used by the routine, clearing various counters, and performing any other control functions required by the particular routine. For this particular routine, the constants used are all 1 bits in location 100 and other memory locations being loaded with the predetermined sum for each add operation to be performed.
   b. The accumulator (also referred to as the working register) is cleared, and the pass counter is reset.
   c. The contents of memory location 100 (all 1s) is added to the cleared accumulator. Upon completion of this addition the accumulator should contain all 1s.
   d. The contents of the accumulator are compared with the memory location containing the predetermined results of this particular addition (a constant loaded in step a).

e. If the accumulator is not equal to the predetermined sum, the test routine determines the failing bit or bits and stores this failure data in a specified memory area. All error information is printed out as well as other failure indications that have been programmed into this particular test routine. If a failure did occur, the program would halt. You would then analyze the printout and other failure indications to determine the required corrective action. After taking the necessary corrective action, you would depress the continue pushbutton (PB) or its equivalent to get back to step b, connector 6. The same addition check would be cycled to confirm the corrective action.

f. If the sum of the first addition was equal to its predetermined sum, the pass counter is checked to determine if it had been stepped to 1. The pass counter used in the flow diagram has two primary functions:

   1. The count in the pass counter determines whether the program

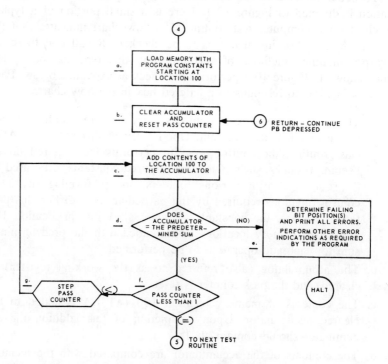

Fig. 10-1. Flow Chart (ADD)

branches (jumps) to step 6 of the flow diagram or to the next test routine.

2. Its count is also used to determine what predetermined sum, from the memory constants, will be used to compare the results of a particular pass. For example, when the pass counter is equal to 0, the predetermined sum used will be equal to all 1s. When the pass counter is equal to 1, the predetermined sum used will be equal to the sum acquired when all 1s are added to all 1s.

g. The pass counter is stepped to 1 and the program branches to step c. The second check (which, by the way, will be different variations) of the add class instruction is now performed. Location 100 is now added to an accumulator that contains all 1s. Recall that after the first pass in the routine the sum in the accumulator is all 1s and as the computer operation returns to step c from g, the accumulator is not cleared. Therefore, during this pass all 1 bits from location 100 are added to all 1 bits in the accumulator. During this pass in addition to checking, the circuitry checked in the first pass, the carry, overflow, and end-around-carry circuitry is also checked. If an error occurs during this second pass, the program halts. After you have taken the necessary corrective action, you would continue the program by depressing the continue pushbutton. The program would return to the first pass cycle through the entire routine again. Whenever step f is reached and the pass counter is equal to 1, the program will branch to the next test routine (this is indicated at connector 5 of Figure 10-1).

10-2.2 *Flow Chart (ADD) with Loop*

Let's suppose that you were running a maintenance program that contained a class test routine similar to the one just discussed. The routine continued to fail during the first pass. You've taken all the corrective action indicated by the printout and other failure indications, to no avail. What do you do now? What about setting up a loop in the area of the routine that is failing? With it in use you would then be able to scope the addition operation from point to point. Will it work? Looping a routine while scoping the circuitry being exercised is one of the best (if not the best) troubleshooting techniques for isolating a failure when all other techniques have failed. How do you set up a loop? Do you have to be a programmer to set it up? To answer these questions, let's set up a loop in Figure 10-1. We will assume that our failure is occurring in the addition process at step c. Next we take a look at the program writeup to determine where to insert an unconditioned branch instruction. An unconditional branch instruction causes a program routine to jump to the address it specifies regardless of program conditions. Actually, for this particular routine, all you need to do is determine (from the program writeup) the memory location of the first instruction at step b. Once you determine these locations, you would change the halt instruction to an unconditional branch. The address portion of this unconditional branch instruction would contain the address of the first instruction in step b.

The maintenance program associated with many computer systems makes provisions for establishing a loop upon request. As a matter of fact, many program writeups contain instructions for establishing loops. These instructions are so detailed as to include an explanation of routines that cannot be looped because of interaction with the maintenance-control portion of the program. Whenever a loop (other than a program-directed loop) is to be used in a portion of a test routine, considerations must be made to be sure that no interruptions of other portions of the routine or control program are caused. In other words, set up a loop within a maintenance program only after analyzing the flow of the particular program.

10-3   Memory Test Program

A memory-test type of program includes test routines that exercise all memory modules in a particular system in an attempt to verify their operation. Maintenance-program techniques used by memory test programs perform step-by-step checks of each function associated with the module being tested. These functional tests include routines designed to uncover faults resulting from marginal operation of the particular storage media and logic circuitry. The routines used various test patterns to exercise the storage media and logic circuits as rigidly as possible. A few of these test routines are described below. These are typical of many of the memory test programs being used today.

10-3.1   *Memory Access and Logic Circuitry Test*

The first portion of this routine tests the ability to gain access to and write all 0s in specified memory locations. The data are then read and checked for correctness. In the second portion of this routine the operation of the first portion is repeated using all 1s instead of 0s.

10-3.2   *Beat-Test Routines*

These are two basic beat tests. The first writes all 0s in each address of the memory module under test, and then one address is beat with 1s. Beat is the process of performing the same operation (writing data in this case) several times. All addresses but the one beat are then read and checked for a 1 bit. The second beat test writes all 1s into the memory module under test, and one address is beat with 0s. All the addresses but the one beat will be checked for 0s. A routine of this type can check for disturbance of the storage media and the sense-amplifier sensitivity levels.

10-3.3 Core Plane Cross-Talk Test Routine

Cross-talk is the term used to express the effect that adjacent memory cores and core planes have on each other during the write and read operation. The cross-talk test uses a special test pattern to check each core within a memory module for possible failure resulting from cross-talk. Basically this special pattern is made up by alternately writing all 1s and 0s throughout the entire memory module so that facing core planes contain opposite test patterns. The contents of each location are read and checked for correctness.

10-3.4 Addressing Test Routine

The primary function of this test routine is to check the address registers and decoders. Normally, this testing is accomplished by storing the address of each memory location into its respective memory location. Once the entire memory is loaded into its respective memory location, a read and compare process of each memory address is accomplished. Refer to Figure 10-2 for a flow chart of a typical addressing test routine. An explanation of the flow chart follows.

a. Entry to step a is from the control portion of the memory test program. The control program performs the required housekeeping routine, such as loading required constants to be used by the addressing routine, clearing the address counter, and performing any other control functions that are required by the addressing routine.

b. The first memory location to be checked is read from memory. Each time the routine returns to this step a different address will be read from memory and checked.

c. The contents of each memory location will be checked at this step to determine if its contents are equal to its own memory address.

d. The correct address of the memory location read from memory and the erroneous address contained in that memory location are stored for the error analysis.

e. The error-computing routine will determine the failing bit position(s) and if possible the faulty addressing circuitry.

f. The address of the memory location just checked is looked at

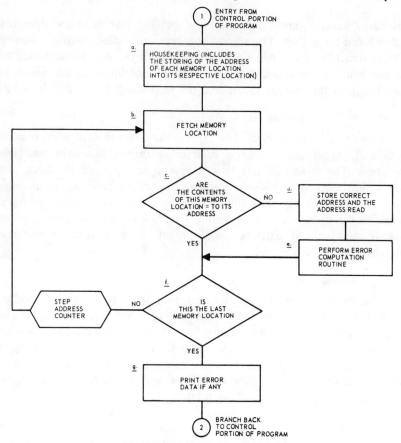

Fig. 10-2. Address Test Routine

to determine if it is the last location in the memory module under test. If it is not the last location to be checked, the address counter is stepped and the routine branches back to step b of the flow chart. If the last memory location has been checked, the routine will branch to the print-error routine at step g. Once all stored error data have been printed, the routine will branch back to the control portion of the memory test program.

10-4 Input-Output Test Programs

An I/O test program is normally made up of several individual programs used to test the various peripheral equipment associated with a computer system. Several of the earlier computer systems employed separate test programs for each of its peripherals. I/O test programs perform operations on such peripheral equipment as:

1. I/O keyboards.
2. Card readers.
3. Card punches.
4. Printers.
5. Message processors (or composers).
6. Magnetic drums and discs.
7. Magnetic-tape drives.
8. Paper-tape punches and readers.

The following flow charts, along with their explanations, should enforce understanding of typical I/O test programs.

10-4.1 Card-Reader and Tape-Drive Test Program

Refer to Figure 10-3. For this particular test five cards are punched in binary format. Each card contains 24 words (30 octal).

a. Step a of the test checks for a reader-ready condition (e.g., cards in hopper, power on). If in error, an operator alert will occur (light will come on); once corrected, the program will continue.

b. Read one card and check-sum. A check-sum is a check in which groups of digits are summed. That sum is checked against a previously computed sum to verify the data read.

c. If a check-sum error occurs, a printout occurs, identifying the error. After appropriate corrective action the program continues.

d. If the last card has not been read, return to step a. A determination for the last card being read could be made by checking a word counter for a count of 120 (five cards with 24 words each.) This type of counter is stepped as each word is written or read. Thus its count will indicate whether the desired number of words has been operated on.

e. As at step a, a check is made for the ready condition of the particular I/O device. If the tape drive is not ready or if it is file-protected (this condition prevents writing on tape), a printout or other indication is produced.

f. Tape is positioned to effect a write operation of 120 words. Other setup conditions, such as clearing certain counters, would also be performed at this time.

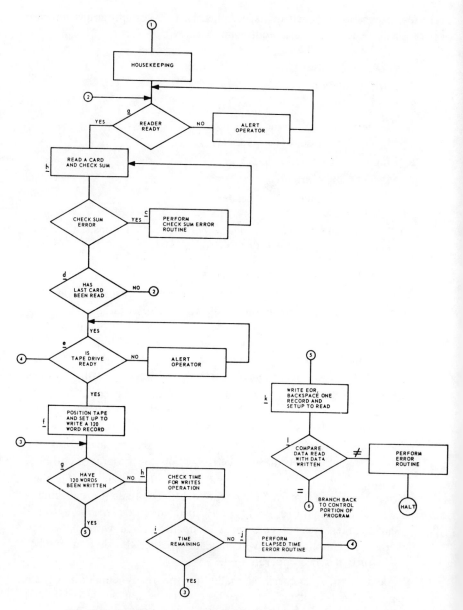

Fig. 10-3. Card Reader and Tape Drive Test Program Flow Chart

g. At this step a check is made to see if 120 words have been written. The word counter used in step d could also be used for this check.

h. The programmer knows what operation, what device, and how many times the operation is to be performed. He also knows how much time is required to perform a certain operation with a given I/O device. With these facts the programmer can check the device ability to perform a given operation in a specific amount of time. In this flow the programmer set up to write one record on tape that consisted of 120 words. At step h he will check the tape drive's ability to complete the write operation in the time allotted.

i. If the time remains to complete the operation, return to step g and check to see if 120 words have been written.

j. The elapsed-time error routine would first determine if, in fact, 120 words were written (check made of the word counter). If 120 words were not written, you would be informed of the number of words actually written and the total time used to write them. Depending on the system, other information could be provided to the maintenance repairman at this time. Once corrective action has been completed, the program continues the test at step e. If the test runs to completion without an error, the corrective action was proper.

k. An end-of-record (EOR) indicator would be written on the tape if 120 words were written in the allotted time. The tape would then be backspaced one record and a read operation effected.

l. At this time the data read from the tape would be compared with the data entered from the cards. A printout of all failures is produced. Once appropriate corrective action has been taken, reload and rerun this test to affirm corrective action. If all data compared at this step, the test would continue on the card-punch test indicated by connector 6.

10-4.2 Card-Punch Test Program

Refer to Figure 10-4. This test will determine whether the card punch can perform its function correctly.

a. At step *a* check to ensure that the punch is ready. You will be alerted by the punch if their condition is not right.

b. Five cards will be punched in binary format. The data that will be punched are the same data read from the tape at step *h* of Figure 10-3, which are the original data read in from the card reader at step b of Figure 10-3.

c. Have five cards been punched? This can be accomplished as before, by checking a word counter to see if it has been stepped to 120.

d. As in the last test, step h, the time allotted by the programmer for the I/O device to perform its operation is checked.

e. If time remains to complete this punch operation, return to step c and check to see if five cards have been punched.

f. An elapsed-time error routine would be used to first determine whether 120 words were actually punched. If they were not punched, the number of words punched and the total time used would be printed out. After taking the appropriate corrective action, the program can be reentered at step a.

g. At this step the operator would be informed to check the cards punched against the cards read at step b of Figure 10-4. If he noted punching errors, he would determine the corrective action

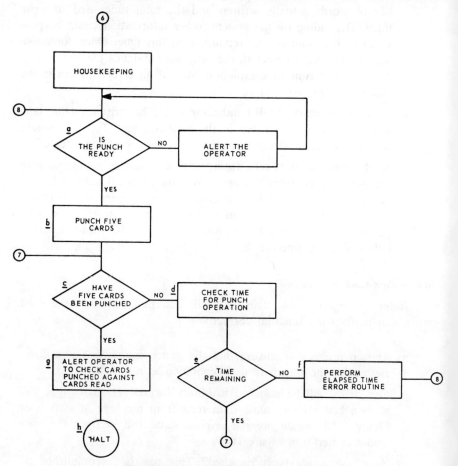

Fig. 10-4. Card-Punch-Test Flow Chart

needed. The test would be recycled, as explained in the particular program writeup, after completing the corrective action.

  h. A halt is indicated here, but the particular program could branch off to another test of still another I/O device.

The maintenance program used by computer-maintenance personnel contain many similarities. With experience in their use and experience in interpretation of them, the similarities are significant. These characteristics aid personnel in isolating failures more rapidly.

Using the two previous problems as an example, suppose that the last test failed because the word counter had not stepped. Both tests used the I/O word counter. The first test successfully completed its function; however, the punch test failed. The logic would indicate that the word counter is at fault. But would it really be the best place to start? Think! Did the counter work well on the first test for the tape test and reader test? It did. More likely the punch control circuitry failed to generate a control signed to the word counter and that is probably why it fails to step.

Familiarity with routines and their similarities provides a broad background of experience. Being able to interpret them regardless of their particular formatting is the key to understanding.

TEST QUESTIONS

1. What are the most significant characteristics of a maintenance program?

2. What are the three failure classifications?

3. What is the start-big programming technique?

4. Does the diagnostic program verify that a specific portion of the system is functional?

5. Can you explain the significance of the sequencing in a computer test program?

6. What significance does the number 4 have in Figure 10-1?

7. What troubleshooting aid can be made from looping a routine or subroutine?

8. What is the purpose of a beat test?

11

Programming and Interpreting
the Printout

In this final chapter on the use of programs to aid in maintenance of computer systems, we discuss a variety of machine printouts. In every case the printout provides information about the computer's ability to operate. In most cases the printout identifies the defective component. However, the printout from the electrographic printer does not. Its printout verifies the system operation only.

The variety of printouts from machines is so great that there had to be some common ground on which all were based. Research soon identified that there was a common basis, although the products were different. This section identifies the bases that are most useful to a technician who has the responsibility for maintaining an electronic computer system. It does not present an in-depth study of one or more pieces of equipment; rather, it presents knowledge of the common areas in order to make the technician more knowledgeable and put him in a more favorable position with his subordinates. The section provides a discussion under the following subsections:

1. Forms of printouts.
2. Features of printouts.
3. Locating program data.

11-1   Forms of Printouts

Many devices provide printed data which the technician uses to analyze the quality and operational capability of the computer system. Each device is designed for a specific purpose and so its printed data look different and have different formats. For those of you who have extensive experience in computer work centers, this subject is merely a review, and for you who work in centers that do not have these devices, this subject may be new. In either case, the material is relevant to the subject of *interpret program printouts*. Each of the following examples provides printed data which, when interpreted:

1. Assess the system's status.
2. Provide data about reliability.
3. Lead to future maintenance actions.

11-1.1   *Punch Card*

Figure 11-1 shows a typical punch card, including punching notations for numerals, letters, and special characters. This card can be interpreted very easily by reading the data punched as printed matter across the top of the card. Eighty columns on the card can be punched, as shown in Figure 11-1. Each column has 12 punching positions—one each for the digits 1 to 9, and one each for the zones 0, 11, and 12. The 11-zone punch is sometimes referred to as X. As illustrated, digits are recorded by punching a single hole in the corresponding digit or zero position of the desired column.

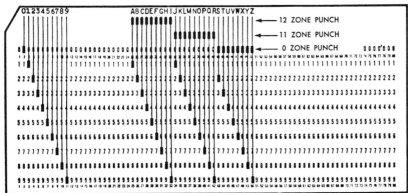

Fig. 11-1. Punch Card

A letter is a combination of one zone punch and one digit punch in the desired column. For example, A is the 12-zone and digit-1 punches, N is the 11-zone (X) and digit-5 punches, and Z is the 0-zone (zero) and digit-9 punches. Some machines also have special-character keys on their keyboard.

A special character is represented by one, two, or three holes in the desired column, as shown in Figure 11-1. Punching of two or three holes in one column for a letter or special character is automatic when the corresponding key is pressed.

11-1.2 Paper Tape

Figure 11-2 provides one example of a paper tape. This example shows seven rows and a center sprocket hole. Tapes are designed to have five, six, seven, and eight rows, plus a sprocket row. Usually the rows are binary-coded as in Figure 11-2, where a hole represents a binary 1 and no hole represents a binary 0.

This paper tape has tracks designated P, B, A, 8, 4, 2, and 1. Each character on an accompanying keyboard, when depressed, generates a binary code, which, in turn, activates punches in the correct columns. As an example, if an operator depresses a digit 7, punches in rows 1, 2, and 3 (binary 4) are activated and 8, A, B, and P are inhibited. Using either a table of codes or memorizing the appropriate codes (listed in reference manuals) makes possible the interpretation paper tape as a form of printout.

11-1.3 Teleprinter Printout

The following example is only one of many possible printouts from this type of printer:

```
ACDF
ALT-COMP TEST USING COMP = 1 MEM = 1 CC = 4
TEST = 000 PCR = 01 0576
EM NO SC
FLEXO TEST USING COMP = 2 MEM = 7 CC = 1
TEST = 002 PCR = 06 3671
IP DR 0001044632460010 STATUS = 10
RS DR 0000000000000000 STATUS = 00
```

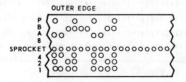

Fig. 11-2. Paper Tape

The characteristics of these printers are such that their speed (lines per minute) and line (number of characters) capabilities vary according to the needs of the system (Figure 11-3).

11-1.4 Keyboard/Printer Printout

The following example shows a keyboard printout. This output is received under the control of a print subroutine which directs the keyboard printer to print selected data. It is another form of printing which can convey its meaning to a technician.

CHANGE COMPUTER CARD GROUP CR0030
COMPUTER ERROR TABLE

START	ADR	OF	ACT	EXP	ACT	EXP
ADR	TST	OP	ACCM	ACCM	INDICS	INDICS
020263	021145	000000	400000	00600	002000	

11-1.5 Electrographic Printout

The following example shows a typical printout from this type of printer. The copy produced from a burning process is controlled by a memory decoder unit. Activation of sensors (amplifiers) provides conduction of wipers to commutators, resulting in burning of the paper. By selection of the appropriate amplifiers and timing, all characters and digits in normal writing are produced.

00 DPCO3 AO1 040620000	Senders address and date
ABC CNTR	Address Receive Msg.
as of 06 Apr 72	
This is a Test for DPCO3	Message part
01 DPCO2 AO1 040620000	
ABC CNTR	
as of 06 Apr 72	
This is a test for DPCO2	
02 DPCO1 AO1 040620000	
as of 06 Apr 72	
This is a text of DPCO1	
UNCLASSIFIED	page 1 of 1

11-1.6 Display Printout

The following example shows one of many different printouts used in a display unit. There are many different types of units and more of

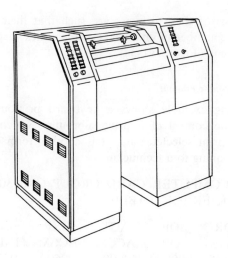

Fig. 11-3. Teleprinter

printouts. Printouts of this type are used most frequently with digital information display equipment. Remember the study of the charactron and typotron and the integrated (ROM) circuit units described in Chapter 5.

DT IS NOW IN PROGRESS. ADDRESS SECTION
IS BEING CHECKED AUTOMATICALLY. TO CHECK
VIK, DUPLICATE THE CHARACTERS BELOW IN
THE ADJACENT UNDERLINED SPACES. ENTER SC
IN THE LAST MESSAGE SPACE. IF DT INDI

2	A	B	C	D	E		CATOR STAYS RED, OBSERVE
3	F	G	H	I	J		THE AXC MAINTENANCE PANEL
4	K	L	M	N	O		FOR ERROR INDICATIONS. IF
5	P	Q	R	S	T		DT INDICATOR TURNS GREEN,
6	U	V	W	X	Y		TEST IS SUCCESSFUL. RESET
7	Z	(	)	/	,		IT TO THE WHITE IDLE CON-
8		1	2	3			DITION. THE CRT DISPLAY
9	4	5	6	7	8	9	SHALL THEN EXTINGUISH.

From these examples we see that in many of the format variations used the variations are a result of the design feature of the data. Regardless of the design of the machine or the format of the printout, certain characteristics of printouts must be included. These characteristics are the common elements that we must look for and use as a bridge when learning new systems.

11-2   Features of Printouts

The most widely used of all printouts is that produced by the teleprinter. Therefore, we discuss it fully. In addition, we cover the keyboard
printer punch, electrographic printer, and punch card.

11-2.1   *Teleprinter Printout Features*

The following items are considered essential printouts for uniformity
in program printouts. Maintenance-prgoram printouts of error detection
and error isolation normally provide them. They are the:

1. Program heading.
2. Results of program run.
3. Error information—data failure, control failures, and so on.
4. Indicated repair statements.

The following examples point out the differences in error printouts
from system to system. The identification of the four printout essentials are
presented. They are identified on each printout as follows: 1 = Program
Headings; 2 = Results of Program Run; 3 = Error Information; 4 =
Indicated Repair Statements.

Teleprinter Maintenance Program Printouts Example 1:

THE FOLLOWING PROGRAM WILL BE OPERATED UNDER
CONTROL OF SMCP 3

   CDS 1L TAPES MC 1L 2606
   A COMPLETE DIAGNOSTIC AND MARGINAL CHECK-
   ING TEST OF THE TAPE DRIVES, TAPE ADAPTER
   UNIT, AND ASSOCIATED CIRCUITRY.

1 +—+—+—+—+—+—+—+—+—+—+—+—+—+—
   SS1-OFF SS2-OFF SS3-OFF SS4-OFF BSW 0.10100 1.00000
   NOW TESTING LOGICAL DRIVE 3, WHICH IS PHYSICAL
   DRIVE — — —.

2   4. . . .E. .2. . . . #150-040 FAILURE MC WORD 005
    PRESCRIBED 40 ROUTINE 2

3   06447   TAPE DRIVE NO. 3
    REWIND DIDNT GIVE DISCONNECT

    THESE PUS WEREMARGINED AND COULD CAUSE
    ERROR. 13BJ

THESE PUS WERE MARGINED BUT WOULD NOR-
MALLY NOT CAUSE ERROR. 13BS 13BL 13AP 13AJ

4   13AH 13BT 13BD 13BF 13BE
THESE PUS WERE NOT MARGINED BUT COULD CAUSE
ERROR. 13BH 13 BG
+—+—+—+—+—+—+—+—+—+—+—+—+—+—+—+—

This particular printout has all the essential information. The program heading information 1 is complete to the extent that it even indicates the setup condition of the program [i.e., Sense Switch (SS1 through SS4) and B Switch (BSw) settings]. The result of the program run 2 identifies that a margin voltage check failure using margin word 005 occurred. Also, it identifies that the failure was within marginal group 4, circuit line selection E2, marginal voltage +150 V. The failure occurred at the prescribed margin of −40 V while cycling a particular test routine, routine 2. The error information 3 identifies that the tape unit number 3 failed; the brief explanation of how it failed shows that the rewind did not give a "disconnect" signal to the computer control. The indicated repair action 4 includes identification of the plug-in units (PUS) that could have possibly caused the margin failure.

Teleprinter Maintenance Program Printout Example II:
MTU DIAG TEST USING COMP-1 MEM=8 CC=1   1
TEST=005 PCR=076152
                      4
DESC. NO 001
CONTROL WD = 04   3
IP DR 0041040732110254 STATUS = 00
RS DR 0000000732522274 STATUS = 01   2
EX DR 0000000732522274 STATUS = 01
TEST WORD = 0404040404040404
WORD READ = 0101010101010101   3
FAULTY MODULE MTU 4, INTERFACE WITH CC1   1

This printout is for test 5 of the magnetic tape unit (MTU). This printout is provided by the maintenance diagnostic programs. The program heading 1 shows that computer 1 (COMP), memory-8 (MEM), and controller comparator 1 (CC) were used during the test. The controller comparator is an I/O control unit. Also included as part of the program heading (last entry above) is the faulty module number (MTU-4) and the number of the controller comparator (CC-1) it was interfaced with. Depending on the particular diagnostic test, the results of the program run 2 will consist of the in-process (IP), result (RS), and expected result (EX) descriptors (DR) processed during the test. Basically, descriptors are used to set up, initiate and control, or terminate data transfers between core memory and the terminal devices. Along with each descriptor will be an indication of certain status conditions (e.g., status 00 indicates that the particular I/O operation was initiated satisfactorily, and status 01 indicates end of record). The error information 3 indicates that a data-comparison error occurred while reading tape drive unit 4. The 0 in the control word (WD) specifies a read operation, and the 4 specifies tape drive unit 4. If an error had been detected during the write operation, the control-word printout would contain a 7 in place of the 0. The test word indicates what was written on the tape. The word "read" indicates what was actually read back from the same tape. The indicated repair statements 4 provided in this type of printout must be used in conjunction with specific diagnostic tables contained in the service manual. Normally the test number, contents of the program count register (PCR), and the descriptor number (DESC. NO.) are used with the diagnostic tables to determine the required corrective action. The corrective action indicated by the diagnostic tables can include, but is not limited to, the replacement of plug-in assemblies.

11-2.2   *Keyboard-Printer-Punch Printout Features*

The printer portion of this unit provides a printout consisting of the same four basic areas as the teleprinter. However, as the example that follows shows, areas 3 and 4 are subordinated in area 2 .

```
KPP MAGNETIC TAPE SYNCHRONIZER (MTS) DIAGNOSTIC
PROGRAM EXAMPLE III.
THE MTS DIAGNOSTIC PROGRAM HAS THE FOLLOW-
ING SENSE SWITCH OPTIONS
SW1—LOOP ON ERROR
SW2—LOOP ON INTERMITTENT ERROR
SW3—LOOP ON SYNCHRONIZER
SW4—INHIBIT ERROR PRINTOUT
SW5—ON AND OFF TO CONTINUE     1
SW8—OUTPUT ERROR TABLE
MOUNT SCRATCH TAPE WITH WRITE ENABLE RING
AND DIAL UNIT ZERO. PLACE UNIT AT LOAD POINT.
PRESS UNIT ZERO ON LINE AND OTHER UNITS LOCAL.
TYPE IN 7 TO CONTINUE
CHANGE MTS CARDS CRR000        4
MTS ERROR TABLE
```

MTS COM	ACT STA	EXP STA	ACT DAT	EXP DAT		
511400	000000	500000	000000	000000	3	2

The program heading information 1 for the above magnetic-tape-diagnostic-program printout includes the sense-control-switch (SW) options for the magnetic-tape-synchronizer (MTS) portion of the program. An example of the use of these switches would be SW8 ON to provide the MTS error table, SW1 ON to loop on error, or SW4 ON to inhibit the error printout while looping. Other information included here is the mounting of a scratch tape for writing and reading of test data (with a write enable ring in place to allow writing), and the identification of zero being dialed on the tape drive to be tested. A note is included in the program heading to remind the operator to ensure that the scratch tape is at load point. If the tape were not at load point, an error indication would occur during the MTS portion of this diagnostic. Also, the tape driver is placed to an on-line status, and other tape-drive units are placed to local (effectively, off-line). The test is started by typing in a 7 at the keyboard-printer-punch (KPP). The MTS test is the first test to be cycled. The magnetic-tape synchronizer includes such circuitry as tape control and computer interface circuitry. The results of the program run 2 include both error information and indicated repair action. The error information 3 includes detailed program data associated with the MTS test. MTS COM indicates the MTS *command word* generated by the program. ACT STA is the *actual status word* received from the MTS. EXP STA is the *expected status word* based on the preliminary setup conditions. ACT DAT is an indication of the *actual data* received, and EXP DAT indicates the *expected data*. Normally this error table would contain other information; however, what we have presented should suffice in giving you an idea of the printouts associated with this diagnostic program. The indicated repair statement 4, change MTS CARDS CRR000, would be used with a functional card group table (located in the appropriate reference manual) to determine the cards that should be changed. Before jumping into the middle of the MTS and pulling cards, let's take a closer look at the error table. It is apparent from the actual and expected data indications that we did not have a data failure. However, in checking the status tables and the status word, the actual and expected status indicates that the tape-drive unit under test was dialed to another setting, (5), not zero. Recall that the program heading called for the tape drive to be dialed to zero. In other words, an operator error was the cause of this failure and not card group CRR000. Once zero has been dialed into the drive under test, the program can be recycled.

Although these three printouts employ different formats for presenting failure information, they maintain uniformity in that each printout contains the four essentials: program heading, results, error information, and indicated repair statements. Once you are able to identify and interpret these four essentials in your system's printouts, the job of maintaining the particular computer system will be simplified.

11-2.3 *Electrographic Printout Features*

Referring again to the example in Section 11-1.5, notice the characteristics of this message. The printout is formatted by title and section heading. It differs from previous printouts in that it does not display a diagnosis of the fault. However, it can be used to determine validity and reliability of the machine it is used for. It consists of the following:

1. Heading. This is preceded by the start characters 00.
2. Part. The body of the message is composed of parts. In this example parts 01 and 02 are shown.
3. Character forms. In an actual printout of the machine, parts of the message, such as part number (00, 01, 02), are automatically inserted. Other data are entered by operators when the program allows for it. Each character is generated automatically by a series of dots (7 high and 5 across). Error detection is possible by examination of the printout for missing rows or columns of dots, or missing parts of messages.
4. Closing. The bottom of each page is identified with "page # of #."

11-3 Locating Program Data

The final discussion on the subject of interpreting program printouts is where to find the information. We know that specific technical and reference manuals contain the programs used in a system. In each case a datum is provided that relates to a technician's understanding and use of the program's:

1. Purpose.
2. Procedures.
3. Flow charting.
4. Results and expected results.
5. Test points (where they are needed).
6. Special test equipment.

11-3.1 *The Service Manual*

The most frequently used source for obtaining program information is the service manual of the system or end item. Layouts in these manuals provide the program information as follows:

1. Title.
2. Description or purpose.
3. Table of step instructions with breakdown, including:
   a. Step notations.
   b. Actions.
   c. Control settings.
   d. Test equipment or test points.
   e. Results.
   f. Performance standards.
4. Flow charts.
5. Reference to other technical data.

The chapters most frequently used in these manuals are those on operations, and service or maintenance. Recall from your previous training that most of the maintenance instructions are contained in the service chapter. Quite logically, any data pertinent to program purpose, function, and control will be found there. Consideration of the variety of programs, their explanations, and interpretations must be included when correlating the computer printouts.

11-3.2 Areas of Similarities in Printouts

Interpretation of printouts, as explained in this text, identifies that printout similarities exist in the areas of:

1. Basic program format.
2. Purpose.
3. Maintenance devices.
4. Technical reference location.
5. Technical reference layout (tabular form, flow charting).
6. Descriptions in service manuals.

TEST QUESTIONS

1. A maintenance-program printout can provide what three useful features?

2. If an alpha character B is punched into a card, which columns are punched?

3. What is the total number of punches that can be punched in a row on a card?

4. Does paper-tape punching use the binary code?

5. What are the four major parts of a printout?

6. In a series of technical reference manuals about a computer, which chapter will usually contain information about program printouts?

12

Troubleshooting

In the previous chapters you gained an insight into the tasks needed to maintain a computer system. While performing the maintenance inspections and tasks associated with the particular system, one important fact should become apparent to you: *Successful mission accomplishment of a computer system is dependent on a system of scheduled maintenance inspections performed by competent maintenance personnel.* Wouldn't it be great if the effective performance of all scheduled maintenance guaranteed equipment with no problems? Of course, this is not the case, since equipment failures can occur at any time. However, effective accomplishment of the scheduled maintenance inspections minimizes equipment failure. When a failure does occur in your system, you are going to be responsible for troubleshooting, that is, for isolating and correcting the problem as fast as you can in order to return the system to the performance of its primary mission.

Troubleshooting, as we once knew it, has taken on a new dimension. With the advent of the computer and all its shortcuts and wonders came a new age of troubleshooting. The computer figures our pay, works our math problems, and makes our life as a maintenance repairman somewhat of a breeze. Yes, the computer can do all these things as long as it func-

284

tions properly. But, brilliant as it is, the computer (just like all of us) still has its problems. This is where you come in. All of a sudden this electronic brain (that has practically taken our job and made us look ridiculous when compared to its ability and speed in working math problems) has failed, and it is now at your mercy. As any good technician dedicated to his profession, you will respond by curing its ills. Isn't this ironic? You may not be as fast or possess the abilities of that computer, but without you it is nothing more than several miles of wire and a maze of electronic hardware completely within your power. Now, while you are savoring all this great feeling of power and pride, keep in mind that you will maintain your superiority only as long as you are able to maintain proficiency in troubleshooting the system.

In every computer system there are many troubleshooting aids designed to make your job of isolating failures easier. Some of the more important troubleshooting aids you might use on the job are:

1. Fault indicators.
2. System and unit testers.
3. Performance test standards.
4. Diagnostic programs.
5. Flow diagrams.
6. Specialized test equipment.

The various troubleshooting techniques presented in this chapter are representative of those used in troubleshooting the majority of computer systems maintained by computer maintenance personnel. The computer system you are maintaining, together with your personal abilities, will dictate the troubleshooting technique or techniques you adopt and excel in using. The troubleshooting techniques we are going to present fall within four basic task elements:

1. Analyzing logic and wiring diagrams.
2. Analyzing oscilloscope waveforms and patterns, and signal tracing with an oscilloscope.
3. Using and interpreting fault location guides and facility panels (Chapter 13).
4. Using the group-removal-and-replacement method of pluggable units (Chapter 13).

12-1 Troubleshooting Considerations

The basic troubleshooting procedures used in computer maintenance are generally quite logical. A good technician will attack a problem by asking and trying to answer some simple questions. His first questions normally concern the causes of the trouble. As each question is answered, he eliminates some possible sources of trouble; step by step he decreases the areas he must troubleshoot. How far he is able to proceed depends upon his knowledge of the equipment and his ability to troubleshoot. His knowledge may permit him to locate the exact component that is causing the trouble, or it may only permit him to isolate the trouble to a cabinet or rack. However, with only a limited knowledge of the equipment and by using the correct procedure, the troubleshooter (you) will probably find the more obvious troubles.

12-1.1 Know Your Equipment

Remember, there is no substitute for familiarity with the equipment when it comes to troubleshooting a system. If you are not familiar with your equipment to the extent that you can analyze its operation, interpret its indicators, read its printouts, and analyze its programs, you will have difficulty in isolating a failure within that equipment.

12-1.2 Think Before You Act

The most important step of any troubleshooting effort is to think before you act. Ask yourself, "What are the symptoms, and what is most likely causing the trouble?" By asking and trying to answer these two questions, you will be following a logical sequence of steps which will lead you to the cause of the trouble.

12-1.3 Establish a General Troubleshooting Procedure

The word "general" as used here means all-encompassing. Establish a troubleshooting procedure that can be followed regardless of the particular hardware failure. Figure 12-1 presents a general troubleshooting procedure that can be used for just about any hardware failure encountered within a computer system. The directions given in blocks 1 through 5 are steps to be used in locating the trouble, and the directions given in blocks 6 and 7 are steps used in repairing the unit. Steps 2, 3, 4, and 5 may sometimes be eliminated, but steps 6 and 7 must always be followed. Later in this chapter we expand this general troubleshooting procedure by incorporating specific troubleshooting techniques in steps 1 through 5. When incorporated into a troubleshooting procedure, the troubleshooting

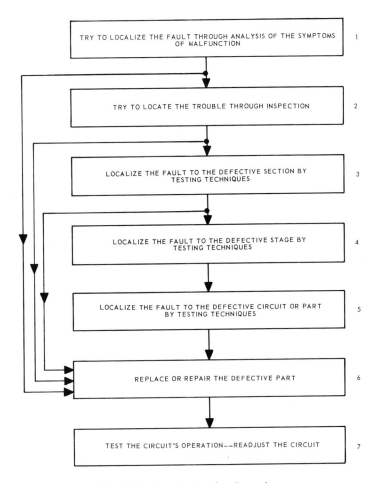

Fig. 12-1. Troubleshooting Procedures

techniques presented in the paragraphs that follow simplify the trouble-shooting effort.

12-2 Troubleshooting with Logic and Wiring Diagrams

A computer is no more than a combination of simple devices which perform a few basic operations. The complexity arises from the fact that the logic is not standardized but varies according to the manufacturer. In 1960, MIL-STD-806A was developed and approved by the Department of Defense for the preparation of logic diagrams. Unfortunately, many computer systems were manufactured prior to this date; consequently, nonstandard logic symbols are still quite common. A point to remember is that the symbol representation varies from manufacturer to manufacturer, but the basic principle of using similar symbols remains the same. Stated simply, no matter how it is disguised, an AND gate, for example, remains an AND gate.

The manufacturers that have adopted the military standard have merely adopted the symbology but do not fully utilize the basic concepts. Figure 12-2 shows some of the variations of symbology that have been developed from MIL-STD-806B. A manufacturer of a particular system converted all its logic to MIL-STD-806B; however, the particular system used *negative logic* voltage levels exclusively (thus requiring input and output state indicators on logic symbols). However, the manufacturer decided to eliminate all state indicators. If troubleshooting this particular system using its logic, you have to take for granted that the indicators are there. The idea worked until technicians from other computer systems were assigned to this system and applied the true principles of MIL-STD-806B. They found that without the presence of the state indicators, the system took a complete reversal and would not operate according to the standards they knew. It is apparent from this one example that the technician's responsibility of recognizing the various types of logic becomes rather difficult. In order to broaden your knowledge, a variety of manufacturers' logic symbols are included in Figure 12-2 together with their logic function (title).

12-3 Troubleshooting with Boolean Algebra

Recall from your school days that boolean algebra is a form of logic that uses mathematical symbols to describe logical processes. This type of logic was named in honor of George Boole, an English mathematician, who developed it in 1854. No practical use was made of this new type of logic unit 1938. Then C. E. Shannon, a research assistant at the Massachusetts Institute of Technology, discovered that this form of logic was perfect for indicating the logical functions of computer and telephone switching circuits. There are several advantages in having a mathematical technique for describing these circuits; it is far more convenient to calculate with equations than with schematics or logical diagrams. Just as an ordinary algebraic equation can be simplified using basic theories, equations describing logical conclusions for arithmetic operations, logical decisions, and switching networks can also be simplified.

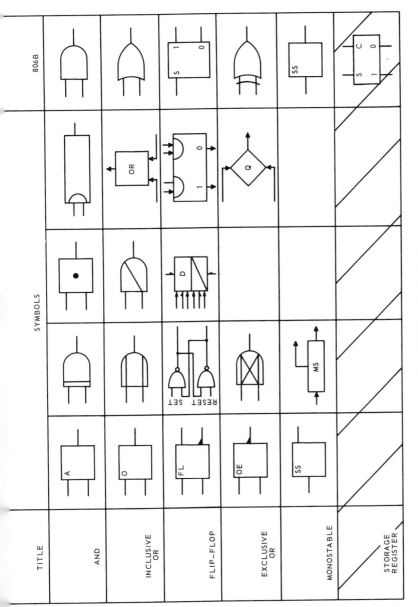

Fig. 12-2. Logic Symbols

289

This enables the designer to devise the simplest logic to perform a function. It also enables you, the technician, to understand and troubleshoot with the logic, thus achieving efficiency of repair and maximum operational availability. Normally, troubleshooting with boolean algebra involves the development and use of a boolean equation or truth table.

12-3.1 Developing Boolean Equations

A boolean equation is developed from certain fundamental ideas encompassing logical conditions and operations. Logical conditions are called *variables* and are *represented by letters.* Logical operations are called *functions* and are *represented by symbols.* When a variable is used in a normal algebraic formula, it is assumed that the variable may take any numerical value. For example, in the equation 3A plus 6B equals C, the A, B, and C may range through the entire field of numbers. However, the variables used in boolean equations have a unique characteristic in that they may only assume one of two possible values, *high* or *low*, and these in turn may be represented by a *true* or *false* condition. For review purposes, let's consider the development of a boolean equation for the circuits shown in Figures 12-3 and Figure 12-4. Figure 12-3 illustrates two AND gates feeding an OR gate, thus becoming an overall OR function. Note the lack of signs of grouping within the final equation. Figure 12-4 shows two OR gates feeding an AND gate, thus becoming an overall AND function. In this case, signs of grouping (as shown in Figure 12-4) are used to retain circuit integrity. In developing the boolean equations for each of the figures, we start at the input and work toward the output. This is a good rule to remember, especially when you attempt to develop a boolean equation during a troubleshooting period. Based on your previous technical school training, the boolean equations just developed should not seem all that difficult to you. What about developing a boolean equation for a circuit such as presented in Figure 12-5? Could you do it? To be sure you can, the next paragraph explains how to develop this equation.

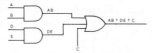

Fig. 12-3. Overall OR Function

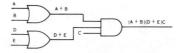

Fig. 12-4. Overall AND Function

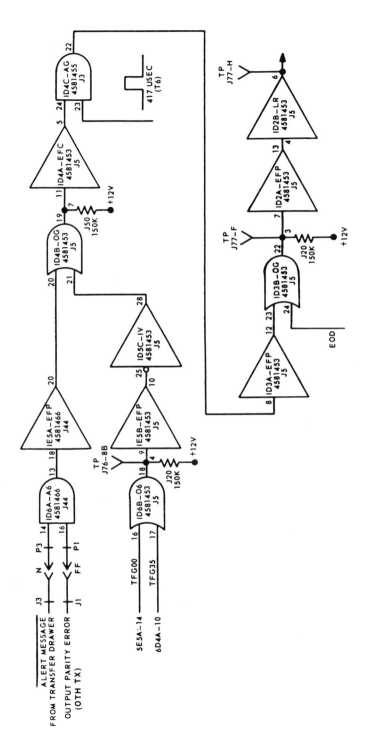

Fig. 12-5. Logic Circuit

291

The circuit you are looking at in Figure 12-5 is a stepping circuit used to develop output pulses that in turn step a counter. In analyzing this circuit, a determination as to the output's origin and its duration must be made. As stated earlier, a boolean equation is developed from the input to the output. We will develop the boolean equation by beginning at AND gate J44-13. J44 develops an output at pin 13 for its input signals: Alert Message · (· indicates *and*) OPE OTH TX (Output Parity Error signal from the Other Transmitter). Note the line above the signal "Alert Message." It is called the *viculum* and it indicates the *absence* of the signal Alert Message. OR gate J5-18 provides TFG00 + (+ indicates *or*) TFG35; observe that this expression is fed to Inverter J5-28, which NOTS (inverts) the expression, thus providing TFG00 · TFG35 (TFG stands for Timing Format Generator) as pin J5-21. At J5-19, the signal (Alert Message · OPE OTH TX) + (TFG00 · TFG35) is produced. This signal primes pin 24 of AND gate J3-22. J3-23 is primed by T6 (Time 6 pulse), which produces an output at J3-22 as long as pin 24 is satisfied. The output of an AND gate is determined by the duration of its *shortest input*. In this particular stepping circuit, timing pulse T6 determines the duration of the output at J3-22. This time duration is 417 μs. The 417-μs output at J3-22 is written (Alert Message · OPE OTH TX) + (TFG00 · TFG35)T6. To complete the equation, we find at pin 24 of OR gate J5-22 a signal that, when present, replaces the entire equation thus far developed; this signal is EOD (end of date). The remainder of this stepping circuit consists of nothing more than an emitter follower and level restorer. Now, the output's origin and duration are known, as is the boolean equation for this stepping circuit. The complete boolean equation reads ((Alert Message · OPE OTH TX) + (TFG00 · TFG35)T6) + EOD.

Now that the boolean equation for the stepping circuit is completed, let's determine its effectiveness in troubleshooting. For example, to determine that the stepping circuit is functioning properly, an oscilloscope would be used to check TP J77-H for a pulse that is 417 μs in duration. If this pulse is not present, the next logical step would be to check TP J77-F and eliminate the possibility of the emitter follower (EFP J5) and level restorer (LR J5) being defective. Should the pulse be present at TP J77-F and not present at TP J77-H, card J5 would be changed. However, if the pulse is not present at J77-F, the boolean expression must be analyzed to determine which logical function provides the normal stepping pulses. The first portion of the equation (Alert Message · OPE OTH TX) can be eliminated because it is an error condition that normally is not present. Another stepping condition is EOD, which occurs only at the end of a transmission or the reception of a message. At the point in analyzing this boolean equation it becomes apparent that the normal stepping pulses are provided when the format generator *is not* at TFG00 and TFG35. The troubleshooting approach at this point would be concentrated on the function (TFG00 · TFG35)T6. A check would be made at the timing-pulse generator for T6 pulses. If T6 pulses are being generated, a check of TP J76-B would be made to determine the *absence* of TFG00 and TFG35. The absence of TFG00 and TFG35 at TP J76-B would indicate that the problem circuitry is between TP J76-B and TP J77-F (in other words, the timing frequency generator should be functioning properly). At this point, cards J3 and J5 would be replaced.

12-3.2 *Developing Truth Tables*

Another means of troubleshooting by use of the boolean equation is to disregard the full equation and develop what is known as a truth table. A table of this nature is nothing more than a means of determining an output by considering all inputs and their variables. In Figure 12-6 a truth table has been developed for the output of a very common computer circuit—the full adder. The circuit inputs consist of X, Y (the addends), and C (a carry input from a previous stage). The outputs are represented by S (the sum) and Co (the carry out). Look over this truth table carefully and note the binary inputs and outputs. What is happening in lines 1 through 8? Binary math? That's part of it. Something else is there—something very important to a truth table. The definition of a truth table should give you your answer. A truth table is a means of determining an output by considering all inputs and their variables. For example, in line 1 of Figure 12-6, $0 + 0 + 0 = 0$, with a carry of 0; in line 8, $1 + 1 + 1 = 1$, with a carry of 1. Now, look at all the inputs between lines 1 and 8. Here are all the other variables possible for the inputs X, Y, and C. This answers the question of what is happening in lines 1 through 8 of the truth table. A determination of the output from a full adder circuit is being made by considering all its inputs and their variables. Now the big question is, How can a truth table help you in your troubleshooting efforts?

When troubleshooting, the true value of a truth table is its identification of all input variables along with their outputs. The easiest way for you to see this is by setting up a hypothetical troubleshooting problem. Let's suppose that a failure occurs within your computer system X, and the failing card (the full adder circuit in Figure 12-6) is identified and replaced. While we are supposing, let's go further and involve you. That's right, you are the technician assigned to perform the bench check. First you read over the failure document. It reads: "Card failed during diagnostic program routines of the ADD class instructions." Not much to

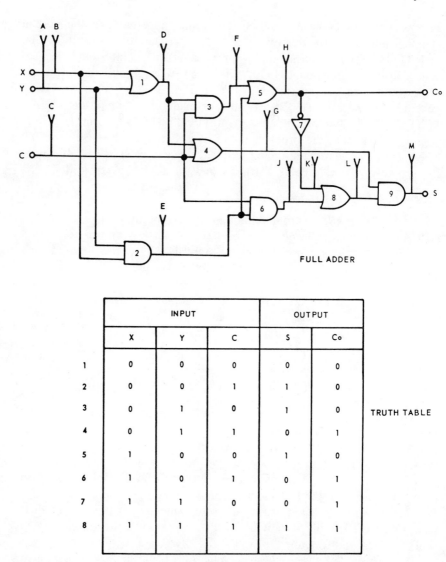

Fig. 12-6. Truth Table

go on, is it? You look over the logic diagram and develop a truth table. Systematically you set up your tester to provide the inputs identified in each line (1 through 8) of the truth table. After setting up each test, you check TP-H and TP-M for the output indicated by the truth table. Let's further suppose that each output checks until line 8; here you find no output at TP-M. Now you perform the following checks and get the results indicated:

1. TP-G—output OK.
2. TP-L—no output.
3. TP-J—no output.
4. TP-E—output OK.
5. TP-C—output OK.

From the results of the above checks it is apparent that AND gate 6 is failing [i.e., with two good inputs (TP-E and TP-C) it produced an erroneous output at TP-J]. Also, by starting at the output and checking each TP back to the input, the gates that were functioning properly were identified as well as the faulty gate. Now, you must admit that the truth table helped the troubleshooting effort. Actually, once we knew that only line 8 was failing, the contents of the truth table pointed to AND gate 6. What does this mean? For one thing, all the checks made after we found the failing variables (line 8) were not necessary.

You might be questioning the statement that indicated the contents of the truth table pointed to AND gate 6 once line 8 was identified as failing. Let's analyze that statement to determine its validity. The only time an error occurred was during the addition of 1 and 1 with a carry in of 1. Looking at the logic, it becomes apparent that the only gate affecting the sum (S) output, when adding the inputs of line 8, is AND gate 6. This is true because its upper leg is conditioned by the carry input, and its lower leg is conditioned by the ANDed function of $X \cdot Y$ from AND gate 2. Also, you must keep in mind that the tests (lines 1 through 7 performed prior to line 8) were successful.

Before leaving our hypothetical troubleshooting problem, let's regress to when you were looking at the card's failure document. Suppose that the repairman who ran the diagnostic program identified (on the failure document) that the failing program routine was attempting to add 1 and 1 with a carry in of 1. Just think how much easier it would have been for you to bench-check the card with this information on the failure document. The repairman who prepared the document could have acquired this exact failure information by consulting the diagnostic program writeup. Now when you hear your supervisor say, "Put *all* the failure data on the failure documents," you will know why it is needed.

12-4 Troubleshooting with Logic Analysis

A fine line is drawn between troubleshooting with boolean equations and logic analysis. First you devise your boolean equation and then you use it in your testing to determine if each function is present. It is during this testing and application of your boolean equation that logic analysis takes place.

12-4.1 Functional-Area Approach

The primary purpose of the equipment in electronic computer systems is the processing of data. This is accomplished through a logical flow of data, which, in turn, is accomplished through the functioning of the equipment's circuitry. The basic functions of these circuits, exclusive of power supplies, are the generation, transmission, conversion, logical manipulation, and storage of signal voltages. When the system fails in the accomplishment of any of these functions, the cause must be found before the repair can be made. This means that you must troubleshoot the system in an effort to isolate the fault to the failing functional area and then to the failing component within this functional area. The logical method of isolating a fault is through a process of elimination of the functional areas that are performing properly. This is normally accomplished through careful analysis of the malfunction's symptoms. The effectiveness of this analysis depends upon your knowledge of the functional operation and data flow within the computer system. Once a failure is isolated to a specific functional area, further analysis of the circuitry within this area is required to isolate the malfunction to the failing component. Another name for this functional-area approach is the block-diagram approach to troubleshooting.

12-4.2 Block-Diagram Approach

For an example of the block-diagram approach to troubleshooting, refer to Figure 12-7. Here we have a block diagram of a demodulator unit. Let's suppose that its output is absent and you are attempting to isolate the failing function (e.g., AGC, filter). What approach would you take in troubleshooting this demodulator? Look over the following steps and compare them to the troubleshooting approach you would use.

1. Check for the presence of the data input to the AGC circuit.

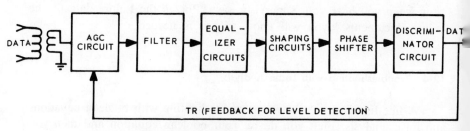

Fig. 12-7. Block Diagram of Functions

2. Check the data output of the equalizer circuit. The results of this check will isolate the failure to the first or second half of the circuits in the demodulator.

3. The first half of the circuits (i.e., the AGC, filter, and equalizer functions) would be suspect if *no data appeared* at the output of the equalizer. By checking the input and output of these first three blocks, you should be able to isolate the failure to one of them.

4. The second half of the circuits (i.e., the shaping, phase shifter, and discriminator functions) would be suspect if *data appeared* at the output of the equalizer. By checking the input and output of these three blocks, you should be able to isolate the failure to one of them.

The method of troubleshooting explained above is sometimes called the *split-half* method; that is, once you determine the absence of an output, you split the circuits in half and check for an output at the halfway point. When you determine that the failing circuit is in the first or second half, you split these circuits in half for further isolation of the failure. This process is continued until the failure is isolated to one function. This split-half method could also be continued once you begin troubleshooting the circuits in the failing block.

12-4.3 Signal-Injection Approach

This method of logic analysis consists of inducing a normal signal (or a signal similar to that which is present under normal operating conditions) to the input of the circuits in question. The circuit conditions that result from this application are then checked at various points, using test equipment such as a vacuum-tube voltmeter, oscilloscope, or any other device that is appropriate for use as a signal indicator. By using these test instruments and injecting a signal into the circuits, you can monitor circuit operation at various stages, and localize the points of origin of such faults as distortion and hum, noise oscillation, or any other abnormal conditions. When this method of logic analysis troubleshooting has revealed a faulty stage, you can further check that stage by making voltage or resistance measurements, or by individually testing circuit components.

A logical procedure along these lines is to first test those components that are easiest to check and those which *experience* has shown to be the most trouble. If a vacuum tube or transistor is involved, it is usually checked first, or, in the case of vacuum tubes, one known to be good is substituted in its place. In most cases a schematic and/or logic diagram is all that is necessary to determine where to insert the signal and where to check for its presence. In other cases, voltage charts or illustrations of waveforms may be needed for comparison purposes. However, in the majority of cases involving logic analysis troubleshooting through signal injection, the important things to remember are these:

1. Narrow the trouble down as far as possible by analysis of the symptoms.
2. Use your schematic diagram and logics.
3. Check waveforms and voltages before checking resistances (resistance checks require that the power be off).
4. Think the problem through before replacing components.
5. Check the records. Do not overlook the importance of your fellow workers' previous experience. The same trouble could have happened to them.

Troubleshooting with boolean algebra and logic analysis is a must in the majority of electronic computer systems. Your ability in using these two methods of troubleshooting increases as you gain experience on the job and become proficient in analyzing waveforms and patterns and signal tracing with an oscilloscope.

12-5   Troubleshooting with Patterns and Waveforms

In this section the objective is to learn how to analyze patterns and waveforms as seen on an oscilloscope, and to use this analysis when troubleshooting. As stated in the introduction to this chapter, this is one of the specific task elements in troubleshooting. The analysis of this task exposes the many different types of digital data patterns and analog waveform presentations you may observe on an oscilloscope during your career in the electronics environment.

12-5.1   Purpose of Measuring Patterns and Waveforms

Two specific reasons are evident for measuring patterns and waveforms. The first is to analyze data content and the second is to determine if a waveform meets the prescribed requirements.

12-5.2   Analyzing Data Content

The digital data content in the variety of systems presently being used and maintained is extremely varied. However, it generally has one common element; it is digital. This means that within a prescribed duty cycle one pulse, or its absence, represents a bit; a group of pulses represents a data word, a byte, or another form of intelligence. Digital data consist of information that is routed, altered, stored, processed, controlled, and displayed by the computer system. Digital data also generate visual intelligence in the form of printouts, displays, mechanical readouts, and automatic functions of the console units. In addition to providing the substance for the program to operate, digital data (converted from punch cards or other inputs) control program sequencing, which, in turn, controls the actions of the computer.

12-5.3 Determining Prescribed Specifications

The data content we have been talking about thus far is digital; therefore, it is in informational pulse form, either voltage or current, representing a language called *binary*. From your studies in school, you know that binary is a two-character (1 and 0) language or number system. Now let's consider these data as containing intelligence indicating the number of aircraft (flight size) and that the total number of positions allowed in a word for storing these data is three. This would mean that low numbers of aircraft in a formation may be cataloged individually and high numbers of them may be grouped under specific numerical headings. For example:

1. For a flight size of 1 to 4 aircraft, the binary count would be equal to its respective count; i.e., 1 aircraft = 001, 2 aircraft = 010, 3 aircraft = 011, and 4 aircraft = 100.

2. For a flight size of 5 to 7 aircraft, the binary count would be equal to 5 (101).

3. For a flight size of 8 to 12 airfcraft, the binary count would be equal to 6 (110).

4. For any flight size consisting of more than 12 aircraft, the binary count would be equal to 7 (111).

By the arrangements shown in this example, it follows that digital data expressed in binary can be interpreted to mean specific information. More significantly, it can be processed, altered, updated, and used in a very simple and accurate form in an electronic computer system.

We also know that digital data are manipulated in parallel and serial form; that they are speeded up, slowed down, shifted, erased, and generated as the requirements dictate. For instance, if a requirement exists to multiply a number by 2, a simple machine operation could accomplish this action. This operation is a left shift. Notice the two examples in Figure 12-8.

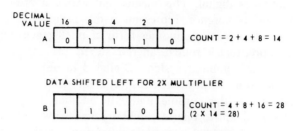

Fig. 12-8. Multiplication Function

A of the figure shows a five-stage counter with a count of 14 in it. By applying a left-shift pulse to the counter, the data bits are moved one position left. This action causes the value of each bit to double, and now the count, as indicated at B of the figure, equals 28.

Manipulation of data also can be accomplished by division of binary. Using the figure 101 again, suppose a right-shift pulse were applied to the counter with the count inserted as shown at A of the figure. What count would result? If you answered 7 (00111), you would be absolutely correct. In other words, the original contents of the counter have been divided by 2.

We can also manipulate the digital count either by addition or subtraction. Using the same figure again, let's add two bits serially, one at a time, to the LSD of the figure and, since the LSD contains a 0, the counter causes a 1 to be stored in its place. Enter the second bit of data into the LSD and, since the LSD, 2-, 4-, and 8-stage now contain a 1, the counter causes a 1 to be stored in the 16-stage and a 0 in each previous stage (i.e., the LSD, 2-, 4-, and 8-stage). What has occurred is that two binary bits have been added to the counter, and it has upcounted from its original count of 14 (01110) to a count of 16 (10000). Subtracting a 1 from a binary counter can be accomplished by a complementing-and-adding process. Refer to Figure 12-9 for this explanation. At A you see the binary configuration for 45. B represents 45 in complement form. C represents the result of adding 1 to the complement (B) of 45. D represents the answer, 44, which is actually the complement of C.

In the previous paragraphs we discussed digital data as patterns containing intelligence. In the discussion that follows we must also include analog voltage current waveforms that do not contain intelligence. Stating that analog waveforms do not contain intelligence may need further explanation. Digital data, as we have discussed, are readily interpreted into word data, such as range of aircraft, flight size, or computer instructions. Analog waveforms do not contain this translatable information. However, each waveform is, in itself, capable of transmitting an image to the human

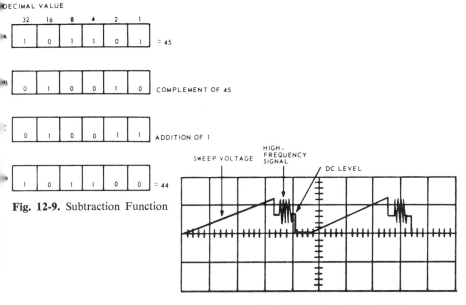

Fig. 12-9. Subtraction Function

Fig. 12-10. Time-Share Display

brain and causing a specific reaction. For instance, consider a console using *time sharing* for its display cycle—where the first part of the display is a sweep voltage and the second part is a dc level with some high-frequency signal riding on it, as shown in Figure 12-10. The image displayed is converted by the human mind into the functional operation of the circuits involved in providing the sweep voltage, dc level, and the high-frequency signal. Therefore, if any portion of the waveform is distorted or missing, that portion should convey a message to the repairman. What message? Well, if the sweep voltage were distorted, the logical circuit to suspect first would be the sweep generator.

If a display as seen on the scope reflects a high or low basic frequency, examination of the waveform requires use of the scope controls to verify the frequency accuracy. This is most often accomplished by measuring the time of one cycle and then applying the formula frequency = 1/time. On the other hand, if a display is known to contain either amplitude- or frequency-modulated data, single-pulse examination would not reveal any significant information other than to facilitate the measurement of the carrier frequency. Examination of *multiple cycles* reveals that data are, or are not, being received. For instance, in A of Figure 12-11 a basic reference signal without any data is depicted. All cycles are the same pulse width and amplitude. Now insert *amplitude-modulated data* onto the basic reference frequency and *increase the num-*

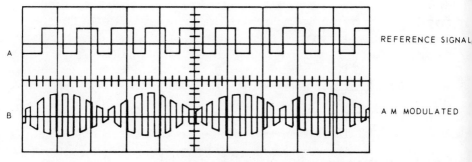

Fig. 12-11. Amplitude Modulation

ber of cycles per centimeter on the scope, and the waveform would appear
as it does at B of the figure. If the signal carrier were *frequency-modulated,*
the signal as seen on the scope would show *no change in amplitude* as
it did with amplitude modulation. However, it would show considerable
change in frequency, since *frequency modulation requires the algebraic
summation of the data and carrier frequency.* It should be apparent, then,
that knowing what effect amplitude and frequency modulation have on
the carrier frequency is an aid when analyzing waveforms as a troubleshooting technique.

12-5.4 Reading Techniques for Digital-Data Patterns

With the purposes of measuring data foremost in mind, let's consider
the next element of the task in analyzing patterns and waveforms, i.e.,
"reading the data."

Oscilloscope displays provide for a left-to-right sweep presentation of
digital data. Therefore, when scoping serial input data with the least significant digit (LSD) as the first input, it will appear on the left of the scope.
Look at examples A and B of Figure 12-12. Each word is generated by a
system that uses positive logic. Although consisting of a different number

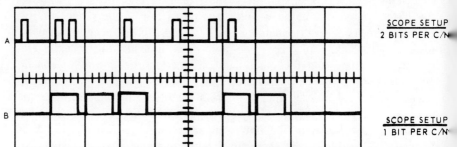

Fig. 12-12. Digital-Data Displays

of digits, they show data starting on the left. For our discussion, assume that A of Figure 12-12 depicts a 16-bit serial input word (LSD at the left) with two bits per centimeter. The data content of this display shows a binary configuration of 1011001001011000. Since the word is 16 bits long and there are just two bits per centimeter, only the first 8 centimeters are considered. Let's further assume that the first 13 bits (i.e., 1011001001011) represent range data. The LSD is equal to ¼ mile, and the MSD (bit 12) is equal to 512 miles. The sign bit (bit 13) indicates which direction, east or west (0 = east and 1 = west), an aircraft is from the radar site. The maximum range that could be represented by the range bits (bit 1 through 12) is 1023¾ miles. The data shown indicate an aircraft with a range of 364½ miles west of the site. For our example, this range is computed by totaling the decimal values represented by each binary 0 since the sign bit is a 1 (indicating negative). This, in effect, is determining the one's compliment. In our example, the total range value computes to 659¼ miles; subtracting this from the maximum range of 1023¾ results in an actual range of 364½ miles. If the sign bit had been 0, the actual range would have been computed by totaling the decimal values represented by each binary 1; this computes to 659¼ miles.

In example B of Figure 12-12 the data displayed are a fieldata code consisting of eight positions—one bit per centimeter. The first six bits of this particular fieldata code are used to represent an alpha or numeric character. Bit position seven of the code indicates whether the character is alpha or numeric (i.e., 1 = alpha and 0 = numeric). Bit position eight is the parity bit; *odd parity* is used. From the listing below, identify the alpha or numeric character represented in binary form using the reading technique of LSD on the left and MSD on the right.

Bit position:	1	2	3	4	5	6	7	8		
	0	0	1	1	0	0	1	0	=	G
	1	0	1	1	0	0	1	1	=	H
	0	1	1	1	0	0	1	1	=	J
	0	1	1	0	0	0	0	1	=	6
	1	0	0	1	0	0	0	1	=	9

The correct answer is alpha character I. Notice how each alpha character is assigned a binary code (first six positions) that is one value higher than the previous (i.e., G = 12, H = 13, I = 14, J = 15, etc.). Once again the reading technique was from the left of the scope to the right. By now you might be asking yourself, "How do you always obtain the LSD of a word in the first centimeter of the scope display?"

Oscilloscope synchronization plays an important role in reading a data display. It provides the basis for selection of a sweep start time coincident with the first bit of a data word or any other selected bit. By selection of a timing reference signal and use of external horizontal sweep, the LSD bit is placed in the first centimeter of the scope.

12-5.5 Reading Technique for Analog Waveforms

Analog waveforms are usually easier to acquire and interpret than digital patterns. This is so primarily because analog waveforms are performed more frequently with less alteration. Primary techniques in reading analog waveforms require extensive knowledge in the use of the oscilloscope. For example, you'll need to be knowledgeable in the:

1. Synchronization of the scope.
2. Use of the dc and ac voltage selection on the vertical preamplifier.
3. Proper selection of sweep speeds.

To successfully read a waveform, knowledge and understanding of its generation make the job easier. For instance, in the actual reading of the waveform the dc level of an ac sine wave is its midpoint and normally is equal to 0 volts dc. However, any ac waveform may be caused to ride a dc potential other than 0 volts. When this occurs, use the dc switch and volts-per-centimeter control on the scope's vertical preamplifier to determine and validate the accuracy of your reading.

The average dc level of a square wave is normally 0 volts dc; however, in a rectangular waveform, this average dc level is dependent upon which part of the alternation is above or below the 0 volts dc reference for the

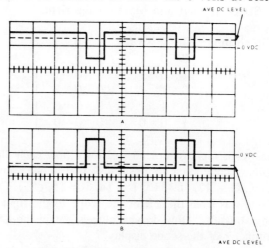

Fig. 12-13. Determining the dc Level

longer period of time. Figure 12-13 shows examples of the average dc level within rectangular waveforms. Notice in detail A of the figure that the positive portion is longer in duration when compared with the negative portion. This leads to an average dc level at a point above 0 volts dc reference. Now notice that in the B section, the situation is reversed (i.e., the negative portion of the waveform is longer than the positive) and the average of dc level is below the 0 volts dc reference. These waveforms show examples of amplifier or other circuit outputs which allow signals to be displayed without clamping to a base line. However, if the circuit generating these waveforms is designed for 0 volts dc clamping and the average dc level is other than 0 volts, you know that a circuit defect exists. Before continuing with the development of our objective in this section, let's examine a few figures of various patterns and waveforms and determine whether they are or are not correct.

12-5.6 *Interpreting Patterns or Waveforms*

We have provided four figures for your interpretation. Preceding each figure you will find a description of the scope of presentation. Your job is to read and interpret the description, study the scope of presentation, and determine whether it is correct or not. If the presentation is incorrect, record the reason it is incorrect in the space provided.

Problem 1: A radar return from a height finder has been converted into digital form and stored. Flight plans for the particular aircraft specify its altitude at 10,500 feet. The storage space allowed for height within the data word is the first 9 bits of a 16-bit word (two bits per centimeter). The LSD of height is equal to 375 feet. An ordinary binary counter is used to accumulate these height data. Now refer to Figure 12-14 and determine if its oscilloscope presentation depicts the description given. Your answer:

_____

_____

_____

Problem 2: While performing a bench check of a keyboard, the letter K was depressed and the configuration displayed on the scope was as shown in Figure 12-15. For this problem, determine what the correct bit configuration is for the letter K by referring back to the page (in this section) that presented the bit configuration for letters G through J (one bit

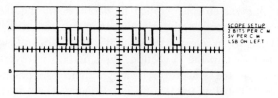

Fig. 12-14. Height Display Data

per centimeter). Your answer:

_____

_____

_____

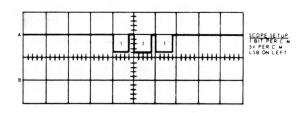

Fig. 12-15. Character Display Data

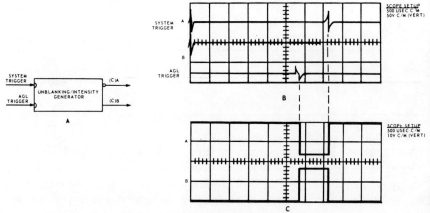

Fig. 12-16. CRT Unblanking/Blanking Waveform

Problem 3: A display cycle of a particular CRT is developed from a range of 0 to 210 miles. An unblanking intensity pulse (provided by the unblanking/intensity generator shown in section A of Figure 12-16) provides this display cycle by unblanking the CRT. The two elements controlling the generator are shown in sections A and B of the figure. They are *system trigger* and *AGL* (automatic gate length) *trigger*. System trigger occurs at range zero, and AGL trigger occurs after it (at 210 miles). System trigger amplitude is 35 V (±10 V) and AGL trigger amplitude is 15 V (±2 V). The output amplitude from the unblanking/intensity generator is 18 V. CRT unblanking occurs from system trigger to AGL trigger, and blanking occurs from the AGL trigger. Based on these specifications you are to determine if the unblanking/intensity generator output (as shown in section C of Figure 12-16) is correct. Your answer:

_____

_____

_____

Problem 4: The waveform shown in Figure 12-17 represents the output of an integrator circuit. The parameters for the standard are shown in section A of Figure 12-17. Compare these with the waveforms displayed in section B and record your findings in the space provided. Note that the pulse width is measured from the start of rise time to the 50 percent point of the fall time. Your answer:

_____

_____

_____

Answer to Problem 1: With a height flight plan specifying 10,500 feet, the proper binary configuration for the data word would appear as follows:

75	750	1,500	3,000	6,000	12,000	24,000	48,000	96,000	= 10,500 ft
0	0	1	1	1	0	0	0	0	
SD								MSD	

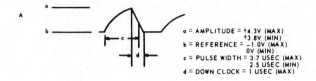

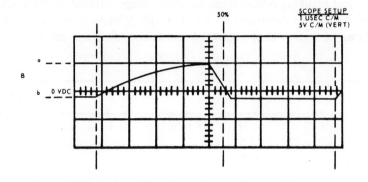

Fig. 12-17. Integrator Output Waveform

The other bits in positions 12, 13, and 16 of Figure 12-14 represent another element of data about the aircraft, not the height.

Answer to Problem 2: The display as seen in Figure 12-15 is incorrect. The letter K has a binary value that is equal to 16 decimals (000010). The character is alpha, so bit seven is a 1, and parity bit (bit position eight) is a 1, indicating odd parity; however, the figure shows a 1 in bit position six, indicating and improper output.

Answer to Problem 3: The waveforms are correct. System trigger turns on the unblanking/intensity generator. At turn-on time output B goes low; this low is used to gate the data to be displayed to the CRT. The unblanking pulse, A, goes high at turn-on time and brings the CRT out of cutoff. At AGL trigger time (210 miles after system trigger) the generator output is switched, thus ending the display cycle.

Answer to Problem 4: The integrator output waveform does not meet specifications. Its amplitude exceeds the maximum of 4.3 V. Its base

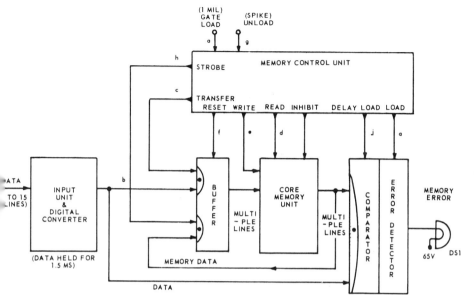

Fig. 12-18. Memory-Unit Block Diagram

line is good. The pulse width exceeds the maximum limits of 3.7 μs. The fall time is within the specifications.

With the solutions to the four problems given, our study of patterns and waveforms is concluded. The study you made in the section on logic analysis, coupled with this one, provides you with the tools to proceed with troubleshooting tasks.

12-6 Troubleshooting with Signal-Tracing Techniques

Let's combine the techniques of analyzing logic, patterns, and wave-forms into the technique of signal tracing. This will be accomplished by troubleshooting a typical computer malfunction. Since you are working in a computer-system environment, the chances are that you have some type of memory unit. As you know, every memory unit has a control unit. For our troubleshooting problem, a memory that is used to store and validate input data has been selected. The block diagram for this memory is shown in Figure 12-18. As you can see, the memory consists of the following:

1. Input unit with converter.
2. Buffer.
3. Memory control unit.

4. Core memory unit.
5. Comparator and error detector with lamp.

Using our figure, we can now set the scene for the malfunction. As data came in, the error light went on, but using the reset switch, the error light went out. This error light didn't come on again until later in the day. This indicates an *intermittent error condition*. Troubleshooting an inter-mittent error can cause a person to become quite frustrated. However, before the intermittent error turns into a more-entrenched error, there is a certain amount that you can accomplish. As a matter of fact, this is where you can really make money.

In the discussion that follows, correlate the letters in parentheses with those in the block diagram. The *gate load level* signal (a) conditions the memory control unit and error detector for 1 ms. This is the time required to validate and store an input character into a memory address. *Data* (b) are loaded into the buffer register with a *transfer pulse* (c). The memory address to be written into is cleared with a *read pulse* (e). The buffer is reset with a *reset pulse* (f), which is developed from the *unload pulse* (g). The buffer is then loaded with data (the same data just written into core) from core by a *strobe pulse* (h) (see memory data), which is also devel-oped by the unload pulse. The same memory address is cleared again with a read pulse, and the data is loaded into a second cycle along with the *gate load level signal* for the actual detection of errors. If validation occurs on a bit-by-bit check, the error light remains off.

12-7 Analyzing Probable Trouble Areas

The block diagram shows four distinct areas in which error could occur and give an error indication:

1. Buffer register.
2. Core.
3. Comparator/error detector.
4. Control unit.

12-7.1 *Buffer Register*

If a stage of the buffer fails, proper comparison cannot take place. Also, a faulty control signal feeding the buffer (i.e., reset, transfer, or strobe) will result in a failure indication.

12-7.2 Core Unit

A defective core is possible but highly unlikely. Cores seldom fail, but don't rule out the possibility altogether. More likely, though, one of the control signals that affect the condition of the core (i.e., read, write, and inhibit) is defective.

12-7.3 Comparator/Error Detector

A defective leg of a comparator circuit could cause an error indication. Also, the error-light control circuit could be defective, causing the error light to turn on.

12-7.4 Control Unit

If any one of the pulses feeding or generated by the control unit becomes defective, the operation is impeded and an error indication occurs. Considering the fact that this unit receives, generates, and distributes the pulses that directly affect the core, wouldn't you say that it would be a primary suspect when the error light came on?

12-8 Determining Priority Order of Failure Probability

A definite priority (indicated as follows) is apparent when certain characteristics of the four areas listed above are considered:

1. Memory control unit.
2. Buffer or comparator.
3. Core.

12-8.1 Memory Control Unit

This unit contains six pulse generators: transfer, write, read, inhibit, and strobe. Generators are likely places to suspect a failure because they usually have extensive circuits. If one fails, the signal may be lost, differentiated, or distorted.

12-8.2 Buffer or Comparator

The buffer and the comparator present equal possibilities for failure. A buffer usually contains a bistable device made up of more than one stage that is vulnerable to failure. If the multiple input gates to these units employ diodes, you can place these diodes high on your list of probable failures when an error occurs. In comparators, AND, OR, EXCLUSIVE OR, F/Fs, or other comparison devices are used. Frequently the transistors or diodes used in comparators open or short between their junctions. Also, a possibility for error exists when a F/F, setting to the *one* state, is used to provide the ground for the error lamp. A relay may also provide this ground to the lamp. Either type of switching without proper control could cause the error light to come on.

12-8.3   Cores

As a rule, cores do not break down and fail. However, the wiring of the cores (for addressing, inhibiting, and sensing) may short or open. More often than not, the current driver circuits fail in a memory unit. Based on these facts, we can suspect that the cores themselves are least likely to cause a failure, and the current driver circuits are most likely to cause a failure.

12-9   Selecting the Approach

Using the priority order above, we see that no verification of the buffer, core, or comparator is possible without verification of control unit operation. Therefore, the analysis must proceed by examining the logic of the control unit.

12-9.1   Determining the Control Signal

Three considerations are to be made and determined from analysis of the memory control unit logic:

1. Width of the pulses.
2. Polarity of the signals.
3. Sequence of operation for load and unload.

Figure 12-19 includes a logic diagram of the control unit and timing charts for the load and unload sequence. As we continue to signal trace the techniques of logic, patterns, and waveform analysis, we should begin to determine which signals must be verified first, second, third, and so on. At the same time a listing of the boards involved in the entire unit should be acquired or made, and along the side should be noted conditions that might suggest changing it. Let's analyze each of the signals:

TRANSFER SIGNALS
Notes:

1. Pulse width 4 μs.
2. Card A14, monostable multivibrator.
3. Card A12, inverter amplifier.

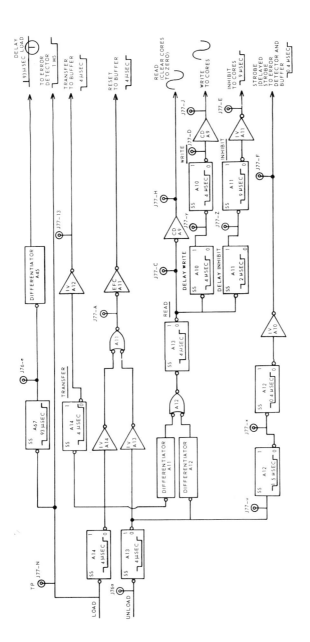

Fig. 12-19. Memory Control Unit

313

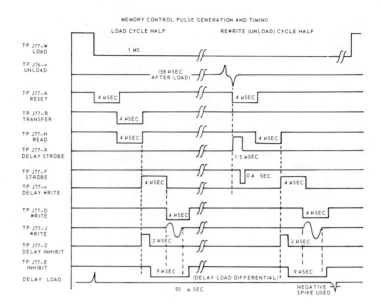

MEMORY CONTROL PULSE GENERATION AND TIMING

Remarks:

1. Transfer pulse begins at the end of load pulse and continues for 4 μs.
2. *Load* must be present before transfer occurs.
3. Results if *transfer* does not generate but load is present:
   a. Error light will turn on.
   b. Data will not be gated into buffer; therefore, memory loads all 0s because the *reset* cleared the buffer.

RESET SIGNAL
Notes:

1. Pulse width 4 μs, starting with *load* or *unload*.
2. Card A14, monostable section and inverter section.
3. Card A11, OR gate (one leg), and inverter section.
4. Card A13, monostable multivibrator section and inverter section.

Remarks:

1. *Reset* pulse begins with *load* and ends at beginning of *transfer*.

2. Results of reset do not generate.
   a. Error light will turn on.
   b. Data loaded into buffer will combine with previously loaded data.
   c. Core memory will load invalid data with buffer, and comparison of data in the error detector unit results in error correlation.

READ SIGNAL
Notes:

1. Pulse width 4 μs, starting and ending with *transfer pulse.*
2. Card A11, differentiator section.
3. Card A12, OR gate (one leg).
4. Card A13, monostable multivibrator.
5. Card A9, current driver.

Remarks:

1. *Read* signal is converted to a current pulse, which causes all the cores to reset to the ZERO state.
2. Read controls the generation of *write* and *inhibit.*
3. Results if read is not generated:
   a. Memory will not clear.
   b. *Write* and *inhibit* will not be loaded into core.
   c. Data stored in buffer cannot be loaded into core.
   d. Error light will come on because core data and input data do not correlate.

WRITE SIGNAL
Notes:

1. *Write delay* pulse width 4 μs (starting at the end of *read*).
2. Write pulse width 4 μs (starting with the end of write delay).
3. Card A10, two sections of monostable multivibrator are used.
4. Card A9, current driver section.

Remarks:

1. *Write* signal is converted into a current pulse used to load the data.
2. Results if write or write delay generators malfunction:
   a. Memory cores will always be zero, *read* will reset them.

b. Correlation will be improper because on the *unload* (rewrite) cycle, data stored in buffer and loaded in memory will be 0s.

c. Error light will come on.

INHIBIT SIGNAL
Notes:

1. *Inhibit* pulse width 9 μs.
2. *Inhibit delay* pulse width 2 μs.
3. Inhibit delay pulse starts at the end of *read*.
4. Card A11, two sections of monostable multivibrator and inverter are used.

Remarks:

1. *Inhibit* signal restricts the buffer data (zero bits) from loading into cores because of its polarity.
2. Results if *inhibit* or *delay inhibit* generators malfunction:
   a. Improper data load to core memory.
   b. Possible switch of cores when data bits are zero in buffer.
   c. Possible switch of all cores in memory because of write current.
   d. No correlation in detector circuit, resulting in error-light indication.

STROBE AND DELAY STROBE
Notes:

1. *Delay strobe* pulse width 1.5 μs.
2. *Strobe* pulse width 0.4 μs.
3. Card A12, two sections of monostable multivibrator.
4. Card A10, inverter section.

Remarks:

1. *Delay strobe* causes generation of strobe to occur during a *read* (memory) reset. The strobe pulse transfers the memory core's data through drivers back into input buffer storage.
2. Results if strobe is not generated:
   a. Rewrite into core is incomplete.
   b. Memory core unit will contain 0s.
   c. No correlation in detector circuit, resulting in error indication.

12-9.2 Analyzing the Conditions

If any unit (buffer, core comparator, or control) fails in any part of the circuit, the error circuit provides a visual sign. The primary reason for this is because input data are routed to the comparators for later use in the comparison cycle. Further analysis shows that any one control signal, including *unload,* provides a visible error indication. However, the load signal not being present (even if data are to be stored) inhibits all memory action. This is true for two reasons:

1. Without load no transfer or reset action can occur; therefore, the buffers cannot be cleared and loaded.
2. Without load, the error detector cannot sample the comparator output. With this logic and function analysis completed, a set of notes similar to the items we listed above, predicting the failing component or assembly, is possible.

12-9.3 Isolating the Malfunction

In this hypothetical problem, an intermittent error was indicated. From the logic analysis, we understand that:

1. Load must have been present.
2. Correlation did not occur.

Unfortunately, no further positive prediction can be made. However, some probable hypotheses can be assumed:

1. Core memory is good.
2. Error-detector circuit is good because manual reset extinguished the lamp.
3. Buffer and comparator may have a failed component.
4. Most likely area to validate first is the *memory control unit.*

12-10 Validating the Memory Control Unit

Now comes the time for the use of the oscilloscope and the physical signal tracing. Assume that each test point is available while the unit is in an operational configuration. By synchronizing the scope (preferably a memoscope) on load, each of the pulses generated by the memory control unit can be checked. Further, each pulse can be checked for pulse width and other relationships. Since the problem is intermittent, the complete absence of a pulse is unlikely. But, examining each pulse for its desired characteristics *may* provide a clue. Signal deterioration is often a prelude to signal failure.

If you find such a clue, write a note about it, draw its measured waveform, and ask yourself: Does the pulse width exceed its parameter? Does it have too short a pulse width? Is the pulse amplitude too low or too high? Is clamping or base reference voltage proper? Ask any question that may lead you to develop an opinion or cause you to select a specific approach when the failure becomes *solid*. If you find the slightest clue, write it down and list the specific assemblies (PCB) involved. If you are proved right later, you will know just what cards to remove. If all signals look, measure, and recur as specified in the performance standard, begin the same procedure for the buffer, then the comparator, and finally the sense amplifier and address control cards within the core memory unit. As we stated earlier, do not discount the cores themselves as a possibility; just consider the possibility highly unlikely.

The example just completed shows one instance in which the oscilloscope can be used in troubleshooting. We could present numerous other examples of different parts of systems where the oscilloscope is used for signal tracing during troubleshooting periods. Rather than do that, let's develop some problems in certain areas of a computer system and determine when the oscilloscope may be used.

12-11 Determining When To Use the Oscilloscope

If someone tells you that the scope will be used for every troubleshooting problem encountered, don't you believe it. Just because you get an error indication doesn't mean at all that you must scope the computer.

Problem 1: Look at the repairman in Figure 12-20. He saw something on the display unit that triggered his trouble button. Can you pick out what he saw? If you see the retrace from the map outline, you've got it. Our repairman walks back to the console. He takes a real close look at the display and finds retrace from the *track dot, tag,* and *symbol* (A in Figure 12-20). Where is the trouble? This is no time for an oscilloscope since he already has what amounts to one in front of him. Why not use it? Okay, now our man goes through several tests with the console itself. The checks he makes include:

1. Reducing intensity with the front-panel intensity control. The re-

Fig. 12-20. Display Problem

trace gets lighter and, just before losing all signal, it disappears. That won't help.

2. Selecting different operating modes. All have the same indications. The problem seems to be localized to the Z-axis (unblanking/intensity) and might include:

 a. High voltage.

 b. Improper voltage levels in intensity or unblanking.

 c. Improper timing. (Consider this as an unlikely possibility because the symbols seem to be proper.)

Our repairman knows that with the front-panel intensity control at maximum, no retrace should be visible. Without going into voltage levels (because of the variety of them), it is apparent that retrace is a function of blanking/unblanking. Further, retrace occurs at the end of a sweep cycle when the generators are allowed a short period of time to return to their starting point. If blanking is improper, the return energy produced by the generators is amplified and presented as *retrace*.

Our man now knows where to look. What should he do next? Get the oscilloscope? Not yet. First, examine the logic and alignments to see which control is involved in the blanking/unblanking circuit. Then ask:

1. What cards are involved?
2. What controls are involved?
3. Is there an alignment for correcting this problem?
4. Can the work be accomplished on line?

He answers these questions, and then he gets the oscilloscope. From his list of test points he quickly and accurately measures the controlling waveforms and records his findings. From his findings he researches the alignment for the waveform test point that is improper. He compares the waveform with the standard. Can the *pot* or *variable capacitor* range far enough to correct the problem? These data should be available in his own notes or can be located in the pertinent reference manual. A quick look verifies a misalignment or a malfunction. If misaligned, realign; if a malfunction, change the card and then align. Problem solved—coffee time.

In this problem the oscilloscope came into play after research and display manipulation were completed. A definite precise area was identified in the research as *most probable*. Verification of opinions and conclusions was performed quickly and accurately with the oscilloscope performance standards and notes about the signal area.

Problem 2: While the computer is cycling, a failure occurs. From this study of program diagnostics the problem must first be localized. Clearly, then, this is not the time to use the oscilloscope. However, it is the time to run the diagnostics. Selection of the proper diagnostic may be possible if interpretation from error lamps, failure printouts, and operational printouts provide a clue. In any event, running the diagnostics is the first logic step—not troubleshooting with the oscilloscope.

Interpretation of the diagnostic printout may identify the exact card or card group replacement that will correct the malfunction. Should this be the case, the oscilloscope would not be used. However, if the card replacement does not succeed, than what? Back to the drawing board and on with more function and logic analysis while recycling the diagnostic. Only this time the diagnostic will have a loop set up in it, allowing us to check the functional area suspected to be failing. The function and logic analysis identifies data peculiar to the circuit. It also identifies specific waveforms, data patterns, and voltage amplitudes.

With the probabilities listed, additional cards listed, specifications for the patterns and waveforms at hand, and a loop program (manual or software) set up, the oscilloscope can now be used. The loop that is set up with the aid of the diagnostic allows point-to-point signal tracing. The oscilloscope is used to verify each point, and, at these points, you can make a comparison of measured data or waveforms with the specifications.

If you are beginning to think that signal tracing with an oscilloscope is a last-ditch troubleshooting technique, don't. Troubleshooting with the oscilloscope is indeed a technique used after considerable study and analysis. Exercising the equipment, researching technical data, and applying the knowledge of their functions to components are usually accomplished first. These elements may take from a few seconds to many hours to accomplish. Your expertise on the equipment may be so good that you know just what action is required and that signal tracing pin 17 of card A5 will provide the solution. Or, your expertise and notes may have been leading you to the conclusion that pot R5 is deteriorating, and a scope display will verify it.

Referring back to the introduction to this chapter, where the term "Think" was introduced, applies extremely well to the use of the oscilloscope when troubleshooting. Think the problem out before you jump into the middle of it with a scope. Analyze the problem and its symptoms; check the fault and facility panel for the various error indications that normally accompany equipment failure. The indications provided by this panel can give you a definite starting point for troubleshooting.

TEST QUESTIONS

1. Why must steps 1 through 5 of the troubleshooting procedures be considered in any troubleshooting plan?

2. Can you draw the standard symbols for the following logic functions?
   a. AND   c. Inverter   e. Register
   b. OR   d. Amplifier

3. Is the term $AB + C$ that of an OR or AND function?

4. Why can truth tables be a troubleshooting device?

5. What is the functional-area approach to troubleshooting with logic analysis?

6. When point-to-point troubleshooting using block diagrams, what method is often used by technicians?

7. What is the purpose of measuring patterns or waveforms?

8. What type of register operation is required for a number to be multiplied?

9. What is frequency modulation?

10. What is meant by the "average dc level of an ac waveform"?

11. In the signal-tracing technique discussed in the text, is the block-diagram analysis placed first for a specific reason?

12. What decisions can a technician obtain by determining a priority order of failure probability?

13. Why could a logic analysis lead to isolation of the exact part that is malfunctioning?

14. Even though an oscilloscope is to be used, what steps in troubleshooting can minimize its use?

13

System Troubleshooting

In Chapter 12 we explored some of the troubleshooting techniques common in point-to-point signal tracing. Considerations of when to use block-diagram examination, to the proper time for using the oscilloscope, were discussed. Some systems are designed to use these methods of isolating and correcting defective component. Other systems are designed to use a systems approach to troubleshooting.

This chapter examines two techniques that can be used in system troubleshooting. The first one is the technique of finding a faulty component by use of the system's fault indicators. From the earliest system to the present, fault indicators have been used. Only more recently, though, has the actual component (assembly) been able to be identified. Earlier designs of functions incorporated many printed circuit cards or multiple assemblies, and the indicators reflected operation of the entire function. Newer systems, because of state-of-the-art improvements, use fewer cards or assemblies; therefore, the indicator often identifies a specific component.

The second technique is an adaptation of the split-half method of troubleshooting discussed earlier. The primary difference is that cards are removed in a group and replaced with cards known to be good. This method is known as the group-removal-and-replacement technique of troubleshooting. This technique also requires use of the fault indicator.

13-1 Analyze Fault-Location Indicators

Fault indicators, as the term implies, identify (through the use of various types of lamps) where the malfunction occurred within the system. An indicator may be installed anywhere that it is convenient for visual observation. In order for the indicators to convey any meaning to maintenance personnel, they must be appropriately labeled, and the labels or labeling must be kept in readable condition.

If you are working on a computer system, you should be somewhat familiar with its fault-indicator assembly. Therefore, a study of selected fault-indicator assemblies of different systems would be of little use to you here, especially when analysis proves they are all the same in principle. This text is used to present a study of these units in terms of their:

1. Uses.
2. Types.
3. Technical reference information.

13-1.1 *Use of the Fault-Indicator Assembly*

The two uses provided by the fault-indicator assembly are the identification of a failing function or subfunction and the identification of correct or incorrect data flow. Regardless of the extent of coverage the indicator has on a panel, only one of these two uses is possible. For both uses to be present on a panel, a minimum of two indicators must be used. Let's examine this thought more thoroughly.

A fault indicator or data-flow indicator lamp is frequently located on the panel or assembly containing the circuit it represents. This arrangement is convenient for verification of that function or subfunction of the system. It does, however, have a distinct limitation; that is, inspection of each cabinet, rack, chassis, or drawer is necessary to locate the inoperative function. This system is cumbersome, time consuming, and inefficient. To overcome this limitation, additional indicators are installed at a centralized, convenient location within the system. Notice the words *additional indicators*. The need for primary indicators, those located at the function, is necessary in addition to those remoted to the more convenient location. Some of the most used locations of convenience are:

1. Front doors of cabinets.
2. Fault and facility panels.
3. Fault indicator and confidence consoles.

Thus far we have established that each function or subfunction within a system will likely have an indication of operation or failure. Further, because of the volume of circuits and placement of units, a conveniently located assembly is made. This assembly, called by various names, provides at a glance the status of all or most of the equipment within the system. We also identified the two uses for this assembly. Let's examine each.

13-1.2 *Identify the Status of the Function*

The indicators are positioned in groups that are associated with specific functions of the equipment. Figure 13-1 illustrates this arrangement. The block to the right represents a portion of the central fault panel. It has a functional title, *Computer Arith Control,* and has 10 lamps, representing indications of subfunctions within the arithmetic control unit. For explanation and use in this study, only the *Logic Sign Check* indicator is examined. Before identifying when the lamp would light, review the other elements of the figure. Only cabinet 53 is involved, but within the cabinet, racks A2, A4, A5, and A6 provide some control over the logic sign check fault indicator. The light will turn on when an incorrect *sign check* (parity) error occurs from a subfunction in rack:

1. A2 when A2-DS1 lights.
2. A5 when A5-DS1 lights.
3. A4 when A4-DS1 lights.
4. A6 when A6-DS1 lights.

Shown in the figure are five additional fault indicators for rack A6. They are DS2, 3, 4, 5, and 6. If one or more than one of these indicators turn on, the rack A6-Ds 1 lamp also lights.

Lamps A2-DS1, A4-Ds1, A5-DS1, and A6-DS1 are rack lights and receive their inputs from circuit indications. The breakout of racks A2, A4, and A5 is similar to that indicated for rack A6 in the figure. For this study, the detail in the figure is sufficient. If any rack light comes on, it provides the necessary input to the cabinet light, which, in turn, provides the input to the fault indicator—Logic Sign Check located in the Arith Control area of the fault facility panel. From this indication, we determine that a problem exists in the arithmetic control circuits and, as a trouble-

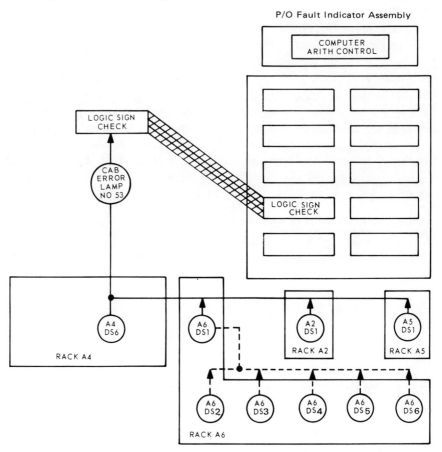

Fig. 13-1. Function Indicator

shooting aid, the fault indicator has directed attention to a local area. But what about data flow?

13-1.3 *Identify the Status of Data Flow*

Circuit lamps installed on panels are used in various methods to identify data flow. In Figure 13-2 four lamps are used to display the status of a transmitter (XMT A or B) during transmission time. In this system only one lamp is on at a given time. For example, when data are being transmitted by XMT A, a sequence is repeated each time data are transmitted and, upon completion of the cycle, lamp A returns to the ON state.

Another example of data flow is that of lamps associated with a

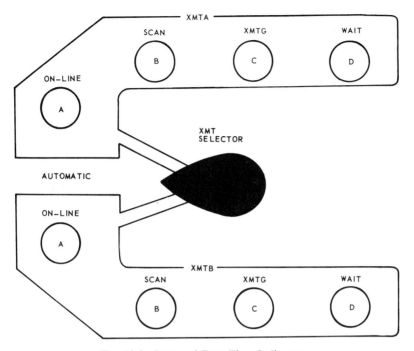

Fig. 13-2. Status of Data-Flow Indicators

register or counter. In a register, grouping of its lamp provides a display which, when read, reveals the date stored. This is contrasted with counter operations, where each lamp turns on and off at a predetermined rate. The experienced repairman can look at the lamps of a register or counter and determine if the count is correct in the register or that the counter is stepping correctly. All these examples show the second use of fault-location indicators (i.e., data flow). To give you some idea of the more common equipment configurations of fault-indicator assemblies, we will identify various types.

13-1.4 *Types of Indicator Panels*

Figure 13-3 portrays many of the different arrangements of indicators used for the two purposes stated. For identification, correlate their use indicated below with that portion of Figure 13-3; each letter corresponds to a callout letter in the figure.

a. Counter and registers, in operation.

b. Information registers, displaying memory core data.

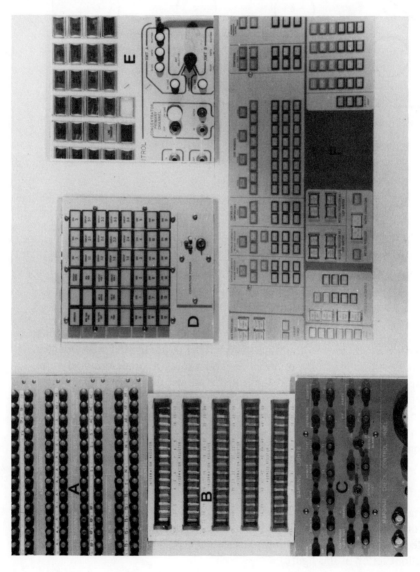

Fig. 13-3. Types of Indicator Panels

  c. Confidence indicators, detecting fault conditions.

  d. Status panel, displaying status of the computer and associated equipment.

  e. Fault and facility panel, showing fault status (upper portion) and data transfer (lower portion).

  f. Confidence indicator console panel, indicating the status of the entire system.

13-1.5 Technical Reference Information

Many portions of the reference material describe or identify each of the indicators on the panel, board, drawer, assembly, or cabinet. The parts of reference manuals that provide data for interpretation and information on the use of indicators are listed below.

1. Circuits and diagrams manual.
2. Operations chapter of the service manual.
3. Principles-of-operation chapter of the service manual.
4. Maintenance chapter of the service manual.
5. Fault-location guides: within the operations chapter.
6. Control and indicator tables: within the operations chapter.

Figure 13-4 shows three examples of the various methods by which indicator lamps are shown in technical manuals. These three examples are not the only methods used, but they represent the extreme. Section A of the figure shows all the indicator lights, their locations, their purposes, and their connections. When any one of these lights turns on, the RE-CEIVE light also turns on. Section B of the figure shows a portion of a table which identifies each lamp on a status panel, by number, title, and color. Under the *function* heading of the table, a brief description of the lamp's purpose is given. Finally, in section C of the figure, the indicators show a rack (36A2, rack A3) error light as well as the functional error lights. Notice that any functional error causes an output from a higher-order sensing unit (input or output) to the higher-order sensing unit within the cabinet. For example, the figure indicates that an input unit error causes an output from the higher-order Battery Data Link Sensor, which, in turn, provides an input to the rack A3 sensor.

It is evident that the repairman's job of troubleshooting is simplified when the system's reference material contains fault-detection information as outlined in Figure 13-4. Simplified, that is, if he knows how to use the information in working back through the error indicators to the end item

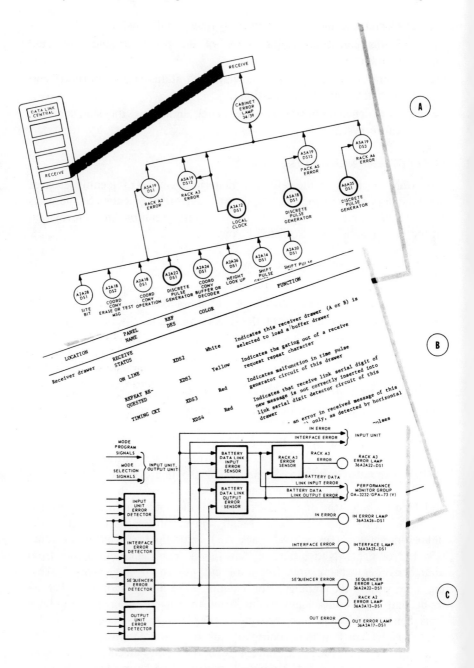

Fig. 13-4. Fault-Location Guides

—the failing unit. Once at the failing unit he must know how to troubleshoot it; he surely cannot remove and replace all the circuit cards within the failing unit, or can he? Depending on the computer system, *group removal and replacement* is an acceptable and adaptable method of corrective maintenance.

13-2   Group-Removal-and-Replacement Troubleshooting Technique

Certain computer systems are built on a simplex mode that does not allow the maintenance man much time for repair. In this case, an accepted method of troubleshooting is *group removal and replacement* of circuit cards. For instance, if you are called to repair a malfunction, your first action would probably be to analyze the symptoms by use of fault lights, printouts, facility lights, and so on. Let's suppose that the fault indications showed a timing error. You now have one of two approaches to choose. First, with a schematic or block diagram, isolate the error to a certain area or group of cards. Second, use charts that identify the trouble symptom and list the cards to be removed. For systems designed to use the group-removal-and-replacement technique, the second method is faster. For example, in Figure 13-5, a chart shows equipment arranged by "alarm groups." The equipment is arranged this way for repair purposes. Each group contains from 3 to 14 cards. The group-removal-and-replacement concept dictates that removal and replacement is restricted to one-half of the cards, not to exceed seven. If after removal and replacement of the prescribed cards the trouble has been cleared, the cards are taken to the card tester for checkout and location of the faulty component. If the trouble still exists within the group, removal and replacement of the second half of the cards is performed.

13-2.1   *Alarm Group Chart*

Let's try a sample case using the alarm group chart. While checking system operation, you find a fault light indicating an azimuth counter error. Referring to the block diagrams, you find that the failing circuit is located in rack A1 (see Figure 13-5). Turning to the alarm condition charts in the technical references you note the page that lists rack A1. The rack number and alphanumeric designator are, in most cases, in the lower center of the page within the text. The azimuth counter circuit is shown as being located in the lower one third of the chart, almost in the center. The chart gives the following information:

1. Rack (A1).
2. Row (the card is located in 700).
3. Card number (21 thru 30).
4. Type of card.

The malfunction is in rack A1, row 700, cards 21 through 30. Note that the card types vary from inverter (INV) to single-shot (SSA). This is important to note because it tells you immediately that your remove-and-

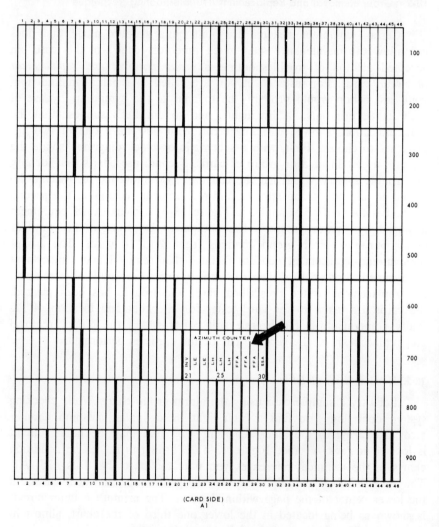

(CARD SIDE)
A1

Fig. 13-5. Card Location Guide

replace action is going to involve different card types. Therefore, you must be extra careful in getting the right card with the right part number in the right location. You may be thinking that this is no big thing; it isn't until you get careless and insert the wrong card in a location. Normally, when this happens you can expect maximum smoke and/or more downtime. But what really hurts is the fact that you feel like a dwarf among giants and look for a hole to hide your head in. Now you remove and replace cards 21 through 25 (half of the cards) and, if this clears the fault indications, you have removed the faulty card, and the equipment is again operational. If this action does not eliminate the problem, you would then remove and replace cards 26 through 30.

13-2.2 Group Removal Using Diagnostic Test

Another type of remove-and-replace technique is that used in conjunction with a diagnostic test. A message as indicated below is provided by a control program once the diagnostic is called in from the storage media. You respond to this message for program operation. Note that the printout is in two parts. The first part indicates program options, and the second part [titled "Enter Data Control Unit (DCU) and Console Configuration"] contains pertinent information regarding the running of the diagnostic.

a. *Display Diagnostic Program*

Definition of Sense Switch Functions

SW1 LOOP ON SOLID ERROR
SW2 LOOP ON INTERMITTENT ERROR
SW4 INHIBIT TYPEOUT
SW5 CONTINUE TEST
SW6 INHIBIT ELECTRONICS CONSOLE TEST
SW7 INHIBIT DISPLAY BUFFER AND DCU TEST
SW8 DUMP ERROR TABLE

b. *ENTER DCU AND CONSOLE CONFIGURATION*

Y   IF UNIT IS IN THE SYSTEM
N   IF NOT IN SYSTEM
*   TO TERMINATE AND LEAVE REMAINING ENTRIES UNCHANGED
/   TO RESPECIFY
D   TO DISPLAY CURRENT CONFIGURATION
DCU   CONSOLE
01 02 03 04 05 06 07 08 09 10 11 12 13 14

Card Group	Rack	Row	Slot	Part Number
B405	DBSG	10	32	1570471
		10	33	1570471
		10	34	1570471
		10	35	1570471
		10	36	1570471
B406	DBSG	10	33	1570471
		10	36	1570471
B502	DBSG	10	26	1570468
		10	35	1570471
		10	36	1570471
		10	38	1570470
		10	45	1570480
B503	DBSG	10	38	1570470
B504	DBSG	10	38	1570470
B505	DBSG	10	34	1570471
		10	38	1570470
B506	DBSG	10	34	1570471
B507	DBSG	10	33	1570471
B508	DBSG	10	33	1570471
B509	DBSG	10	32	1570471
B510	DBSG	10	32	1570471

Card Group	Rack	Row	Slot	Part Number
B601*	DBSG	10	39	1570472
		10	40	1570473
		10	41	1570477
		10	45	1570480
		10	46	1570475
B701* see NOTE A	DBSG	10	33	1570471
	AROSG	9	43	1570380
B801 see NOTE A	DBSG	10	14	1571163
		10	26	1570468
		10	29	1570169
		10	33	1570471
		10	35	1570471
		10	39	1570472
		10	40	1570473
		10	42	1570479
		10	43	1570474
		10	47	1570476
	PPISG	8	40	1570386
B802	DBSG	10	36	1570471
		10	40	1570473
		10	41	1570477
B803 see NOTE A	DBSG	10	15	1570469
		10	42	1570479
		10	44	1570478
	AROSG	9	24	1570376
		9	25	1570376
		9	26	1570378
		9	27	1570378
		9	39	1570378

Fig. 13-6. Card Group Chart (Self-Test)

One of the five characters listed in this second part of the message is .printed out for each DCU and console. Each response for a unit is a single typed entry. The diagnostic test performs the required checks in accordance with your selection. If a solid error is detected (e.g., in a loop and solid error check), a message, printed on the keyboard, reads: Change DISPLAY CARD GROUP XXXXXX CON XX. On the actual printout, the Xs would be replaced by a letter or a decimal number. Figure 13-6 shows that the alphanumeric code printed is a card group. Let's assume that card group B802 is typed out. Referring to the self-test chart (Figure 13-6) you look for card group B802. The columns next to the card group designate the rack DBSG, row A10, and cards A36 through A41. Additional information given in the chart identifies the part numbers of the cards involved. This information is provided for two primary reasons. First, for replacement purposes, and second, for reference purposes, to find out from a parts list the type of card.

We have presented only two examples of the group-removal-and-replacement technique of troubleshooting. There are other applications, but their techniques are the same in principle. It is probable that this technique of group removal and replacement will be the front runner in the newer systems, especially where integrated circuits and modular units are involved. This technique provides for quick restoration of equipment. Therefore, it is an effective technique that is often used on simplex equipment. Be on guard, though, since a card removed as faulty but not repaired creates a catastrophic situation. If you or your fellow workers fail to uphold the integrity of the quality of maintenance, the system fails.

TEST QUESTIONS

1. What is the value of the indicator lamp as a troubleshooting device?

2. What are the two uses of the fault-indicator assembly?

3. Which of the following usually has an indicator lamp?
 a. Circuit   c. Cabinet
 b. Function   d. Rack jacks

4. If lamps are used with a counter, can a technician determine the proper operation? Explain.

5. Using the group-removal-and-replacement technique of troubleshooting, what is the maximum number of cards that usually changes at one time?

6. If personnel integrity is lax during use of the group-removal-and-replacement method, what problem can occur?

14

Special-Purpose Test Equipment

The theme of this book has been to examine any and all possible types of tasks that would provide the technician with knowledge he may use to maintain a computer or communications system. To aid in these tasks the industry itself recognizes that simplified maintenance tasks provide many desirable effects. First the design of the system plays an important role.

14-1 Computer-System Design Considerations

Most modern computers are manufactured by the use of assemblies. The smallest of these assemblies is usually the printer circuit card. All cards look very similar in that they have components mounted on one side and have all runs attached to the end that plugs into a socket. An example is shown in Figure 14-1.

Some of these assemblies have modular components installed on them; some are encapsulated. What is most significant is this second factor. They are designed to have from 1 to 30 or more logic functions incorporated on one card. A card may, for example, contain AND gates,

OR gates, and inverters. Or it may contain an ADDER circuit. Or it may contain a complete register. Because computers use these logic functions, cards are designed to include them. Then, by use of interconnecting wires, logic gates are connected to other logic circuits. Therefore, a complete computer can be built with a limited number of cards. Once all the different logic functions which are to be used in a system are identified, they are laid out on various cards. The cards are manufactured. Because of these factors:

1. Many gates can be placed on one card.
2. Cards are designed as plug-in units.
3. Each card can be designated by type depending upon which logic function or functions it contains.

You see now that with a few cards interconnected, a great variety of circuitry can be obtained. And because of the few different kinds of cards used in a system, the card tester became a troubleshooting aid.

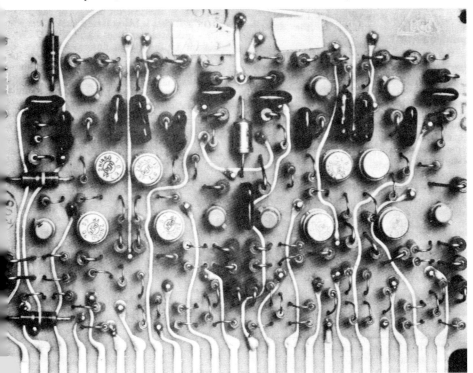

Fig. 14-1. Printed Circuit Card

14-2 Card Testers

The card tester, as its name implies, tests cards for a given system. Its objective is to validate good cards and identify faulty ones so that they can be repaired. If a system is designed so that all its circuits can be placed on one type (size and shape) of card, its card checker would require only one socket. If cards of more than one shape are used, a socket for each type of card must be included on the card tester.

On older computer systems various voltages were used to represent binary values. For instance, one part of the system might use negative logic, where −5 V equals a logic 1 and 0 V equals a logic 0. Another part of the system might use +12 V for a logic 1 and 0 V for a logic 0 (positive logic). In this type of system two card checkers were built primarily because of voltage requirements. In the newer systems a standard voltage may be used (one voltage throughout). In addition, one polarity is usually used, either positive or negative logic. This makes for ease of maintaining a system and also ease of developing a card tester. Presented below are three examples of card testers. Each looks different, but while you read and study the material, discover the similarities in purpose, operations, and results obtained.

14-3 Card Tester, TS1996

The TS1996 card tester is designed to test five differently shaped printed-circuit plug-in assemblies. The technical reference manual indicates which socket is to be used. However, examination of the various sockets clearly shows that only one type (size) of card can fit. This card tester supplies the necessary voltages and signals to the card under test which the card would receive under normal operating conditions. Figure 14-2 shows the front view of the tester with a card inserted.

14-3.1 Characteristics of the Machine

The tester consists of some basic elements. They are:

1. 120-V ac input power unit.
2. Power input, card tester unit, which applies regulated dc voltages to the card test.
3. Card jacks (receptacles), of which there are five.
4. Test circuit selector switches, of which there are 30.
5. Test jack output, for sampling signals and voltage levels of the card under test circuits.
6. GEN, Input, which is a plug for connecting a signal generator.

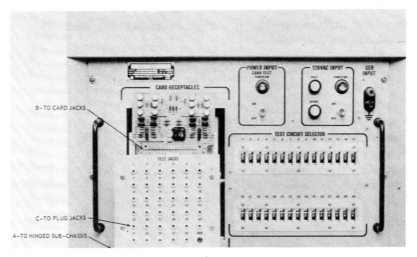

Fig. 14-2. TS1996, Front View (Courtesy of ITT)

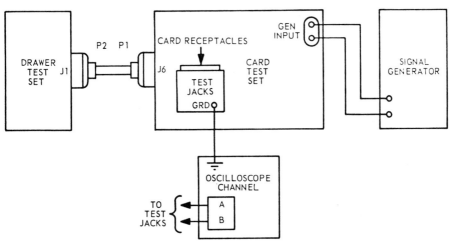

Fig. 14-3. Bench Setup, TS1996 (Courtesy of ITT)

Each of the circuit selector knobs (1 through 30) has a multilevel switch attached. Switch position A (as shown) is the OFF position. Switch position B provides dc voltage, C may provide a pulse, D a level, E an ac signal, and so on.

This test set is usually used with other standard test equipment, the oscilloscope and signal generator. The oscilloscope measures the signal at various test points on the card by use of the test jacks. The signal generator provides sine-wave and square-wave signals at selected frequencies for the card under test. Figure 14-3 shows a bench setup. The unit, drawer test set (to be covered later), also provides selected signals for card operations.

14-3.2 *Typical Check Made with the Tester*

At the beginning of a performance test, the hinged card receptacle subchassis is pulled out from the front panel of the set. The printed card to be tested is inserted into its proper socket. There is a lamp located behind the assembly (card) which provides a shadow of the etched printed wiring on its reverse side. The component side is to the front. This light enables the technician to locate wiring junctions and defects or breaks in the etching.

Each test procedure includes the circuit description and schematic diagram of the card. In addition, it provides instruction for testing the card and wave shapes, voltage levels, and rise and fall signal times. Figure 14-4 shows an example of the testing procedure of a card.

Prior to turning on power, the instructions call for position test circuit selector switches in various positions (see step 5): switch 1 to position C, 2 to position D, 4 to position I, and so on. The signal generator must be ON

Step	Operation of Test Equipment	Point of Test	Performance Standard
5	Set POWER INPUT ON-OFF switch to OFF. Set TEST CIRCUIT SELECTOR switches to the following: 1-C, 2-D, 4-I, 5-J, 7-D, 15-B, 18-B, 24-F, 25-F, 26-I, 28-D, 29-C, and 30-I. Set all others to A.		
6	Set POWER INPUT ON-OFF switch to ON. Adjust oscilloscope horizontal display for 50 usec/CM.	2, 24	Waveform 5 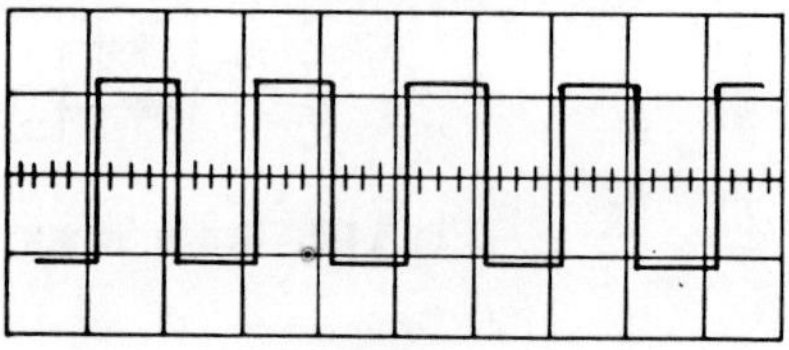

$$V_o = 0 \pm 1V$$

$$V_1 = -11 \pm 1V$$

$$T_d = 50 \text{ usec}$$

$$T_r = 1.5 \text{ usec}$$

$$T_f = 1.5 \text{ usec}$$

Fig. 14-4. Test Procedure, TS1996 (Courtesy of ITT)

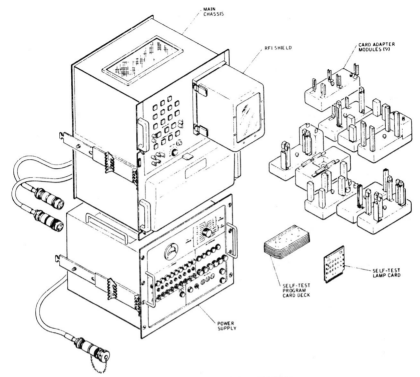

Fig. 14-5. Card Test Set, TSM109

and operating at a selected frequency (a previous step in the procedure). Power is applied next, and measurement of waveform 5 is taken at test jacks 2 and 24. If the waveform has all the qualifications listed below waveform 5 (V0, V1, Td, Tr, To, and Tf), the card is good. If any part of the test fails, the circuit schematic and description will provide clues to the failing component. Then replacement components can be exchanged for defective ones.

14-4 Card Test Set, TSM109

The TSM109 card test set shown in Figure 14-5 is designed to test a variety of cards which have been manufactured in a variety of shapes. In order to have one machine capable of testing the variety of cards, a different method from the previous card tester was selected. In this set adapter modules designed for specific cards have been built. The rear of the adapter module fits a common jack on the test set. In place of the selector switches used on the TS1996, punched cards (in pairs) program voltages and signals to the card under test.

The principles of operation are developed under a GO–NO/GO concept. During the sequential operational steps the set performs the GO signal, allowing the test to continue. When a failure occurs, a NO/GO signal is generated and a halt occurs in the program. With a failure the input and output data and voltage signals may be sampled by use of one or more of the 80 test points. These test points are located next to the card being tested.

14-4.1 Characteristics of the Machine

The machine consists of the following functional elements:

1. Programmer.
2. Digital signal comparator.
3. Clock pulse control.
4. Analog signal synthesizer.
5. Digital signal synthesizer.
6. Level changers.
7. Loads.
8. Power supply.
9. Card readers and adapter modules.

These elements make up the entire operating parts of the test set. Each title specifies what part of the function performs in the set.

In addition, the control panel, as shown in Figure 14-6, shows all the modes of operation, and the unit on the right houses the card under test. For automatic operation the start pushbutton (PB) is used, and each step of the test that is correctly completed results in a GO indication. For a single-step mode, the SINGLE CLOCK and STEP (PBs) are used. In cases where a loop is required, the loop (PB) is used. If an error is sensed while in the loop, the NO/GO OVERRIDE (PB) may be depressed, and the operation will continue without a halt.

The MOD 64 lamps indicate the step of the test being performed. The program voltage lamps indicate which voltage sources are being selected by the program cards for the test.

14-4.2 Typical Test with the Machine

A suspect faulty card is examined for its part number. A correlation is made with the reference manual. The proper adapter module and reader cards (punched cards) are selected. The cards are inserted in the machine.

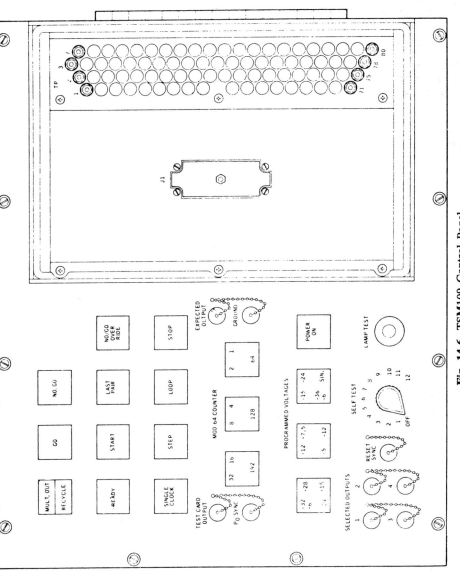

Fig. 14-6. TSM109 Control Panel

One card connects the adapter to the bus interface, and the other card connects the bus to the program control. With these units in place, the suspect card is installed in its proper jack. Power is applied to the set. If the correct reader cards and adapter module are properly in place, the READY lamp lights. Depressing the START (PB) initiates the automatic program by starting the MOD 64 counter. As each check is made, the GO lamp lights. The MOD 64 counter steps and the next test is made. This process continues until a failure occurs. When a failure happens, the NO/GO light comes on and the program halts. The MOD 64 counter contains the number of the failing step. Manual control is assumed. A loop may be selected, in which case the program runs continuously, but halts at each failure and must be restarted. Or a loop and NO/GO OVERRIDE may be used together, in which case the program runs continuously. Finally a manual step-by-step check may be made by selection of the SINGLE CLOCK and STEP (PB) switches.

14-5 Card Tester, GPM50

Probably the most eleborate card tester ever developed is the GPM50. This tester incorporates many special features; however, it provides the same service as the TS1996. It validates cards that are good, and it identifies components on cards that are bad. This test set is capable of checking approximately 95 percent of all components on each card semi-automatically. A paper tape has been prepared for each different type of card. This tape controls the tester's operation. The remaining 5 percent of the components are checked manually. Each card is subjected to a series of tasks. Usually resistance and impedance checks are performed first, then a voltage check is made, and finally a dynamic check is made with signals at their usual operating levels and frequencies.

14-5.1 Characteristics of the Machine

Figure 14-7 shows the GPM50 card tester. Four cabinets are bolted together. They are, from left to right:

1. The program and decoding cabinet.
2. The viewing and switching cabinet.
3. The simulator and display cabinet.
4. The manual test and power cabinet.

A tape with a test program in binary coded form is loaded into the programming and decoding cabinet. The tape is decoded by this unit and the results of the decoding provide control for each phase of testing for

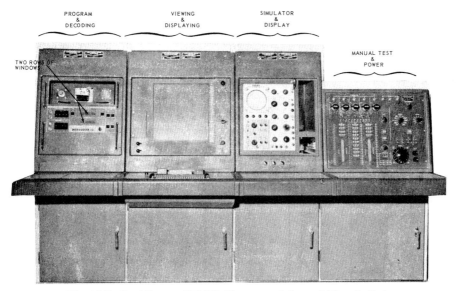

Fig. 14-7. Card Tester, GPM50 (Courtesy of General Electric Co.)

the card under test. Note the arrows on the figure. These windows have nixie lamps and provide a special readout feature. The upper row displays the step of the test if a halt occurs. The lower row displays the out-of-tolerance measurement. By using the test number the operator can refer to reference instructions about the test and correlate a failure with a logic or schematic reference.

The viewing and switching (second cabinet) provide two features. First, the display portion (large square screen) displays a microfilm of the card under test. Some of the features included are the schematic, voltage levels, and pulse shapes. On the lower shelf are the receptacles for the cards. More than one is provided because of the different sizes of cards. Also included on the lower shelf is a simulator control panel. This unit consists of switches which program the required signals and levels for the manual portion of the tests.

The third section of the test set incorporates an oscilloscope which provides a capability to view waveforms produced from the card being tested. If a signal has to be verified, the oscilloscope is used. Instructions accompanying the tape program indicate which waveforms are to be used. The illustrations included in the display-unit microfilm list the waveforms.

The fourth cabinet contains the power supply for the entire tester and also contains control switches if a card is to be checked manually.

14-5.2 *Typical Check with the Tester*

After the card that is to be tested is identified, it is inserted in the proper receptacle. Its paper tape is selected from the library of tapes. The tape is inserted in the program unit and power is turned on.

The operator depresses the start pushbutton and the automatic programming begins. Resistance and impedance checks are performed by the machine. A halt occurs if any portion of the test fails. If no failure occurs, a halt occurs at the end of the test.

At that time the operator knows that the resistance and impedance are correct. With the use of his instruction manual he knows if he must simulate any voltage or signals; then he depresses the start pushbutton again and the static (voltage) checks are made. If all goes well, the dynamic phase follows the static check.

The dynamic checks are those which exercise the circuits in a very similar way to the way they operate in the computer. They may be either digital (square wave) or analog, such as a display sweep waveform. If a halt occurs before the end of the test, the failing signal can be measured in the oscilloscope and its optimum form can be compared with the one in microfilm. Some of the displays seen on the oscilloscope are automatically presented by control of the tape program.

14-6 Power-Supply Test Set, TS1846

One of the most important pieces of equipment in any data-processing system is its power supply. Without the power supply, the system is of no use. Therefore, it is very important to be able to repair the power supplies quickly. This keeps downtime to a minimum.

The test set shown in Figure 14-8 represents testers that may be used to maintain four types of power supplies. This test set is used to analyze power-supply operation, to set overload calibration, and to isolate malfunctions.

14-6.1 Characteristics of the Machine

The functional elements of the test set include the *variable power transformer circuit* (ac input), the resistive load circuits (transient and static load), and the monitor meter circuit. All are shown in Figure 14-8. The elements that operate to perform a specific function or a group of related functions are described as follows.

1. Variable power to transformer circuit. This circuit is used to control the input voltage to the power supply under test. In this way, the regulation of a power supply under varying input voltage conditions may be determined.

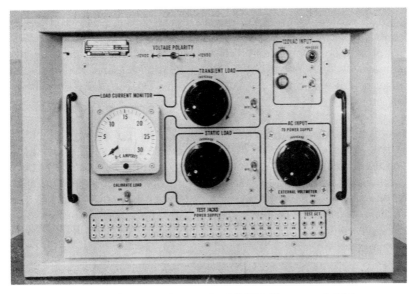

Fig. 14-8. Power-Supply Test Set, TS1846 (Courtesy of ITT)

2. Resistive load circuits. The +12-V or −12-V output of the power supply under test is applied to various configurations of fixed and variable load resistors which comprise the resistive load circuits of the test set. The resistive load circuits are used in the performance of static load tests, transient load tests, and overload calibration tests.

3. Monitor meter circuit. This circuit is connected in series with the output of the power supply under test and the selected resistive load circuits. An ammeter in the monitor circuit indicates the amount of current drain required to actuate the overload protective circuit of the power supply under test. The ammeter is also used to set current drains on a power supply when testing the power-supply voltage regulation.

14-6.2 *Typical Check with the Machine*

For this discussion let's talk in terms of what each part of the operation does while checking a power supply.

AC INPUT. The ac input function provides a variable ac voltage for the power supply under test. This voltage is available by turning the front panel 120-V ac input ON/OFF switch to ON. Then control T1 on the front panel ac input to the power supply is adjusted to the required voltage.

VOLTAGE POLARITY. The front-panel VOLTAGE POLARITY switch permits a positive or negative voltage from a power supply under test to be appropriately applied to the test-set circuitry without changing interequipment cabling conncetions. Also, this switch ensures that the correct voltage polarity is applied at all times to the LOAD CURRENT MONITOR meter.

STATIC LOAD. The STATIC LOAD function provides a variable load for a power supply under test. Placing the front-panel STATIC LOAD ON/OFF switch to the ON position and varying the STATIC LOAD control causes a resistive load to be presented to the power supply under test. This variable resistive load presents static load in a range of 50 to 100 percent of the power-supply rated output. The power-supply dc output and ripple voltages are checked under maximum load conditions using an external meter or scope.

TRANSIENT LOAD. The front-panel TRANSIENT LOAD provides step exercise to the power supply under test in order to observe its recovery time. When the TRANSIENT LOAD ON/OFF switch is placed in the ON position, the TRANSIENT LOAD control is adjusted to provide a load of 20 to 80 percent of the rated output. Once the control is adjusted to a desired load, the TRANSIENT ON/OFF switch is repeatedly cycled between ON and OFF positions to provide a transient load. During this time, an oscilloscope is used to observe the recovery time of the power supply.

CALIBRATE LOAD. The front-panel CALIBRATE LOAD ON/OFF switch, in conjunction with the static load circuitry, provides for overload testing. While adjusting the static load control for a depressing resistance, the meter is observed for the maximum current indication before a sudden reduction in power supply output occurs as a result of the overload protection circuits of the power supply under test. An oscilloscope is also used during this test to observe the sudden reduction in the power-supply output.

TEST JACKS. The test set has a bank of front-panel TEST JACKS divided into two groups: power supply and test set. There are 50 test jacks, A through HH, associated with the power supply under test. Some or all of these test points are made available by using various types of interequipment cables connected between the test set and power supply. There are six test jacks, 3 through 8, associated with the TEST SET group, which permits access to test points within the test set. Both groups of test jacks are used with auxiliary test equipment to monitor voltage levels and waveforms.

14-7 Drawer Tester, AN/FYM2

The tester shown in Figure 14-9 is used for testing and troubleshooting drawer assemblies of a communications system. The tester is programmed

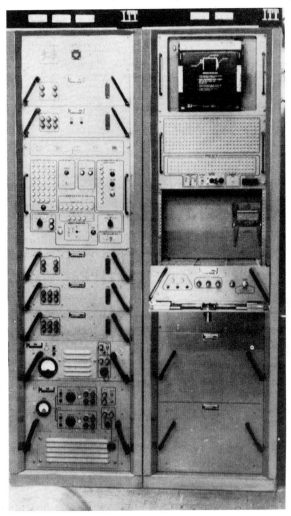

Fig. 14-9. Test Set, FYM2 (Courtesy of ITT)

by a plug-in patch panel which routes signals developed by the test set to the drawer under test. The testing is sequential, step by step. A failure at any step is indicated by an error lamp on the indicator panel. And in many instances the step of the failure is indicated in binary form on the indicator panel.

14-7.1 Characteristics of the Machine

The tester is made of two cabinets. The one on the left (Figure 14-9) is the control and display console. The one on the right is the programmer and storage console.

The control and display console includes (from the floor up):

1. 12-V dc power supply.
2. Lamp power supply.
3. Two processor drawers (signal).
4. Receiver/comparator drawer.
5. Indicator panel.
6. Generator/controller drawer.
7. Transmitter drawer.

Each of the drawers, as its name implies, provides a function for testing a suspect drawer. The generator drawer generates required signals and the transmitter drawer sends them to the drawer under test. Results are processed and sent to the receiver/comparator, where indications are developed for display on the indicator panel.

The programmer and storage console consists of (from the floor up):

1. Two storage drawers for program patch panels.
2. Test shelf (with a drawer to be tested in place).
3. Test-jack panel.
4. Program patch panel.

14-7.2 Typical Check with the Machine

When a system malfunction has been isolated to a particular drawer assembly, the suspect drawer is mounted on the test ledge. The appropriate pluggable programmer is selected and mounted on the programmer panel. One or more pluggable programmers are available for each of the drawers the test set will test.

The drawer test set checks each drawer by automatically exercising each circuit in the drawer in a preprogrammed sequence. The input and output signals of the drawer are evaluated at each programmed step by the comparator circuits. Each satisfactory response initiates a GO (sequence advance) signal, which causes the drawer test set to advance one step and automatically evaluate the next programmed function. In some instances circuit complexity makes it impractical to perform the entire test automatically. Auxiliary test equipment (an oscilloscope) is connected to the tester to make the necessary additional checks manually. During these manual operations, the automatic sequencing of the test steps is interrupted and resumed thereafter. The manual mode of operation may be selected anytime for examination of waveforms.

AUTOMATIC TEST. Figure 14-10 shows a block diagram of the automatic test setup. Signals produced by the test set signal generator for each test step are applied, through the patch programmer, to appropriate inputs

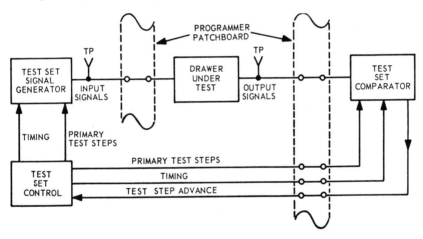

Fig. 14-10. Block Diagram of Automatic Test

of the drawer under test. The output signals produced by the drawer are then coupled through the patch programmer to the test set comparator, which samples the drawer outputs at each step to determine whether they are of proper quality and in proper relationship with the signals from the test set control. If the comparator accepts the signals, the test set will automatically advance to the next step. If the incoming signal is rejected, the test set will stop and the test lamp will light. Inputs and outputs are then checked to determine the cause of the failure.

MANUAL TEST. Figure 14-11 illustrates use of visual comparison of signals instead of use of the test set comparator to check them. The test set control circuits provide the required control and timing signals that cause the signal generator to activate the drawer under test. The drawer

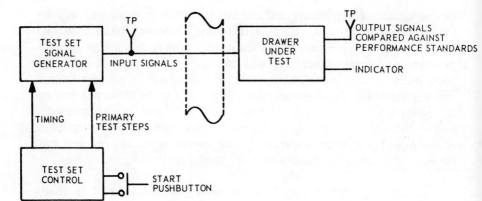

Fig. 14-11. Block Diagram of Manual Test

outputs are then checked at the test point with auxiliary test equipment and compared with prescribed performance standards. If the indications are correct, the START pushbutton is depressed to advance to the next step. If the indications are incorrect, the trouble is then isolated to the defective printed circuit card.

When a malfunction occurs during the performance of a test procedure, it is necessary to determine the location of the trouble by using the following support material:

1. Test block diagrams.
2. Test set signal generator test logic diagrams.
3. Drawer under test logic diagrams.
4. Test set comparator test logic diagrams.

In a system such as this, where an assembly within the test set may fail, a troubleshooting aid is provided in the manual. Figure 14-12 shows the layout which accompanies each test. Note that each of two parts of the test set is identified. They are, on the left, the *signal generator* (1) and, on the right, the *comparator* (3). The center block (2) identifies the drawer under test.

Callouts 4 through 9 provide the following data to assist the operation.

4. The number of the Test Step (100).
5. The particular test drawer (assembly).
6. The specific cards within the drawer which are used during the test step.

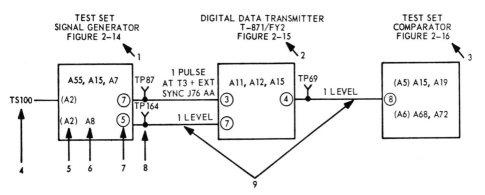

Fig. 14-12. Logic Layout for TS100

7. The logic sheet number where circuitry may be identified.

8. The test points on the test set programmer and storage console.

9. The performance standard to be observed.

The drawer tester enables isolation of the trouble to a card or group card level. If data flow is understood, it is quite possible to isolate the malfunction to a single card component. In most cases, however, suspect cards will need further testing on the card tester.

14-8 Trouble Analyzer

The trouble analyzer shown in Figure 14-13 tests suspected assemblies without their being removed from the equipment cabinet. The analyzer is a small, portable digital device composed of a number of plug-in cards which are identical in most instances to the cards it tests. The meter and indicators on the analyzer work in conjunction with a test probe and probe indicator to provide the operator with simple go or no go results. This set isolates troubles to a faulty card, monitors assembly supply voltages, and aids in the adjustment of delay component cards. An oscilloscope can be used in conjunction with the analyzer while troubleshooting or checking an assembly. If so, the analyzer has SYNC, DATA, and GROUND terminals available for this purpose. Data processors usually process data in both serial and parallel form, and the circuits which process those data must be checked. The trouble analyzer, for example, can compare two serial words bit for bit. One word is produced by the analyzer and is used as a standard. This standard word is processed by the circuits to be tested and then fed back to the analyzer for comparison with the original word.

Other tests performed by this tester are:

1. Logic level.
2. Pulse presence.
3. Clock test.

14-8.1 Characteristics of the Machine

One of the most significant characteristics of the machine is its portability. Instead of bringing a suspect drawer to the test set as in the study of the drawer checker, the tester is brought to the suspect cabinet. On the other hand, a less desirable characteristic is that the equipment may be unable to perform its function; while testing is being performed, that part of the system is out. Three cables are connected to the suspect cabinet. The bottom one shown (Figure 14-13) is used to provide power for the test set. The one connected to the outrigger assembly receives control voltages and data from the functions under test. The cable shown in the center is the probe, which is placed over selected pins while testing is performed.

This tester can be operated in different modes. Figure 14-14 shows a closeup of the control panel of the tester. Note the selection switch below the meter. It indicates three possible operating modes:

1. Rack test.
2. Self-test.
3. Delay-line test.

While in *rack test* or *self-test* the two switches labeled *clock test* and *level test* may be used.

The control switches on the right are used for delay-line adjust and are inoperative when the mode select switch is *not* in delay-line adjust.

14-8.2 Typical Checks Made with the Machine

We identified three types of checks that are made with the machine in the opening paragraph. They were level, pulse presence, and clock. In addition, the set provides an adjustment capability for delay lines. A brief discussion of each test follows.

LEVEL TEST. When the level test is performed, the operator connects the cables to the power and function jacks in the cabinet. He then inserts the probe lead into the test point. He programs the control panel to rack test, and the normal-level switch to level. He then depresses the

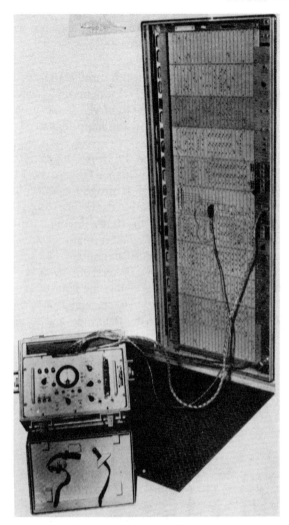

Fig. 14-13. Trouble Analyzer Connected to Equipment
(Courtesy of General Electric Co.)

pushbutton on the probe. If a level is absent, the lamp on the probe lights.

PULSE-PRESENCE TEST. The pulse-presence check uses the same connections. The clock and level test switches are placed on normal. And two indications (SYNC amber lamps, above the mode switch) display the presence of a pulse. If one comes on, it indicates zero frequency (dc). If both come on, it indicates that the presence is between 0 Hz and approximately 16 Hz. If both sync lamps are ON, the pulse presence is between 16 and 100 Hz. Finally, if both sync lamps are ON and the error-probe indicator is OFF, the pulse presence is greater than 100 Hz.

CLOCK TEST. The clock test checks for the presence of the master clock (1 MHz). The control panel clock normal switch is placed in CLOCK, and the level switch is in NORMAL. If the probe light is OFF, the megahertz signal is present; if not, the lamp lights.

DELAY-LINE TEST. A delay-line PCB is plugged into the jack as shown on the right side of the control panel (Figure 14-14). The amount of delay a card is to be adjusted for is programmed with the use of the three delay switches to the left of the card. The top switch shows increments of 10s. The middle switch shows increments of 1s, and the bottom switch shows increments of quarter microseconds. A delay line's adjustment screw is preliminarily set at minimum.

After placing the MIN GAIN, Delay Set, MAX GAIN switch (to the right of meter) to Delay Set (the delay-line adjustment screw is turned until first the *ready* lamp, then the *set* lamp, come on), the *min gain* and *max gain* pots are adjusted, again using the ready and set lamps as guides.

Fig. 14-14. Trouble Analyzer Control Panel (Courtesy of General Electric Co.)

TEST QUESTIONS

1. What characteristics of computer design make possible the card tester?

2. What three functions do all the card testers discussed in this chapter have in common?

3. What is similar in test procedures between the drawer checkers and the card tester TSM109?

4. What are some of the programming techniques used with card and drawer checkers?

5. Does the power-supply test set 1846 check the overload circuitry of a power supply?

Index